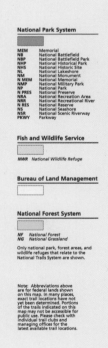

SANTA FE TRAIL
NATIONAL HISTORIC TRAIL

Trail of Tears

TRAIL OF TEARS
NATIONAL HISTORIC TRAIL

Original Route Segment

Begin

NEZ PERCE NEE-ME-POO
NATIONAL HISTORIC TRAIL

PONY EXPRESS TRAIL
1860-1861

W3R

STAR-SPANGLED BANNER
NATIONAL HISTORIC TRAIL

CAPTAIN JOHN SMITH CHESAPEAKE
NATIONAL HISTORIC TRAIL

NATIONAL HISTORIC TRAIL
IDITAROD

JUAN BAUTISTA DE ANZA
NATIONAL HISTORIC TRAIL

EL CAMINO REAL DE LOS TEJAS
NATIONAL HISTORIC TRAIL

KANZA
OCTA
030

OREGON TRAIL
NATIONAL HISTORIC TRAIL

CALIFORNIA TRAIL
NATIONAL HISTORIC TRAIL

COMMEMORATING 200 YEARS
LEWIS AND CLARK
NATIONAL HISTORIC TRAIL
1804 · 2004
LEWIS & CLARK CAMPSITE JUNE 2 - 11, 1805

MORMON PIONEER
NATIONAL HISTORIC TRAIL

HISTORIC

SELMA TO MONTGOMERY
NATIONAL HISTORIC TRAIL

ROUTE

Old Spanish Trail

OLD SPANISH TRAIL
NATIONAL HISTORIC TRAIL

Original Route

ALA KAHAKAI
NATIONAL HISTORIC TRAIL

El Camino Real

EL CAMINO REAL DE TIERRA ADENTRO
NATIONAL HISTORIC TRAIL

Hiking Trail

OVERMOUNTAIN VICTORY
1780
NATIONAL HISTORIC TRAIL

AMERICA'S NATIONAL

HISTORIC TRAILS

IN THE FOOTSTEPS OF HISTORY

KAREN BERGER

Photography by **BART SMITH**

Foreword by **KEN BURNS** and **DAYTON DUNCAN**

RIZZOLI
NEW YORK

New York · Paris · London · Milan

CONTENTS

Foreword

KEN BURNS and DAYTON DUNCAN

The history of the United States is the story of two journeys. One began on July 4, 1776, when a new nation radically declared the self-evident truths of human equality and liberty and set off on the quest—halting, imperfect, still incomplete—to reach the lofty destination of fulfilling its founding ideals. The other is more geographic: a journey—though composed of many journeys, filled with struggle and adventure, heroism and tragedy—across the vast American landscape.

For the last four decades, in our own exploration of our nation's complicated past and in our desire to tell that story—to "map" it through documentary films and books—we have followed both journeys and learned how intertwined they are. We've learned that every place exists not just in coordinates of longitude and latitude, topography and ecosystems, but also in layers of time. To truly understand America and its people requires coming to grips with it all.

Working on *The West*, a documentary series for PBS, brought us to parts of Texas, New Mexico, Arizona, and California, which Spanish missionaries and conquistadors, in search of gold and souls to convert, entered from Mexico long before the United States was founded. To them it was "the north"; to the native people they encountered, who had lived there for untold generations, it was "home," the center of the universe.

Making a film about the Lewis and Clark Expedition took us up the Missouri River, through the Great Plains, over the Rocky Mountains, and to the Pacific Ocean. Like them, we were awed by what Lewis described as "scenes of visionary enchantment." And like them, we were welcomed by the tribes whose friendship and assistance made the expedition's success possible.

California Trail through
City of Rocks National
Reserve, Idaho

FOLLOWING SPREAD: Pacific
Springs ghost town,
Oregon Trail near
South Pass, Wyoming

Mylie Lawyer, an aging Nez Perce woman, told us the story of Watkuweis, who had persuaded her tribe to provide food and shelter to the cold and starving explorers, the first white men to reach their homeland. We also learned the story of how the Nez Perce's hospitality was betrayed 70 years later. In trying to escape an army intent on confining them to a reservation, they embarked on their own desperate journey toward Canada and freedom—a heart-breaking tale that ended with their surrender, just 40 miles from their destination.

In following the route of Horatio Nelson Jackson, who in 1903 became the first person to cross the continent in an automobile, we came to a sage-covered plain just west of South Pass in Wyoming, another great intersection of time and place. Here the Oregon, California, Mormon Pioneer, and Pony Express Trails all left their mark on the American landscape and history. People had passed this way, on foot and by slow-moving wagons, in search of a better life—land to farm, the promise of riches in gold, a refuge from religious persecution—and then as a way to communicate with those they left behind in the East at the pace of a galloping horse.

We were there to tell the story of the dawning of a new age, when American wanderlust found a different way to travel. As we waited for just the right pre-sunset light for filming, we talked with some cowboys who happened along. With the sun finally at the right angle, we mounted our cameraman on the hood of our Suburban, strapped him safely in a bra-like harness, and bounced down the dirt path. One of the ranch hands turned to the other and said, "I'll be getting free drinks at the bar for a month telling this story."

The national historic trails are 19 strands in a grander tapestry that preserves our country's history and landscape—through national parks, national monuments, national scenic trails, national historic sites and battlefields, national wildlife refuges, national seashores and recreation areas, and much more.

Weaving that tapestry began in 1872, with the creation of the world's first national park, Yellowstone.

For the first time in human history, a nation decided that its most magnificent and sacred landscapes should not be the exclusive preserves of the nobility or the well-connected. They would be for *everyone* and for all time.

That idea, we believe, is the Declaration of Independence applied to the land, and like the idea of freedom itself, it has evolved and expanded on its own historical journey. The park system broadened from the protection of majestic landscapes—think of the Grand Canyon or Yosemite—to the preservation of sites that commemorate important moments in our past. This includes reminders of painful episodes in American history—the Japanese internment camp of Manzanar in California, or Sand Creek in Colorado, a peaceful village where Cheyenne Indians were massacred by American soldiers—set aside on the belief that a truly great nation can openly acknowledge its shortcomings and learn from them.

The national historic trails also represent a clear-eyed view of the lessons history can teach. You can retrace the routes taken by Patriot soldiers to secure our nation's independence or by hopeful pioneers to expand our boundaries, as well as routes like the Trail of Tears and the Nez Perce Trail, which show that not all roads in our history have led to freedom and equality, or the Selma to Montgomery Trail, which teaches just how long and difficult the road to freedom can be.

Like the nation itself—a diverse collection of people whose stories connect to tell an epic saga—the historic trails connect those stories to a land epic enough in scale to contain them.

We have followed many of these trails—across landscapes we will never forget, but also across time, getting the chance to "meet" people who traveled the same paths before us. Those personal journeys have deepened our understanding of the larger American journey. "You road I enter upon and look around," the great poet Walt Whitman wrote, "I believe you are not all that is here, I believe that much unseen is also here."

We invite you to follow these trails too. They belong to you. They belong to all of us.

Introduction

KAREN BERGER

What I remember most is the heat: the wind against my skin like a hair dryer turned on high, my breath warming me from inside, not that I needed to be warmed. Underfoot, the desiccated earth cracked into a hardpan mosaic the color of bleached driftwood. Toward the horizon, the undulating light fractured and danced like something Monet would have painted if he had lived in the desert and painted air instead of water.

The trail led along the Sweetwater River in Wyoming. If you are an easterner, which I am, the idea of walking along a river brings forth images of gentle forests, moss-covered stones, and perhaps neat adjoining fields with corn rows and hay bales. But on the eastern rim of the Great Divide Basin, the river was no match for the parched, brown earth. The only green was a thin line of optimistic willows. Every once in a while, a cottonwood promised water and shade, but beyond the river's reach, life scaled back to sagebrush and tumbleweed, the frugalities of scarcity and subsistence.

One hundred and seventy years ago the path that crosses this lonely momentary break in the Rocky Mountains was the 19th-century equivalent of an interstate highway on steroids. The route may not look like a path that anyone would choose as the easiest way to get from here to there, but it was, in fact, exactly that. During the early 1800s, explorers had scoured the American West, looking for a way to take wagons across the Continental Divide. South Pass is what they found. Back then, anyone walking here would have been in the company of an endless train of thousands of emigrants bound for gold, or farm-

land, or religious freedom, or trade, or adventure. Today, four national historic trails commemorate the Oregon settlers, the Mormon pioneers, the California gold rush miners, and the riders of the Pony Express, all of whom used this route to cross from the Atlantic to the Pacific watersheds.

No one travels by wagon train anymore, and today's interstate and railroad cross the Continental Divide south of here. Today's visitors have the landscape to themselves.

The day before, two men in a pickup truck had stopped, demanding to know what we were doing. I told them we were walking.

"No one walks here," they announced. "You'd have to be crazy." And then: "Are you?"

"Are we what?"

"Are y'all crazy?"

I assured them of our sanity, and they drove on, the truck spitting dust and the men shaking their heads.

Since then, I'd seen some wild horses and a few antelope. Every once in a while, a pile of rusted machinery or a chipped concrete foundation stood witness to the fact that someone, at some time, had thought they could wrest wealth, or perhaps just eke out a living, in this inhospitable space. Once I saw an abandoned cabin, its splintered wood dry as the desert grasses. And at South Pass itself, a living history outdoor museum rose from the landscape, complete with mercantile, blacksmith shop, and an honest-to-god gold mine.

In one important way, I was different than my forebears. Like the emigrants, I had left civilization behind. But unlike them, I could easily enough get it

Sweetwater River near former site of Three Crossings Station, Pony Express Trail, Wyoming

FOLLOWING SPREAD: Oregon Trail, just before Parting of the Ways with the California Trail, Idaho

back. If the going got tough, I could hitchhike or walk to a town where I'd find a bed, a bath, a hot meal, and a cool air conditioner.

There were other differences as well. I carried what I needed on my back; they had had wagons to haul their supplies. I had high-tech outdoor equipment—the kind of gear you could take to stay warm on Mount Everest or stay dry in the Amazon; they had wool and cotton and leather. Perhaps most importantly, I had information—about weather, water sources, trail conditions, and resupply opportunities; they only had the grapevine, and each other.

But in the moment, the similarities overcame the differences. I was covering the same 15 or 20 miles a day they would have covered, at the same human speed of 2 to 3 miles per hour. I pulled down my hat the same way they did, to protect myself from the same sun. The same clawing thirst scratched at my throat; the same huge horizons magnified the distance I had yet to cover. Mostly roadless, still sparsely settled, harsh and unforgiving, the land had not much changed since the first Anglo-Americans hauled themselves from the Atlantic part of America to the Pacific on the other side. I was walking in the path of history.

This is the gift of the national historic trails, 19 trails designated by Congress to commemorate and protect the historic routes of travel across the American continent: the chance to walk—or ride, paddle, bicycle, or drive—on the paths of those who came before; the opportunity to learn our national stories while experiencing the landscapes where they took place.

Congress passed the National Trails System Act in 1968, establishing the first national scenic trails, designed for recreation. In 1978, the act was expanded to include trails that played important roles in American history. At this writing, the National Trails System has grown to include 11 national scenic trails, 19 national historic trails, and more than 1,300 other designated recreational trails.

Each of the national historic trails commemorates some aspect of the American story and the American people: Polynesians who settled Hawai'i, Spaniards who colonized the Southwest, English who explored the Eastern Seaboard, soldiers who fought in the Revolutionary War, settlers who crossed the continent

on foot, American Indians who helped enable the spread of European culture and whose lives were uprooted by it, African Americans who marched for freedom.

In the context of national scenic trails, the word "trail" deserves some exploration. Usually, we think of trails from a walker's perspective: a trail is a path from here to there. Consider Bill Bryson, trying to haul himself and an unlikely travel partner over the Appalachian Trail from Georgia to Maine. Or novice hiker Cheryl Strayed, attempting to cross 1,000 miles of western mountains on the Pacific Crest Trail. The trails they were following were specially designed to offer opportunities to hike, to exercise, to get away, to observe wildlife and the landscape—to use recreation to re-create one's relationship with nature.

America's 19 national historic trails are a different matter entirely. All of them offer opportunities to experience the varied environments that have played a role in the American narrative. But even more, these trails place us at the intersection of story and landscape. When we touch the wooden walls of a frontier fort, step in the ruts of wagon wheels, look down at a river from a bridge that wasn't there a hundred years ago, or consider what it would be like to walk, ride a horse, drive a wagon, or march in military formation over an expanse of land, we understand the past in a physical, visceral way.

Trails are about connections. Our historic trails connect us across thousands of miles of distance, from forests and prairies to mountains, deserts, and oceans. They connect people and cultures by recognizing some of the individuals, groups, and cultures that changed the course of our history. And they connect us across time.

In doing so, they challenge our idea of exactly what a trail is.

In his book *On Trails*, Robert Moor explores the difference between traces, paths, and trails. Paths, Moor writes, are forward-looking and intentional. Paths are built—deliberately constructed to take us somewhere. A garden path, writes Moor, would never be called a trail. In that sense, our national historic trails might more properly be called paths—and indeed, the Appalachian Trail is often called "a footpath in the wilderness."

Traces are evidence of what came before—breadcrumbs, as it were, often with little to link them except our imagination. Traces may give us clues about how the land was once used and traversed; they do not necessarily give us the route or the full story. American Indians may have followed the game looking for food, or they may simply have taken the same route because the game followed the easiest route from one place to another. Either way, over time, traces became trails.

Trails tell us where people have gone before. By that definition, our national historic trails are, indeed, trails: a conglomeration of traces and sites and paths and remnants and ruins. Some of them trace back to the earliest indigenous people and the dawn of human history in the United States, and some trace even farther back, to the trails of wild elk, the migration paths of birds on continental journeys, the beaten-down tracks of migrating buffalo. We humans often continue using these trails because we agree with our forebears that the paths they used yesterday are still the best way to cross the land today. Sometimes the routes of our national historic trails are so logical that we put roads on them, or railroads, or interstate highways. I-80 follows part of the Oregon Trail through Nebraska; I-25 follows the Tierra Adentro route up the Rio Grande from El Paso, Texas, to Santa Fe, New Mexico. As a result, in some places, evidence of the past is hard to discern amid the bustle of modern cities, agriculture, and traffic jams. But elsewhere on our national historic trails, the land remains very much the same, with miles of dirt roads uninterrupted by houses, farms, cultivation, electric lines, railroads, or other signs of modern civilization.

Another assumption we make is that trails are strictly linear, connecting one place with another. But most of the national historic trails do not go from point A to point B. Instead, they are networks of trunk trails and high-water routes; spring, summer, fall, and winter routes; shortcuts and alternates that peel off to different destinations.

Unlike a path that tells people where to go, the historic trails reflect where people actually went, whether by plan or by accident or as a result of circumstances. Those trails changed over time, as new needs required new routes, or when better alternates were discovered. Was the water in the Platte River so high one year that a new crossing needed to be found? Did one group of emigrants want to avoid contact with another group? Did a party traveling early in the summer get word that low snow levels that year made a mountain shortcut possible? Was there unrest with American Indians along part of the way? Was a new goldfield discovered, necessitating a new branch at the end of the line? Each of these questions created the possibility of new trails.

As a result, a map of our national historic trails looks as if a stand of trees fell on top of each other. Some of these trees are just trunks, but others have branches and twigs. Some are lying on top of each other, pointed in various directions. Some of them intersect, some run contiguously or parallel for a while, and some are completely isolated.

Another key element of our national historic trails: they were used by trappers, wagoneers, horsemen, sailors, paddlers, walkers, soldiers, and dogsledders, and they sprawled across land and water, over mountains, across plains and deserts, over subtropical lava, and through fields of snow. As such, they represent the enormous panoply of American landscapes, and they embody the idea of multiple use. These trails are not solely for long-distance walkers, or for motorists, or for sailors, or for family travelers; they are for everyone. Sections of the national historic trails can be driven, hiked, paddled, sailed, or experienced on bicycles, horseback, dogsleds, snowshoes, or cross-country skis. All of them offer historic sites: museums, interpretive displays, living history, markers, and visitor centers. In some cases, the lands through which they pass are managed by the National Park Service, the Bureau of Land Management, or the Forest Service, as well as state and local agencies. Many of the sites are managed as cooperative partnerships between federal government agencies, private foundations, museums, and associations of history buffs.

The 19 trails vary immensely. The shortest is 54 miles long, running in one continuous straight line from start to finish. The longest contains more than 5,000 miles of sprawling interconnecting networks

and alternates. The terrain they cover includes virtually every kind of environment and ecosystem in the United States today, from Hawaiian lava fields to Alaskan tundra to the Rocky Mountains to eastern forests to the Great Plains to southwestern deserts.

On some trails it is possible for visitors to become fully immersed in the history. Every five years, for example, Jubilee participants can join the commemorative Voting Rights March from Selma to Montgomery, Alabama. Every fall, a two-week reenactment hike commemorates the Revolutionary War soldiers who hiked from Virginia to Kings Mountain in South Carolina, where one of the most important and least known battles of the American Revolution took place. A Pony Express re-ride of the entire route from St. Joseph, Missouri, to Sacramento, California, takes place annually. At other sites, living history reenactments teach everything from how to cook over a pioneer fire made of buffalo chips to how to shoot a musket, make candles, pull a handcart, or pack a wagon for a 2,000-mile journey. Through the National Park Service's Passport to Your National Parks program—available at visitor centers, living history exhibits, museums, and other historic sites—visitors can keep track of the trails and sites they have visited.

The first four parts of this book cover the 19 trails that Congress has certified as national historic trails. Part One features four trails that follow the routes of Spanish conquest, settlement, and trade in what is now the American Southwest. Four trails in Part Two commemorate historic events on the East Coast from Captain John Smith's 1607–1609 explorations of the Chesapeake Bay through the American Revolution to the end of the War of 1812. Part Three considers Manifest Destiny and America's westward expansion, with seven trails covering the 1803–1806 Lewis and Clark Expedition to explore the Louisiana Territory and possible routes to the Pacific, the great westward migrations of the mid-19th century, and the ancient Native Alaskan routes of travel that allowed American settlers into the Alaskan interior. Four trails in Part Four reflect on American diversity: the stories of Hawai'i's original Polynesian settlers, the forced removal of Cherokee and Nez Perce people from their original homelands, and the civil rights movement.

PREVIOUS SPREAD: Mammoth Hot Springs, Nez Perce Trail, Yellowstone National Park, Wyoming

Fusiliers Redoubt, Washington-Rochambeau Revolutionary Route Trail, Yorktown Battlefield, Colonial National Historical Park, Virginia

As diverse as this collection of trails is, it offers a still-incomplete picture of American history. New trails periodically enter the system, and other trails across the country—managed by trail and history associations as well as local, state, and federal agencies—also honor and interpret important historical events. Part Five considers some of the other trails that commemorate parts of American history that the system of national historic trails has not yet included, among them the American Civil War, the suffrage movement, and the Underground Railroad.

Taken as a group, the national historic trails—and other history-focused trails—are pathways of the imagination. Each trail carries its own stories: some are about excitement and the glory of adventure, of goals set and achieved, or of empire building; and some are mementoes of tragedies and struggle and national wounds that have yet to heal. Most visitors will not walk any of these trails in their entirety. But we can interact with the land as it is now and consider how our forebears interacted with it back in the days of once upon a time—before we had GPS to tell us which way to go, before automobiles and trains and powerboats could carry us there, before towns and interstate rest stops allowed us to resupply.

Today, when we visit the national historic trails—whether to hike or drive or visit a museum or watch a living history display—we may be motivated by a desire for adventure, fun, relaxation, connection with nature, escape, fitness, meditation, healing, or a score of other reasons. Our forebears passed through these lands for as many different reasons: for freedom, for a king, for God, for a protest, for economic opportunity, for adventure, for war. We all have our reasons, both then and now. The national historic trails give us points of intersection across time and distance—a way to connect ourselves to those who came before through our common humanity and our experience of the land.

Monument Valley Tribal Park,
Trail of the Ancients, Arizona-
Utah border

PART ONE

SPANISH SOUTHWEST

In 1976, a famous *New Yorker* cover by Saul Steinberg lampooned Manhattanites. "The View from Ninth Avenue" bustled with shops, traffic, and all the necessities and pleasures of life; the world—or, at least, the relevant world—ended at the Hudson River. Behind it, New Jersey shrank to a thin strip of brown nothing; the rest of the United States was pictured as a flat emptiness occasionally interrupted by a highlight like a mountain range shrunk to the size of an afterthought. Steinberg's New Yorkers were portrayed as being every bit as provincial as anyone who had spent their whole life never leaving the boundaries of a backwater village. • It's all a matter of perspective. Had that map been drawn by a Spaniard in the North America of the 1500s, it would have been centered around Mexico City. From a European

perspective, there was nothing much else to see. Certainly not New York: the Dutch were decades away from bringing trading trinkets to the island whose trees would one day be replaced by skyscrapers. The forebears of the Pilgrims were still wandering Calvinist Europe, hoping to find safe haven on their native side of the Atlantic. And it would be several more generations before the English set foot on the swampy landing of the James River that would become the British toehold in Virginia.

But in Mexico City, our cartographer would find a European worldview as bustling and self-contained as the Ninth Avenue of 1976, complete with imperial ambitions, Christian missionaries, old-world traditions, and coins embossed with pictures of kings and queens. Hernán Cortés had built his new Spanish capital in the ruins of Tenochtitlan, the former capital of Aztec Mexico, at the time already 200 years old. As the commercial, religious, political, and social hub of New Spain, Mexico City would have given our cartographer a lot to draw: the Metropolitan Cathedral,

the Palace of the Archbishop, the Royal and Pontifical University of Mexico, and any number of convents and churches. Perhaps, if culturally inquisitive, our mapmaker would include the Pyramids of the Sun and Moon at ancient Teotihuacan.

But looking toward the outposts of El Norte—the lands to the north—the map would have looked a lot like Steinberg's Midwest and West: empty plains interrupted by a jagged peak, or, perhaps in this case, a lonely mission settlement. As for what would become Texas, New Mexico, Arizona, California, and points north, that was unexplored wilderness, a wash of brown interrupted only by the occasional blue thread of a wispy river. This land of creosote, mesquite, and prickly pear cactus was suited for rattlesnakes, Gila monsters, and lizards, but people? The fictional map would have ended long before crossing the Rio Grande. Warnings from medieval mapmakers might apply: "Here there be monsters."

But monsters did not deter the Spaniards for long. Unlike our provincial Manhattanites, the Spanish settlers did cast a curious eye to the far horizon: their goals were territorial expansion, gold, and converting souls to the Catholic God. Sometimes following ancient American Indian trading routes, sometimes creating their own, they headed outward from Mexico City on a series of roads to their farthest-flung hinterlands, bound for conquering, colonizing, and converting whatever and whomever they found.

With colonization, possession is nine-tenths of the law. It is not enough to plant a flag and make a declaration. The Spaniards may have been the first Europeans to try to colonize the Americas, but as time passed, their claims needed to be bolstered against Johnny-come-lately rivals like the English on the East Coast, the French in Louisiana, and later even the Russians, who would claim Alaska and make forays into Northern California. Colonization required a presence, and a presence required government, defense, and control. At the heart of the Spanish colonial system was a trail of missions and presidios that stretched outward from Mexico City. The national historic trails that commemorate the Spanish exploration and colonization of the Southwest are centered around this system.

PREVIOUS SPREAD: La Cieneguilla Petroglyphs, El Camino Real de Tierra Adentro, New Mexico

BELOW: Horned lizard, Old Spanish Trail, Nevada

OPPOSITE: Old Spanish Trail descending Virgin Hill and Mormon Mesa, Nevada

The Spaniards employed a three-pronged strategy as they moved across the continent. First, they subdued resistance using persuasion when possible, force if necessary, and presidios to maintain and defend their presence. Second, Spanish missionaries took on the job of converting the native population and educating them in the ways of Spanish civilization, which included working as laborers and farmers. And finally, Spanish settlers and their families were lured to regions that needed to be settled with promises of land, payment, a starting stake of livestock and tools, and improved social status.

Each settlement was intended to be self-sufficient. A civilian government had jurisdiction, administered by representatives of the king and backed up by soldiers. The result was a system that could control the local population and defend the settlements. Transportation routes enabled further exploration, new settlements, the exploitation of silver and gold, and trading in everything from livestock to fabrics, leather, tools, and luxuries.

Four national historic trails recognize different aspects of the settlement of New Spain, Mexico, and the region that eventually became the American Southwest. Starting from Mexico City, three roads headed north to cross into what is now Arizona, New Mexico, and Texas. From there, the routes continued on to San Francisco, Santa Fe, and Louisiana's Red River Valley. A fourth road connected Santa Fe with the Pacific coast.

The history of the American Southwest is a history of American Indians, Spaniards, Mexicans, and Anglos coming together, coming apart, fighting, compromising, and ultimately forming a distinct cultural collision zone, its mixed heritage reflected in cuisine, celebrations, languages, vocabulary, music, and arts. The national historic trails commemorate the routes that enabled commerce, intermarriage, and hundreds of years of both conflict and coexistence. The result is a vibrant region that is part cultural mosaic, part melting pot—and entirely unique.

Presidio La Bahia, El Camino
Real de los Tejas, Texas

El Camino Real de Tierra Adentro Trail

The name is a mouthful: El Camino Real de Tierra Adentro. Starting from Mexico City in the mid-16th century, the Royal Road of the Interior Land (the name in English) began by reaching northward some 1,600 miles to New Spain's far northern hinterlands in modern-day Chihuahua in Mexico. It is the oldest European trade route in North America.

In 1598, conquistador Juan de Oñate made this first northern camino even longer, extending it another 400 miles by crossing the Rio Grande near El Paso del Norte—today's El Paso, Texas—and then continuing toward what is now northern New Mexico. The trail has an international component: the US section is 404 miles long, but the approximately 1,200-mile-long segment from El Paso to Mexico City is also recognized as a historic trail in Mexico.

Oñate's initial friendly encounters with local Pueblo people led to an invitation for Spanish settlers to use Ohkay Owingeh (renamed by the settlers as San Juan do los Caballeros) as their first capital of the new Spanish province of Nuevo México. The Spanish colony then moved to San Gabriel before moving again in 1610 to nearby La Villa Real de la Santa Fé: the Royal City of the Holy Faith. The camino thus connected the colonial capital of New Spain with the provincial capital of New Mexico. From 1598, when the route from El Paso to northern New Mexico was first established by the Spanish expedition, to 1880, when the railroads made it obsolete, this camino functioned as a precursor to an interstate highway, carrying supplies, mail, and political news in convoys of mule-drawn wagons. Humans traveled the trail in both directions: newly assigned priests, officials, and settlers headed outbound from Mexico City while retiring officers, traders, and prisoners traveled south to meet their reward—or their punishment.

The challenges of the trail were unpredictable, and changed with the era. Comanche, Apache, Navajo, and Ute warriors sometimes accepted the caravans, but sometimes attacked them, depending on alliances, misalliances, and the vagaries of politics. And the land itself could be a formidable enemy. In New Mexico, water was scarce, so, like the Pueblo people who had created paths for trade and communication, the Oñate Expedition hugged the Rio Grande Valley. Even so, several days past El Paso, travelers faced a Scylla-versus-Charybdis dilemma worthy of Odysseus: a section of the river had water, but was impassable for livestock and wagons. The alternate was a 90-mile waterless shortcut known as the Jornada del Muerto—the Journey of the Dead Man—described by Gaspar Pérez de Villagrá in his epic poem "Historia de la Nueva México" in 1610:

> Four complete days did pass away
> In which we drank no drop of water there,
> And now the horses, being blind,
> Did give themselves most cruel blows
> And bumps against the unseen trees,
> And we, as tired as they,
> Exhaling living fire and spitting forth
> Saliva more viscous than pitch,
> Our hope given up, entirely lost,
> Were almost all wishing for death.

As difficult as the journey was, the path that worked best then still offers the best course for travel

Summerford Mountain,
Jornada del Muerto,
New Mexico

Ohkay Owingeh

Los Alamos

25

⭐ SANTA FE

Gallup

40

40

Albuquerque

40

NEW MEXICO

Bosque

Fort Sumner

Lordsburg

Las Cruces

10

EL CAMINO REAL DE TIERRA ADENTRO

NATIONAL HISTORIC TRAIL

El Paso

N

Socorro

0   50 Miles

MEXICO   TEXAS

10

20

today: I-25 roughly follows the route of the historic camino. (For modern travelers, today's interstate has the benefit of modern technology and bridges—it follows the river.)

The national historic trail offers several opportunities for visitors to hike on and experience sections of the old camino, including sections that overlook the Jornada del Muerto. Of course, to truly experience the land as the Spanish settlers and colonists would have, you need to turn off the air-conditioning. Better yet, start to walk on a dirt road. Drink only from natural water sources, when and if you can find them. (By the way, you will need a filter for that water, and a backup plan in case the water source is dry.) A few miles on a waterless dirt road under the full sun of day should do the trick. Now, multiply your miles until you reach 1,455—the distance between Santa Fe and Mexico City.

There were no highway convenience stores back then, of course, but as the trail developed, so did a system of *parajes*, or rest stops. Spaced every 10 to 20 miles along El Camino Real de Tierra Adentro, these shelters and campsites offered safe places to break from the rigors of the journey, and sometimes to resupply. Visitors to the Jornada del Muerto today might imagine the difficulty of passing through this land in a season when the ephemeral springs, seeps, and puddles were dry—and then imagine the relief and gratitude a traveler would feel upon reaching dependable refreshment at either end.

Another difference between today's travelers and the colonists: the settlers needed to bring supplies not only for the journey, but also enough left over to give them a stake until they could start planting, harvesting, breeding, or trading for their own food in their new homes. So Spanish caravans of soldiers, missionaries, and colonists did not travel lightly. Instead, they lumbered north, slowed by cargo and livestock: cattle, sheep, and goats for meat; oxen, mules, and horses to carry rice and beans, vegetables, salt, and spices.

Caravans were infrequent—at first, only once every few years—but they increased over time to trade with and help sustain the remote missions. Unfortunately, as Spanish presence increased, the initial friendly relations with American Indians deteriorated. The camino came to represent two opposite

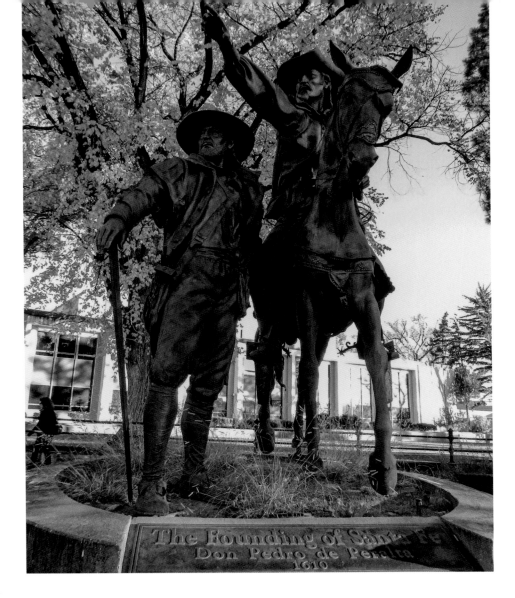

ideas to the Spanish settlers and the indigenous population. For the settlers, the camino was a lifeline to Mexico City, which represented their cultural and religious traditions and the idea of European heritage. But for the Pueblo people, the camino became something else entirely. It was not a route that enabled productive interaction between two equal peoples, but rather a mechanism by which the Spaniards imposed colonization, servitude, and disease. Relations soured into simmering resentment until, finally, tensions exploded. In 1680, a Pueblo uprising drove the Spanish settlers south to El Paso. It was 12 years before they returned, once again using the camino, and reclaimed New Mexico and their capital at Santa Fe.

Sculpture of Don Pedro de Peralta, Santa Fe, New Mexico

For the next 150 years, the camino continued as it began: as a communications and trade route in service of the Spanish crown. When Mexico won its independence from Spain in 1821, the route expanded in importance, becoming part of a burgeoning network of new trade routes that connected Mexico City to Los Angeles and St. Louis. In 1848, when the Southwest was ceded to the United States, the nature and uses of the route changed yet again: it became an international highway between the United States and points south in Mexico. Finally, in 1878, another change came that the camino could not survive: the railroad reached Santa Fe, and the era of the wagon train ended. Boxcars could hold much more cargo than mules and oxen had once hauled in wagons or on their backs. Trains were not only faster for travelers, but also more comfortable. Unused and eroded, the camino sank back into the landscape.

But as the national historic trails show us time after time, good transportation corridors transcend technology. The railroads may have surpassed the wagon trains, but as the era of the automobile began, transportation changed yet again. In 1905, New Mexico Highway 1, the territory's first modern highway, was built roughly along the old route of the camino. Eventually, I-25 followed the same north-south swath through the center of the state. And in 2006, the New Mexico Rail Runner began following the Rio Grande route through central New Mexico to the state capital.

The establishment of the camino as a national historic trail recognizes the multicultural history of a trail that has had hundreds of years of impact. Sometimes recognition of this history is fraught with controversy. For example, the Entrada, an annual pageant that dramatized the Spanish conquistadors reclaiming Santa Fe from the Pueblo people, has recently been discontinued. Revered by the local Hispanic population as part of their history, it was reviled by many indigenous tribes as a symbol of colonialism. At the same time, many New Mexicans today are descendants of some combination of people who arrived or traded using the camino. The national historic trail commemorates these multiple associations with sites interpreting the ongoing history of the Pueblo, Spanish, Mexican, and American people who used the route. It is a living trail that invites the visitor to find a path through the state's historic, cultural, and natural landscapes.

THE ROUTE

El Camino Real de Tierra Adentro National Historic Trail retraces the 404 miles of the royal road that are in the United States, from El Paso, Texas, to Santa Fe, New Mexico. Mexico's portion of the camino is similarly recognized as a cultural route for its role in promoting trade and cultural exchange among Spaniards and other Europeans and American Indians.

Heading north from El Paso, the trail leaves the cityscape behind; the horizon retreats and the sky expands. New Mexico's I-25 roughly follows the old royal road route up the Rio Grande Valley, passing Las Cruces, Engle, Socorro, Albuquerque, and, finally, Santa Fe—though the interstate skips the Journey of the Dead Man shortcut in favor of hugging the banks of the Rio Grande.

A trip on the side roads paralleling the interstate offers the visitor a chance to explore the traces and trail sites that remain and imagine what it might have been like to traverse this inhospitable land before cities and interstates. Long stretches of highway—paved now, instead of packed dirt—pass through rural rangelands covered with creosote and mesquite. Stark sky-island mountain ranges thrust into the sky, and sere plains spread like a prickly sage-gray blanket to the horizon. For a moment, the visitor can escape the development of modern life. Squinting into the distance at a mountain peak 60 or more miles away, it is possible to imagine what it might have been like to know that the distance between here and there must be covered on foot, one step at a time.

Some of the traces—wagon ruts, earthen swales, and gravestones—found on the route of El Camino Real de Tierra Adentro Trail predate both Jamestown and Plymouth Rock. Towns on the route contain centuries-old churches, plazas, and military forts. Also included on the trail are archaeological sites and natural landmarks that told the initial users of the trail how far they had come and how far they had yet to go. Finally, some of the American Indian pueblos that were established along the Rio Grande are still thriving today.

Dry riverbed of Santa Fe River near Agua Fria, New Mexico

FOLLOWING SPREAD:
St. Augustine Church, Isleta Pueblo, New Mexico (top left); Tome Jail, Tome, New Mexico (middle left); Flooded Rio Grande near Belen, New Mexico (bottom left); Descending from La Bajada Mesa along a remnant of Old Route 66, New Mexico (right)

OPPOSITE: View from Old
Highway 85 near Truth or
Consequences, New Mexico

RIGHT: Fort Craig Historic
Site ruins, New Mexico
(top); Socorro Mission-La
Purisima Catholic Church and
Cemetery, Socorro, Texas
(bottom)

LIVING THE HISTORY

Commemorating the old trade and mission route, El Camino Real de Tierra Adentro National Historic Trail features museums, visitor centers, churches, and missions with exhibits and living history displays that celebrate the region's rich multicultural heritage. Many towns on the route retain the character and distinct southwestern architectural style of their Spanish roots. Marked hiking trails on the camino itself as well as trails on adjacent lands give visitors a chance to experience how the land feels underfoot, often in protected areas where the terrain and ecology are similar to what early travelers might have seen. The national historic trail has more than 20 Passport to Your National Parks sites.

El Paso Museum of History, El Paso, Texas

Established in 1974 as the Cavalry Museum, the El Paso Museum of History soon expanded to include all aspects of local history. "The Pass of the North," on the US side of the Rio Grande, and Ciudud Juárez, its sister city on the Mexican side of the river, share a rich 400-year multicultural history, as well as a geographical position of regional importance, as gateways between Mexico and the United States. The museum includes exhibits on the camino and its role in the development of settlements on the northern frontiers of New Spain.

New Mexico Farm and Ranch Heritage Museum, Las Cruces, New Mexico

Ranching and farming were key elements in the Spanish colonial period. The missions were expected to be self-sufficient, raising enough vegetables, legumes, and grain to sustain themselves in the long periods between caravans on the royal road. The museum covers 4,000 years of agriculture and animal husbandry in New Mexico, with permanent exhibits that interpret New Mexico's tricultural history from the earliest American Indian settlements to colonial period homesteads to the modern era, during which New Mexico moved from Spanish to Mexican to American control. The museum and its outdoor exhibits cover 47 acres, including a sheep and goat barn that is a favorite for

families. In addition to the permanent exhibits that show how farms, ranches, and homes were built and managed, and how transportation connected communities, an array of programs, classes, lectures, and demonstrations give visitors an up-close look at different aspects of New Mexican history, crafts, and arts.

Organ Mountains, Las Cruces, New Mexico

Framing Las Cruces and nearby Mesilla, the Organ Mountains provide a scenic backdrop that would have been one of the most dramatic landscapes travelers encountered as they entered what is now southern New Mexico. The Organ Mountains were first documented in 1598 on Oñate's first expedition on what would become the Camino Real. Local landmarks include Paraje Robledo and Robledo Peak, named for Pedro Robledo, who drowned on that first expedition beneath his eponymous peak. The Organ Mountains-Desert Peaks National Monument was added to the National Park System in 2014. A network of hiking trails gives views of the route the camino took through southern New Mexico.

Mesilla Plaza, Mesilla, New Mexico

The now-sleepy town of Mesilla began its life in 1848 when the Treaty of Guadalupe Hidalgo ceded most of New Mexico to the United States. Disgruntled by their new status as Americans, some residents of Doña Ana decided to move to

the other side of the border. But to no avail: the Gadsden Purchase, an American land-purchase agreement with Mexico ratified in 1854, moved the border once more and Mesilla's Mexican residents again found themselves living on American soil. Developing around a central plaza, and protected by the army from Apache attacks, Mesilla became an important military supply center, a trade hub on El Camino Real, and a stop on the Butterfield Overland Mail Route. Mesilla was the biggest city between San Diego and San Antonio, known for its trade, its political influence, and its rowdiness. But in 1881 the Santa Fe Railroad bypassed it. Mesilla lost its hustle and bustle, but not its sense of history. Today, the town plaza is a national historic landmark, with adobe structures, shops featuring traditional New Mexican crafts and jewelry, residential buildings, and restaurants and hotels that hark back to the glory days of the 1860s.

El Cerro de Tomé (Tomé Hill), near Isleta Pueblo, New Mexico

This conical basalt hill was an important geologic feature and natural landmark along El Camino Real de Tierra Adentro. The summit offers views of the Rio Grande Valley. Petroglyphs, a cross on the summit, and a stone shrine attest to the site's history as a spiritual landmark for indigenous people and, later, for the Spanish settlers. Today, the hill hosts a Good Friday pilgrimage and is a year-round destination for recreation and meditation. A small park at the base of the hill features *La Puerta del Sol*, a sculpture by Armando Alvarez that commemorates the camino's role in the settling of the Southwest.

Jornada del Muerto, near Truth or Consequences, New Mexico

Two trails offer hikers a chance to experience some of the challenges of the infamous desert section called the Jornada del Muerto. The 3.8-mile Yost Draw is one of the best-preserved sections of the original camino, with clearly defined pathways and cobblestone ramps that have been etched into the ground over hundreds of years of caravan traffic. The Yost Escarpment Trail is a 1.5-mile interpretive trail that illustrates the challenges of travel through this region. The trail leads to the escarpment edge, with views of the deep arroyos, the varying vegetation, and the route of the camino as it continues north. It is hard to imagine what 16th-century explorers might have made of New Mexico's most recent contribution to the world of transportation: Spaceport America, which is primed to open for commercial space travel, is also visible from the escarpment. Also in this part of the Jornada del Muerto is the short Point of Rocks Trail, a half-mile loop trail to a distinctive basalt outcropping that told southbound camino travelers that water was only 10 more miles away.

Albuquerque Museum, Albuquerque, New Mexico

Located adjacent to Albuquerque's Old Town, this museum focuses on southwestern art and history in general and New Mexico in particular, with exhibits of arms and armor, Hispanic crafts, maps, colonial furnishings, Victorian-era items, decorative arts, and textiles. Exhibits examine the early Spanish settlements, the establishment of the camino, the Pueblo Revolt of 1680, early Hispanic life, the Civil War in New Mexico, the founding of Albuquerque in 1706, the Mexican period, and current American statehood.

Top: Crosses atop El Cerro de Tomé, New Mexico;
Bottom: Sculpture commemorating El Camino Real de Tierra Adentro, base of El Cerro de Tomé, New Mexico

demonstrate how life was lived in the Spanish colonial period; living history festivals and themed weekends bring the period to life with a program of music and dance. One of the highlights is the nearly 50-year-old fall harvest festival that takes place the first weekend of October. Near El Rancho de las Golondrinas, Cieneguilla Recreation Area offers several hiking opportunities, including a short trail to a collection of petroglyphs.

Palace of the Governors, Santa Fe, New Mexico

Built in 1610 on what was to become the main plaza of Santa Fe, the adobe Palace of the Governors is one of the oldest and best-preserved buildings along the camino. Constructed as the seat of Spanish power, it was briefly taken over as living space by the Pueblo people after the Pueblo Revolt. After the Spaniards regained control of Santa Fe, the palace was used as the seat of government for the next 300 years under Spanish, Mexican, and, finally, American rule. Today it serves as a museum that houses an extensive collection of arts, artifacts, photographs, and documents from New Mexico's American Indian, Spanish, Mexican, and Anglo cultures. Outside, the building's shaded portal is used by American Indian artisans to sell handmade jewelry, pottery, and fabrics. Three national historic trails come together here to mark the epicenter of a trade network that linked Santa Fe with Mexico City, San Francisco, and the American heartland via St. Louis.

Museum of Spanish Colonial Art, Santa Fe, New Mexico

This is the only museum in the United States that features the art of the Hispanic Southwest, from colonial-era portraits to contemporary art. The Pueblo Revival–style building contains almost 34,000 works of art, many of which were brought to Santa Fe in a wagon traveling over one of the national historic trails that converged in the town's main plaza.

Coronado Historic Site, Bernalillo, New Mexico

As is true of so many of the national historic trails, the travel routes of settlers and traders on the camino followed long-established paths used by indigenous people, in this case, by Pueblo people who settled in the Rio Grande Valley. In the fall of 1540, a party led by Spanish explorer Francisco Vásquez de Coronado came through here on a quest to survey the region and find the rumored gold-filled Seven Cities of Cibola. While hopes for fortunes in gold were dashed, the Spanish settlers did find the Tiwa pueblo of Kuaua, which had been settled since around AD 1300. At the time one of the largest Pueblo settlements, the earthen pueblos have been excavated and reconstructed as an education site with a museum and visitor center displaying prehistoric and historic American Indian and Spanish colonial artifacts. Also on display are murals found during the excavation, considered to be some of the most important pre-Columbian art in the United States. Reproductions of the murals were also painted on the reconstructed interiors of the kivas to give visitors a sense of what the art would have looked like in its original setting.

El Rancho de las Golondrinas, La Cienega, New Mexico

Just 15 miles south of Santa Fe, El Rancho de las Golondrinas—the Ranch of the Swallows—was an important *paraje* along the camino. Starting in the early 1700s, this stopping place offered respite to travelers who had just completed traversing the Bajada, a steep escarpment with 23 hairpin turns that was one of the major obstacles on the way to Santa Fe. Located on 200 acres in a rural valley, this museum explores the history, heritage, and culture of Spanish colonial New Mexico. Some of its buildings are constructed on original colonial foundations that date from the early 1700s. Others have been relocated and reconstructed from other parts of northern New Mexico. A combination of permanent exhibits and costumed interpreters

Above: El Rancho de las Golondrinas, a living history museum, New Mexico; *Opposite:* Ladder extending from kiva of Kuaua Pueblo, Coronado Historic Site, New Mexico

El Camino Real de los Tejas Trail

2,580 MILES ➤ TEXAS · LOUISIANA

In 1519, Spanish explorers became the first Europeans to map what we now call the Texas Gulf Coast, but it was several years before Spaniards explored the Texas interior. Despite these early explorations, it was a long time—about 160 years—before the Spaniards established a permanent presence in present-day Texas and Louisiana. The English were still nearly 100 years from exploring the Chesapeake Bay; the French were not yet ensconced in Louisiana or Canada; and it would be centuries before the Russians identified themselves as a European power or claimed any part of Alaska.

Busy mining silver, converting American Indians, establishing missions elsewhere—and lacking competition—Spain had neglected its northern territory. The region they called Los Tejas thus lay peacefully ignored until 1685, when a French seaman trying to find the mouth of the Mississippi River overshot his target and landed, by mistake, on the Texas coast.

Word got back to the Spanish government that the French were trying to establish a colony somewhere in Texas. The Spaniards sent expeditions to put things right. It took a few years and several forays, but finally the remains of the French fort were found. It had been destroyed by American Indians, and the French had been killed or hounded out of Texas. And now, realizing there were competing European interests on the continent, the Spaniards put their usual strategy into place. If Texas was their northern frontier, it had to be settled, converted, and defended as such.

The Spanish government did what had worked elsewhere in the Americas: it sent in priests to establish a mission. After a few setbacks—the first missionaries were rejected by American Indians—they retreated, then returned, refining their route of travel, building missions in other places, and following their proven process of settling, converting, and defending. By the early 1700s, they had a bulwark against the English and French, who were by now also firmly entrenched in North America. The Spanish province of Los Tejas had taken its rightful place as the northeast border province of New Spain. El Camino Real de los Tejas was the lifeline that connected southwest Texas (and from there, routes south to Mexico City) to Los Adaes (the province's new capital) and the contested eastern border with French Louisiana.

Despite its royal name, in many places the camino was little more than a track for horses, pack mules, and other animals. But its royal status was uncontested. It connected towns, provincial capitals, presidios, missions, and important economic sites such as mines. The *camino real* designation not only conveyed its importance, but also signified protection for these main arteries for the business of the crown—no matter how pitted, rugged, and primitive.

The Texas camino had the same challenges as all the southwestern caminos: unpredictable receptions from the local inhabitants, a rutted rough track, fierce winds and baking summer heat, and a lack of water. Southern Texas had only a few large rivers (which posed their own difficulties when crossed by wagons). Even more challenging were the long waterless stretches. Names such as *agua verde* (green water), *arroyo seco* (dry creek), and *las lagunillas de mala agua* (ponds of bad water) clearly communicate the settlers' concerns about water—and the agony of non-potable water or no water—across the centuries.

Reconstructed replica of Fort St. Jean Baptiste, Natchitoches, Louisiana

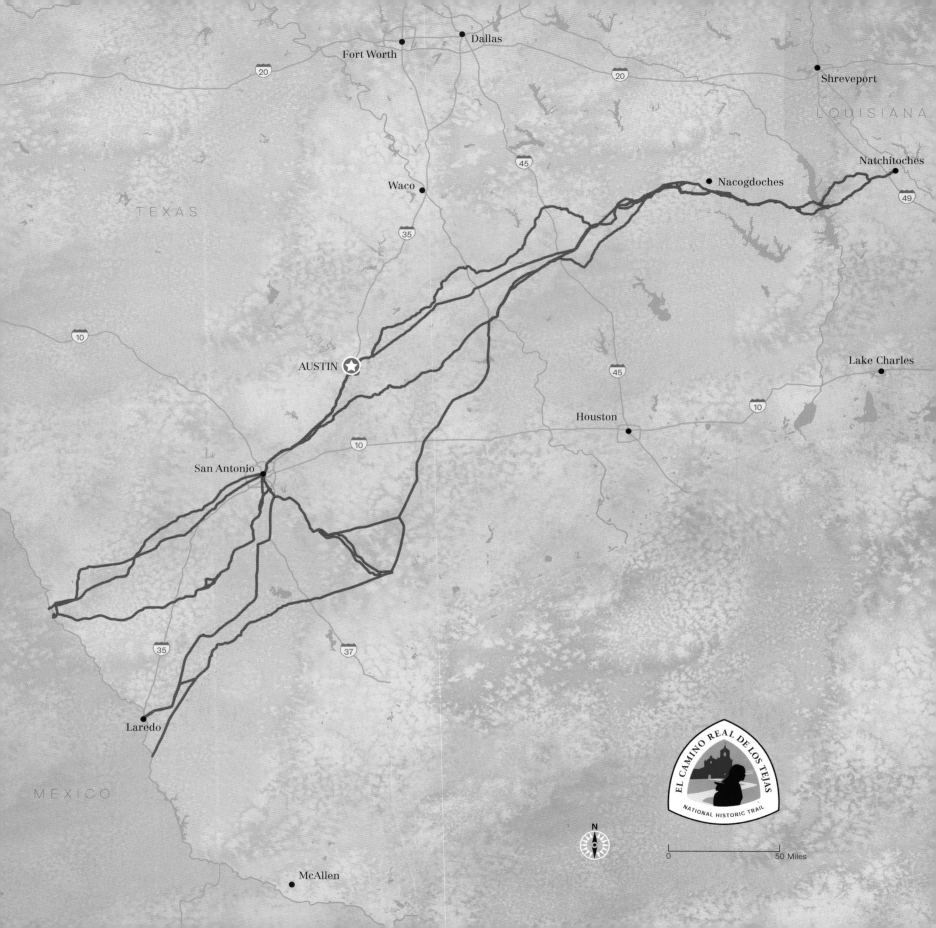

Fort Worth

Dallas

Shreveport

LOUISIANA

20

20

Natchitoches

45

Nacogdoches

49

Waco

TEXAS

35

10

Lake Charles

AUSTIN ✪

45

10

Houston

10

San Antonio

10

35

37

MEXICO

Laredo

EL CAMINO REAL DE LOS TEJAS

NATIONAL HISTORIC TRAIL

McAllen

N

0   50 Miles

In one important way, the Tejas camino was different than its sister royal road to Santa Fe. El Camino Real de Tierra Adentro enabled trade only between Mexico City and its far northern outposts, where the road terminated. The Spanish Texas royal road extended east beyond the northern boundary of present-day Texas to its provincial capital of Los Adaes, thus connecting the Spanish missions with French Louisiana, which had been settled by French and mixed-race Louisiana Creole people before 1800. As a result, traffic and trade reached all the way to Natchitoches in the Red River Valley of present-day Louisiana. Despite Spanish trade and immigration regulations and the route's challenges, the trail—which had been traveled by indigenous people long before European settlement—connected Spanish, American Indian, Mexican, French, Creole, African American, and Anglo-American peoples. And it enabled European culture, influence, trade, and religion to spread.

New Spain's stringent trade restrictions, however, limited who could trade what. The caminos were designed to benefit the mother country and the crown: the people settling the missions were expected to be self-sufficient, and the needs of the native population were not always considered (beyond their perceived need for Catholic salvation). Commerce with American Indian tribes was prohibited, and Anglos were not welcome to immigrate south into Texas.

But after 1821, when Mexico gained independence from Spain, Spanish restrictions on trade and immigration were relaxed. Mexico welcomed new immigrants and installed a much less restrictive trade policy. The camino blossomed into one of the most important trade arteries in the Southwest. Americans flocked to the old camino and south into Texas—which was then still part of Mexico—to seek better opportunities in the lands to the south. The Mexicans would shortly have reason to regret their welcome, as American immigrants ultimately overwhelmed the area and fomented the revolt against Mexico that established Texas first as its own independent republic, and then as an American state.

Texas was booming and the camino could not keep up. As Texas grew into its new American identity, its towns developed beyond the corridors of the

royal road network and the Spanish mission culture. Austin, Galveston, and Houston—not historically on the old camino—became new centers for trade and political influence. As railroads were built to connect these hubs, use of the old camino diminished. Today, modern highways follow the old route, proving—as so many of the national historic trails do—that while conveyances and technology may change, fundamental corridors of travel survive over time, whether used by wildlife, indigenous peoples, settlers in wagons, industrialists on railroads, or truckers on modern superhighways. Although it has been more than a century since wagons and horses covered the route, El Camino Real de los Tejas is not a dusty relic of yesteryear; it has merely adopted the modern form of pavement and lighting to remain a conduit for trade and transport in Texas and into Louisiana.

THE ROUTE

As with many of the Spanish caminos in what is now Mexico and the Southwest, this one needed to provide wagons and traders with navigable passage, manageable river crossings, and enough water for

Outline of the Spanish-controlled Fort Los Adaes, Louisiana

FOLLOWING SPREAD: Lobanillo Swales along El Camino Real de los Tejas, Texas

humans and stock. For centuries, indigenous peoples had been trading between the Great Plains (of today's Midwest) and the Chihuahuan Desert (of today's northern Mexico). El Camino Real de los Tejas followed in these footsteps.

The main line began in present-day Mexico City, staying west of the Sierra Madre Oriental Mountains. Near Guerrero in today's Coahuila in Mexico, the royal road turned northwest to cross into Texas near the Rio Grande. From there—near Laredo, Texas, in the present-day United States—the route quickly evolved into a network, not only to connect different towns and missions, but also to account for changing conditions such as seasonal water availability. Volatile relationships with native populations also forced detours: the Apache, Comanche, and coalitions of other tribes had unpredictable alliances and enmities with each other, as well as changing relationships with the European settlers passing through their lands.

As a result, the approximately 500-mile-long straight-line distance between Guerrero or Laredo in the west and Natchitoches and Los Adaes in the east ballooned into an approximately 2,580-mile network. The sometimes interconnecting, sometimes parallel routes developed a confusing array of names over time: Camino Real de los Tejas, Camino Pita, Camino Arriba (the Upper Presidio Road), Camino de en Medio (the lower Presidio Road), King's Highway, and the San Antonio-Nacogdoches Road or Old San Antonio Road of the mid-19th century. Today's national historic trail is roughly divided into four interconnected segments that represent use during the different time periods: El Camino Real de los Tejas, the Lower Road, the Old San Antonio Road, and the Laredo Road. Beginning at one of three towns on the Rio Grande—Villa de Delores, Laredo, or Guerrero (in Mexico)—the route trends northeast through southern Texas. Most of the routes pass through San Antonio and Nacogdoches, though some detour elsewhere. After crossing the Sabine River (today's border between Louisiana and Texas), the national historic trail continues through western Louisiana (in the time of the camino, it was disputed territory between the French and Spanish Louisiana, inaccurately referred to as the Neutral Strip) before ending at Natchitoches.

LEFT: Ceremonial mound, Caddo Mounds State Historic Site, Texas (top); Mission Tejas State Park, Davy Crockett National Forest, Texas (bottom)

OPPOSITE: Trace of El Camino Real de los Tejas visible in the limestone, McKinney Falls State Park, Texas

FOLLOWING SPREAD: Mission San Antonio de Valero, more commonly known as the Alamo, Texas (left); Arched hallway at Mission Concepción, San Antonio Missions National Historical Park, Texas (middle); Presidio La Bahia, Texas (top right); Mission San Juan Capistrano, San Antonio Missions National Historical Park, Texas (bottom right)

LIVING THE HISTORY

Today's traveler can follow modern-day highways that, long before they were paved, carried wagons and trade goods on the dirt paths that made up the Spanish Texas camino. Texas Highway 21, Texas OSR (the Old San Antonio Road), and Louisiana's Highway 6 roughly follow parts of the historic trail. Roads that today overlay the original camino are marked every 5 miles on the ground with granite markers. Along the way, numerous parks offer chances to hike on the old camino, and a number of original and reconstructed missions are open to the public.

The Republic of the Rio Grande Museum, Laredo, Texas

This museum, the nearby historic La Posada hotel, and the San Agustin Cathedral form a triangle of Laredo's most-visited historic sites. The museum, in a Mexican-style building from the 1830s, re-creates an authentic home from the Mexican period. Once the home of a prominent rancher and mayor, it may have served as a capital for the short-lived Republic of the Rio Grande, one of several revolutionary breakaway movements in the newly independent but troubled Mexican Republic. Laredo is one of the western termini of El Camino Real de los Tejas.

Nuestra Señora del Espíritu Santo de Zuñiga Mission, Goliad, Texas

The Spaniards built this mission in 1749. It became the first major cattle ranch in Texas, important because it supplied food not only for its own residents but also for other missions and settlements in eastern Texas and Louisiana. In 1830, the Franciscan priests closed the mission; 100 years later, it was reconstructed by the Civilian Conservation Corps. Rebuilt to look as it did in the 18th century, it became a state park in 1949. A visitor center is dedicated to the camino. Outdoor activities include fishing, bird-watching, and exploring the landscape on canoeing, kayaking, biking, and hiking trails.

San Antonio Missions National Historical Park and the Alamo, San Antonio, Texas

This river walk takes visitors past six historic Spanish missions. Most of the missions are open to visitors. San Antonio was one of the hubs of the camino in Texas, and most of the trail's alternate routes found their way to this important center. The park's visitor center is located at Mission San José, 5 miles south of downtown. By far the most famous landmark in this area is the Mission San Antonio de Valero, otherwise known as the Alamo. The mission on this site was built in 1724, after having occupied two other locations, and was turned into a secular garrison in 1793. In 1836, the Mexican Army defeated an outnumbered and trapped force of Texans in the Battle of the Alamo. The defeat became a rallying cry for Texan revolutionaries, who won their independence from Mexico later that year—and the Alamo earned its standing as the most mythic landmark in Texas history.

Comanche Lookout, San Antonio, Texas

A prominent landmark for travelers on the royal road, Comanche Lookout had served as a hunting site for indigenous people for at least 10,000 years. The so-called Nacogdoches Road—one route of the camino in the San Antonio region—passed the hill on its way to eastern Texas. During the years of the camino, Apaches and Comanches used the hill as a lookout point from which they could dominate the area, sometimes as hunters and sometimes as wagon train attackers. Today, the park is laced with hiking trails. In addition to the traditional viewpoints, it features a 20th-century fake European-style tower.

Bastrop State Park, Bastrop, Texas

State Highway 21 closely follows one of the routes of the camino. Just off the highway, the sprawling forests of Bastrop State Park contain original swales from the camino. (They are not, however, specifically marked, so ask park staff for help locating them.) The park has hiking and backpacking trails as well as campsites and historic cabins where visitors can stay overnight. Other recreation options include picnicking, golfing, wildlife viewing, and swimming in the pool. Two water trails—one of which is the Camino Real Paddling Trail—offer kayakers and canoeists a chance to explore the region by boat.

Davy Crockett National Forest, near Kennard, Texas

Several miles of the original camino wander through a forest of towering pines in the Davy Crockett National Forest. A diverse ecosystem of deciduous bottomland hardwoods, boggy sloughs, and upland forests offer beautiful fall colors in November and December. The park is divided into several management areas with hiking, backpacking, and horse trails. There is

also a designated wilderness area, giving visitors a glimpse into how the region may have looked when the camino first passed through it.

Caddo Mounds State Historic Site, near Alto, Texas

Prehistoric, American Indian, European, Mexican, and Texan peoples all made their mark on the landscape of the Caddo Mounds, and, sometimes, on each other. The Caddo people selected this site in the Neches River Valley in about AD 800, and, for 500 years, dominated it with their sophisticated ceremonial culture. After about the 13th century, the Caddo appear to have moved toward a less formal social order, although they continued to live here until the 19th century, when pressure and persecution from European American settlement pushed them into Oklahoma. The camino passed by the mounds, known as El Cerrito (the little hill) in the 19th century, then crossed the nearby Neches River just to the north. Trails in the park lead to the

Caddo burial mounds and ceremonial sites, as well as to the camino. A small museum displays precontact artifacts dating from 750 to 1400.

Durst-Taylor Historic House, Nacogdoches, Texas

This 1828 house is another example of Texas as a cultural continuum. Built during the last years of the Mexican period and used in the early years of the Texas Republic, it lies on the foundation of an older Spanish home. But its pier-and-beam foundation and wood framing hail from the Anglo-American architectural styles of the Deep South. It served as the home to a series of businessmen, bankers, and political leaders. Today it is a museum, whose architecture and gardens accurately reflect life in 19th-century Texas.

Cane River National Heritage Area, Natchitoches, Louisiana

Natchitoches is the eastern terminus of El Camino Real de los Tejas. The Cane River

National Heritage Area contains several camino-related museums, interpretive centers, and displays in and around the city, which was founded as a French outpost on the Red River for trade with Spanish-controlled Texas. Fort St. Jean Baptiste State Historic Site was founded to prevent Spanish forces in Texas from advancing east across the border. The fort served as a military outpost under the French, then became a trade center under the Spaniards, who took over the region in 1762. Arrangements can be made here to visit the site of Los Adaes (the original capital of Spanish Texas was located in today's Louisiana). Also in Natchitoches is the Cane River Creole National Historical Park, which contains several plantations that can be visited.

Above, left: Mission Espíritu Santo, Goliad State Park and Historic Site, Texas; *Above, right:* Interior view of Mission Concepción, San Antonio Missions National Historical Park, Texas

Juan Bautista de Anza Trail

1,200 MILES ➤ ARIZONA • CALIFORNIA

They call it the superbloom. In early spring of each year, Southern California's arid plateaus and desert lowlands give way to a profusion of wildflowers as bright and sudden as fireworks. The bloom is a colorful contrast to the usual duns and sages of a land where water is always scarce and life is always hard. Summer days see soaring temperatures, while winter nights drop into single digits. It is precisely because the environment is so challenging that each year—in February or March, no one knows exactly when it will happen—the desert explodes in color. Plants must complete their entire life cycle from shoots to flowers to seeds in a few short weeks, then go dormant to survive the life-sapping temperatures of summer and the bitter cold of a high-desert winter. In some years, snowpack quantity, spring temperatures, and melt-off combine in just the right way, and the deserts and surrounding arid mountains are even more colorful than usual. As with any natural phenomenon, some years, and some places, are better than others. Anza-Borrego Desert State Park is a superbloom showcase.

The superbloom is a lesson in adaptation and survival. The native people who lived here were experts: they understood the vagaries of climate, seasons, and life cycles of the plants and animals. The earliest Europeans to pass this way—Spanish colonists looking for an overland route from central Mexico to Northern California's Pacific coast—had the good sense to solicit the help of the indigenous people. They followed ancient travel routes, which had been developed—like botanical life cycles—in intimate connection with seasonal springs and seeps that could make the difference between life and death.

Today, the journey of these early colonists—who traveled more than 1,000 miles across the Sonoran Desert and the arid mountains and deserts of Southern California to the Pacific coast, then north to what is now San Francisco—is commemorated by the Juan Bautista de Anza National Historic Trail.

The year 1775 was an eventful one in the New World. On the Eastern Seaboard, the Redcoats and Patriots were getting ready to settle the question of American independence. The French had come and gone, having recently lost their claims in Canada to the English, and having ceded the Louisiana Territory to the Spaniards. (They would briefly get it back in 1801 before selling it to the United States in 1803.)

In the meantime, the Spaniards had long since settled New Mexico; claimed Texas and Arizona; started to explore parts of Utah, Colorado, and Nevada; and established a few missions on California's coast. But, though they had had a century-long head start in the Americas, the politics and claims on their northern frontier were changing. In the Pacific Northwest, the British were trading furs and planting flags. In Alaska, the Russians were exploring, trapping, and looking to expand their reach south, perhaps as far as California.

Action begets reaction: with activity building in the Pacific Northwest, the Spaniards needed to protect their northwest hinterlands. A harbor in Northern California would facilitate their cross-Pacific trade in silver and spices. A road would enable them to communicate with and resupply their missions in California. And a defensible settlement and presidio would protect the harbor and their northern border against incursions from the Russians, the British, or anyone else.

Saguaro cacti, Sonoran
Desert National
Monument, Arizona

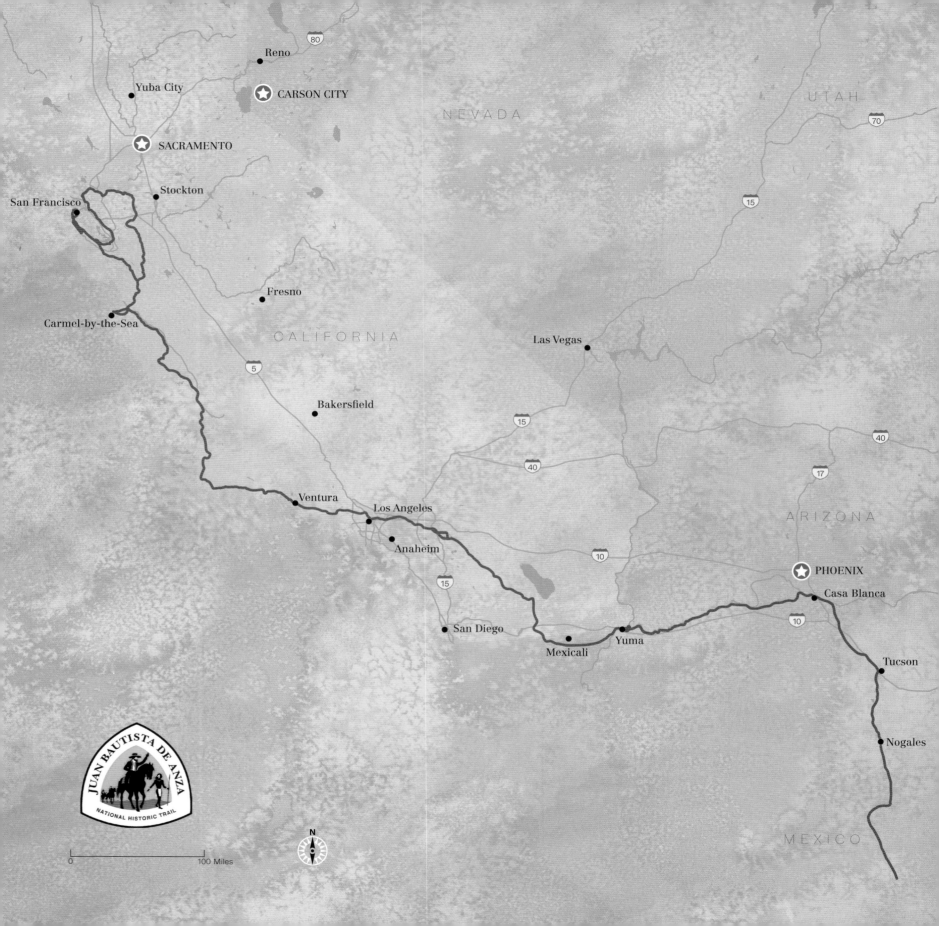

The first hurdle was finding an overland route. A sea route was not promising: Pacific Ocean waters were rough, good harbors were few and far between, and transporting hundreds of cattle (needed to stock the new settlements) on a ship for weeks at a time was even less practical than driving them overland. A land route had its own challenges, including how to transport hundreds of people and all the supplies needed to support them for a 1,000-mile journey through deserts, mountains, canyons, and coastal forests.

In early 1774, Lieutenant Colonel Juan Bautista de Anza, a Basque-descended Criollo (a North American-born Spaniard), applied for the privilege of scouting a route from Nogales, on today's Mexican-American border south of Tucson, Arizona, to New Spain's northernmost mission in Monterey, California. As so often was the case in European explorations of the Americas, Anza was aided by indigenous guides, and the route he identified was based on long-established local travel ways. With success under his belt, Anza was appointed to organize and lead a group of colonists to found a new settlement at a bay north of Monterey in Alta ("high") California.

Anza began recruiting married soldiers with families and other potential settlers in the spring of 1775. Promising rations, salaries, gear, land, and improved social status, he was able to amass a company of traveling colonists—about 30 families totaling approximately 240 people (agreement on the exact number is lost to history). Some of the soldiers returned to Mexico with Anza after delivering the colonists safely; about 190 people stayed to settle in San Francisco. It was a remarkably diverse group: some were Spaniards, some Mexican (at the time defined as people of mixed Spanish and Native Mexican descent), some Afro-Caribbean, and some other combinations of mixed heritages. About 30 percent had African bloodlines. The occupations of the adults included soldiers, clerics, servants, farmers, and blacksmiths. There were also women—eight of them pregnant, four of whom gave birth during the journey—and more than 100 children.

The recruits came from as far away as central Mexico and trekked to the gathering point in San Miguel de Horcasitas (now in Mexico about 175 miles south of the US border). On September 29, 1775, they

departed, heading north, and, about two weeks later, crossed into what is now the United States in Nogales, which is the start of today's 1,200-mile national historic trail. The final shakedown, where the travelers organized wagons, livestock, and supplies, took place at the mission in Tubac, near today's Tucson, Arizona. From there, on October 23, 1775, they struck out into the unknown.

They would have been noticeable: 240 people, some of them walking, some riding horses, sometimes two to a mount. Most of the horses, as well as 200 mules and 28 donkeys, were needed to haul provisions—

Mission San Juan Bautista, California

beans, chili peppers, beef jerky, flour, and corn—sufficient for a five-and-a-half-month journey. About 300 cattle trailed behind; some were destined to become dinner along the way, others to be used to stock the new colony.

The start was not auspicious. While three marriages were celebrated in the first days of the journey, there was also a death on the first night when María Ignacia Manuela Piñuelas Féliz died from complications of childbirth. Journals from the Anza Expedition of 1775–1776 describe the kinds of challenges that make life so difficult here, whether for a flower or a human settler. Water was a constant issue: either too much of it, as in the deep and treacherous crossing of the Colorado River, or on a path that could be made impassible by rain and mud and snow; or too little of it, with stretches of travel that were almost completely dry. In addition, the route challenged travelers with progress-halting sand dunes, biting cold winds, surprise snowstorms, and the first earthquake recorded by Europeans in California. "This morning it was so frigid and the night before was so extremely cold that three saddle animals and five head of cattle were frozen to death," wrote Anza on December 20, 1775. "And the weather was so hard on our people that almost none of them slept, for they spent the night occupied in feeding the fires in order to withstand it." Remarkably, given that the journey included hypothermia, dehydration, and near-starvation, the death of the new mother on the first night was the only one on the entire journey.

Mitigating the difficulties and contributing to the mission's success were the generally friendly relationships Anza had cultivated on his previous trips with indigenous tribes. Seeking to maintain these good relations—and knowing that settlers' lives might depend on them—Anza established severe penalties for anyone caught stealing or harassing American Indian women. And indeed, help from the local population came in the form of physical assistance to cross the Colorado River near Yuma; gifts of beans, squash, watermelon, and corn; and, perhaps most importantly, information about the land and water, and how to travel through the challenging environment and survive.

THE ROUTE

The Juan Bautista de Anza National Historic Trail connects history, culture, and outdoor recreation from Nogales, Arizona, to San Francisco Bay, closely following the actual route of the Anza Expedition. While much of the route can be followed by car on a designated auto-route, a path for nonmotorized recreation—including hiking, biking, and horseback riding—is also being developed. The Anza Trail thus has some of the National Trails System's best opportunities for walking into the past and experiencing large sections of the route and the landscape as they might have been 250 years ago.

The trail starts in Nogales on the Mexican border and heads north to Tucson, where it arcs gently northwest. It continues west and slightly south across the Sonoran Desert of Arizona to the Gila River and then to the crossing of the Colorado River at Yuma. West of Yuma, the route taken by the expedition dipped south of what is now the Mexican-American border south of Mexicali. (Today's national historic trail and autoroute parallel the original route but stay to the north of the border.) Returning to what is today's United States, the expedition trended northwest through Anza-Borrego Desert State Park, which has extensive hiking trail networks. The route then circles east and north around Los Angeles.

From here, the camino roughly followed or paralleled the coastline slightly inland, leading from mission to mission: from San Gabriel to San Luis Obispo, and, finally, on March 10, 1776, arriving at the Presidio of Monte Rey (today's Monterey), where colonists stayed for three months while Anza and an advance party went forward to the San Francisco Bay Area. Anza reached the bay on March 28. Here, today's national historic trail abandons its straight-line point-to-point trajectory and wanders in a wide loop around San Francisco, following the meanderings of the advance party that explored the region in order to determine the right location for its new settlement. They found it. In June 1776, the colonists, led by Anza's second-in-command, Lieutenant José Joaquín Moraga, were given permission to continue their journey and build their new homes—and what would become one of America's most beloved cities.

Saguaro cacti, Picacho Peak State Park, Arizona

FOLLOWING SPREAD: Moonset from Ocotillo Wells, California (top left); Painted Rock Petroglyph Site, Arizona (middle left); Metal sculptures near Borrego Springs, California (bottom left); Anza-Borrego Desert State Park, California (right)

OPPOSITE: Hollister Hills from San Juan Grade Road, California

RIGHT: Golden Gate Bridge, San Francisco, California (top); Juan Bautista de Anza Trail through Alvarado Park, California (bottom)

LIVING THE HISTORY

In addition to dozens of historic markers, museums, and interpretive displays, the Juan Bautista de Anza National Historic Trail features presidios, historic town plazas, missions, and churches, many of which still have active ministries. The National Park Service is working to make as much of the Anza Trail as possible a long-distance nonmotorized pathway that can be experienced by hiking, riding horses, or bicycling. Three hundred miles are currently certified, including paths through the Sonoran Desert National Monument in Arizona and along the Santa Cruz River, where travelers can experience the route in its primitive form. The sites listed here represent a small sample of what is available, from ancient American Indian sites the expedition passed to missions and churches to hiking, biking, and riding trails.

Santa Cruz River Trail from Tumacácori and Tubac Presidio State Historic Park, near Tubac, Arizona

The Mission San José de Tumacácori began in the late 17th century as a "visita"—an outlying mission without a resident priest—and became the head mission of the district in 1771. The expedition celebrated Mass here in the early days of the journey. The trail along the Santa Cruz River passes through a cottonwood-willow riparian landscape similar to that seen by members of the Anza Expedition as they traveled toward Tubac, where Anza had served as the second commander of the Presidio de San Ignacio de Tubac from 1760 to 1776. This was the formal launching point for the Anza Expedition. Each year, a reenactment of the expedition's passage through Tubac takes place during Anza Days.

Anza Trail, Imperial County, California

Some of the landscapes in the Yuha Desert in Imperial County remain very much the same today as they were 250 years ago. The expedition crossed the Colorado River and entered the deserts of upper Baja California and Imperial County in early winter, suffering the double challenge of a lack of water and frigid cold, exacerbated by an early blizzard and an earthquake. Thirty-eight miles of the Anza Trail are marked within Bureau of Land Management lands in the Yuha Desert area west of El Centro. Nearby, the Sonny Bono Salton Sea National Wildlife Refuge offers bird-watching, and designated areas in the Plaster City and Ocotillo Wells State Vehicular Recreation Areas are open to off-road vehicles.

Anza-Borrego Desert State Park, California

This 600,000-acre California state park contains two stretches of the Anza Trail. Interpretive exhibits at the visitor center describe the desert environment and the customs and history of local American Indians. An overnight hike through Coyote Canyon follows the route of the Anza Expedition and passes a monument commemorating the first baby of European descent to be born in California. The historic route travels through Anza-Borrego Desert State Park for roughly 20 miles, providing surprisingly remote desert hiking considering its proximity to Los Angeles. Some portions of the park's trails can also be driven by four-wheel-drive vehicles. The Pacific Crest National Scenic Trail also crosses a section of Anza-Borrego Desert State Park.

Mission San Gabriel Arcángel, California

Near Los Angeles, this was the first mission the colonists reached in Alta California, arriving on January 4, 1776. They remained here for about six weeks while Anza and some of his soldiers went to San Diego to help put down an American Indian uprising. Today, the mission is a working parish with museum exhibits and reenactments about the American Indian and Spanish history of the area. Also available in San Gabriel are city walking tours focusing on the history of the city, the mission, and the American Indian people, as well as ranger-led bird-watching tours in the Whittier Narrows Recreation Area.

El Presidio de Santa Barbara State Historic Park, California

The park includes the site of the original presidio, built in 1782. Some of the soldiers staffing the presidio had been members of the 1775–1776 expedition. Two buildings of the original presidio have been restored. Others have been reconstructed. The site contains adobe buildings from the Spanish, Mexican, and American period. Ongoing archaeological excavations take place, providing new information for the park's displays about life in California.

Mission San Antonio de Padua, Monterey County, California

The mission was founded in 1771. Along the entrance road to the mission, a large wooden sign describes the Anza Expedition's visit to the mission on March 6, 1776. Today, it is a working

parish managed by the Diocese of Monterey. Located on the grounds of Fort Hunter Liggett, the mission includes a museum featuring exhibits on the life of the Salinan people. En route to the mission, travelers can visit Lake San Antonio for recreational activities, including camping, fishing, hiking, and swimming.

Mission Dolores and the Presidio of San Francisco, California

The first goals of the Anza Expedition were to establish a presidio and a mission. After surveying the area around the bay, Anza and his two lieutenants, Moraga and Font, selected the site that would become Nuestra Señora de los Dolores. Local American Indians built the mission, which is the oldest intact building in San Francisco. The presidio was located at the north end of San Francisco, at the base of what is now the Golden Gate Bridge. Today,

the presidio is a national park with hiking and biking trails and trees; in Anza's time, the fort presided over windblown sandy cliffs. The Heritage Gallery at the Presidio Officers' Club has exhibits about the Anza Expedition, the founding of San Francisco, and the presidio's various roles in history, from Spanish, Mexican, and American military uses to a recreation area. The expedition also passed through what would become Golden Gate Park National Recreation Area, which now has trails for walkers and cyclists.

San Francisco Bay Area Trails, California

Several trails in the San Francisco Bay Area are part of the Juan Bautista de Anza Trail. The San Francisco Bay Trail is a walking and bicycling route for the Anza Trail from San José to the San Francisco International Airport. The trail connects several San Mateo County parks, including Coyote Point

Recreation Area, San Mateo Bayfront Park, Burlingame Bayside Park, and Belmont Marina Park. At Alvarado Park in East Richmond, the Anza Trail is a popular hiking trail. Many access points allow hikers to follow various sections of the trail through miles of Bay Area foothills. The East Bay Regional Park District's multiuse 20-mile Delta de Anza Regional Trail commemorates the Anza Expedition with interpretive signs and plaques. The Skyline National Recreation Trail and the Bay Area Ridge Trail, also managed by the East Bay Regional Park District, parallel Anza's route, but stay at higher elevations that offer panoramic views of San Francisco Bay and the route Anza's men would have taken.

Above, left: Bells at Mission San Gabriel Arcángel, California; *Above, right:* Historic buildings at the Presidio, San Francisco, California

Old Spanish Trail

2,700 MILES ➤ NEW MEXICO • COLORADO • UTAH • ARIZONA • NEVADA • CALIFORNIA

What does it take to call a trail "the most arduous in the United States"? Let's leave out recreational hiking trails, many of which are intentionally designed with up-and-downs, rock scrambling, ridge walking, and other challenges people trying to get from here to there quite sensibly avoid. Historic trails are a different animal altogether: they were never intended to be challenging or fun. "Easy" and "boring" were desirable qualities if you were crossing hundreds of miles of southwestern desert and mountains.

Unfortunately for the hundreds of thousands of settlers, traders, trappers, surveyors, wagoneers, explorers, miners, farmers, and religious refugees making their way west in the 19th century, the western American landscape is anything but easy and boring. Many of its trails have legitimate claims to "most difficult." The Chilkoot Trail in Alaska was infamous for ice, snow, and soul-breaking steepness. Canyons on the Columbia River forced Oregon Trail settlers to lower wagons using ropes and pulleys and a fair amount of prayer. And the California Trail's Donner Pass served up an early winter storm that stranded a party of settlers whose survivors became famous for cannibalism.

The Old Spanish National Historic Trail has earned the distinction for difficulty, at least according to historians and editors LeRoy R. and Ann W. Hafen. In their book, *Old Spanish Trail: Santa Fe to Los Angeles*, they called the Old Spanish Trail "the longest, crookedest, most arduous pack mule route in the history of America." Environmental obstacles bedeviled travelers along virtually all of its length. Its high mountains and steep canyons challenged mules,

drivers, and walkers. The plateaus were hardly easier, with deep ravine-like arroyos and waterless stretches that lasted for miles, and sometimes for days.

Mountains and canyons make for dramatic and stunning territory, but routes of travel are about getting somewhere, regardless of what lies in between. In the early 19th century, the "here" and "there" that needed to be linked were the cities and missions of Mexico's northlands. The spokes of the original Spanish roads network had radiated north from Mexico City to reach Natchitoches in the northeast, Santa Fe in the north, and San Francisco in the northwest. Natchitoches already had access to trade routes in Louisiana, and, from there, to points east in the United States. Santa Fe and the California missions were more isolated; settlers needed a way to trade and communicate with one another. Woven cloths from northern New Mexico were wanted on the Pacific coast, horses and mules bred in California were needed in Santa Fe, and American Indian slaves were being trafficked both ways in an active but illicit trade. Legal and illegal, there was money to be made moving people, livestock, and goods from New Mexico to Los Angeles and back.

But finding and traveling on a viable overland route was easier said than done. New Spain's daunting northern frontier had been explored as early as the late 1700s, when Spanish explorers and priests ventured into New Mexico north of Santa Fe, and thence into Colorado and southern Utah. The name "Old Spanish Trail," used by John Frémont during his 1844 topographical expedition guided by Kit Carson, harks back to these early explorations. In point of

Old Spanish Trail descending Virgin Hill and Mormon Mesa, Nevada

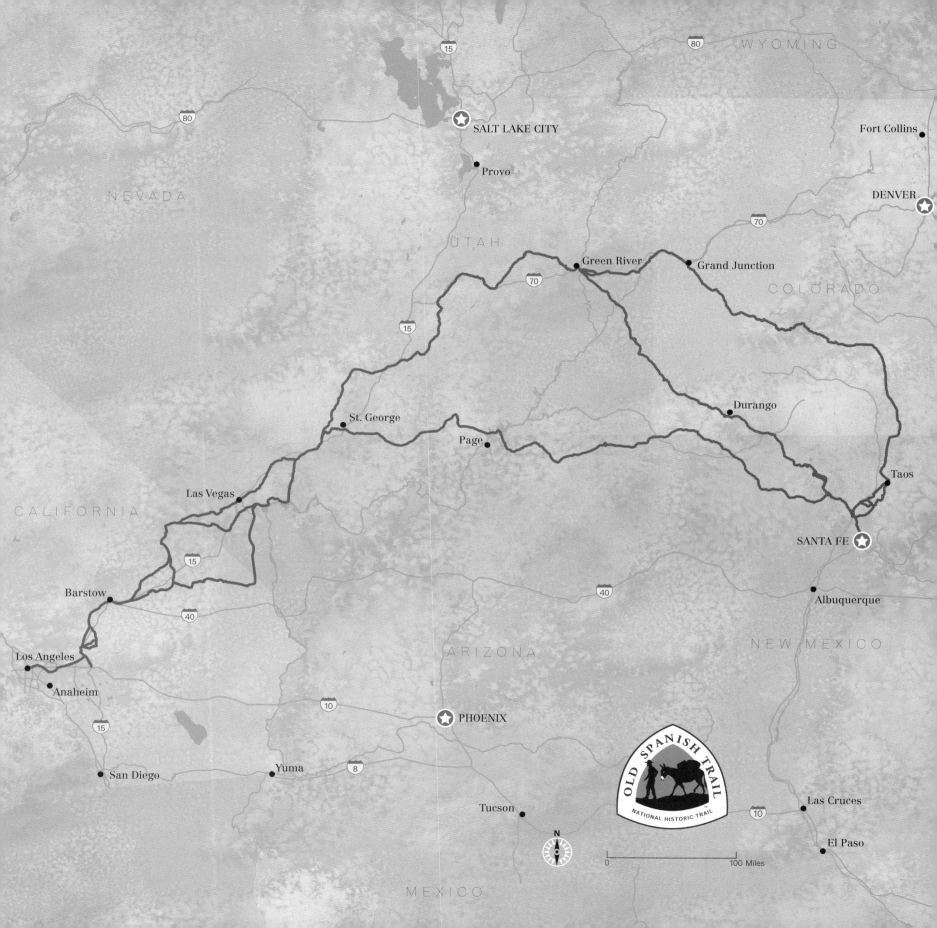

SALT LAKE CITY

Provo

NEVADA

UTAH

Green River

Grand Junction

COLORADO

Fort Collins

DENVER

Durango

St. George

Page

Taos

Las Vegas

CALIFORNIA

SANTA FE

Barstow

Albuquerque

Los Angeles

NEW MEXICO

Anaheim

ARIZONA

PHOENIX

San Diego

Yuma

OLD SPANISH TRAIL
NATIONAL HISTORIC TRAIL

Tucson

Las Cruces

El Paso

N

0   100 Miles

MEXICO

fact, the "Old Spanish Trail" was neither Spanish nor old; it wasn't until 1829, eight years after Mexico gained its independence from Spain, that the route was used for trade from the interior to the coast. A Mexican trader named Antonio Armijo led 60 men on a several-month journey from Abiquiú in northern New Mexico to Los Angeles and determined that a trade route was feasible.

Armijo brought 100 pack mules, not horses: mules were stronger, more sure-footed, could get by on less food and water, and had better instincts for survival and self-preservation in difficult terrain. (In the currency of the day, it took more American Indian–made blankets to buy a mule than to buy a horse.) And there were no wagons. The terrain—a combination of canyons, rivers, arroyos, and mountains—made wagon travel impractical and sometimes impossible. A seemingly endless array of obstacles lined up: sand could trap a wagon and rocks could smash a wheel into firewood. So instead, the traders traveled with pack mules.

Like many of America's national historic trails, the Old Spanish Trail is a braided network. As the trail developed between New Mexico and the coast, so did alternates and extensions. Routes varied according to destination, seasonal conditions, water availability, starting point, purpose, cargo, intermediary stops and trading posts, and pack animals. Relationships with indigenous tribes, both hostile and friendly, also drove the route this way and that. As the network evolved, it combined Armijo's original route with indigenous footpaths and new paths developed by traders and explorers, some of them swinging far north into central Colorado and Utah. Over the next 20 years, the trail was used by Mexican and American traders, fur trappers, missionaries, families, emigrants, horse dealers, and outlaws. Later, military and railroad surveyors made the journey, along with some of the first Anglo families to settle in the Southwest and California and, in one notable case, two toddlers traveling in the saddlebags of a mule.

Use of the route declined after the United States took control of the Southwest in 1848: first came a wagon route to Southern California, and later, the railroads. But the impact of the Old Spanish Trail cannot be overstated: it changed the commerce, communica-

tions, and connections of the Southwest. El Camino Real de Tierra Adentro had connected Santa Fe to Mexico City since the provincial capital was established in 1610. After the Mexican Revolution, the Santa Fe Trail connected New Mexico with Missouri and points east. And now, the Old Spanish Trail connected Santa Fe with the Pacific coast (and, via the route Juan Bautista de Anza had pioneered, to San Francisco as well). These three trails, which met in the plaza in front of the Palace of the Governors in the center of Santa Fe, together created a trade network that linked Mexico, the Southwest, California, and the eastern United States. In recommending that the trail be certified as a national historic trail, the National Park Service concluded that it was "nationally significant within the theme of the Changing Role of the United States in the World Community, and the topics of trade and commerce, during the period of 1829–1848."

THE ROUTE

Using today's highways, the distance between Santa Fe and Los Angeles is on the order of 850 miles. The Old Spanish National Historic Trail is a network of

Palace of the Governors, Santa Fe, New Mexico

2,700 miles of trails, including Armijo's original route, along with later developments and variants through New Mexico, Colorado, Utah, Arizona, Nevada, and California. Because the route was not a wagon route, there are hardly any traces of it left on the land, unlike the thousands of miles of swales left by later traders on the Oregon and California Trails. So, in many cases, the exact route is not known. However, historians do have good descriptions of the general trajectories of most of the variants, which together make up the national historic trail.

Armijo's original route followed a fairly straight line—as much as the land permitted—along the border between New Mexico and Colorado, and then along the border between Arizona and Utah. Trade routes into Colorado and Utah arched north. The Northern Route took a northwest path from Santa Fe through Durango. The North Branch Route was the longer option, heading straight north through Taos, and crossing the Continental Divide at 10,000-foot Cochetopa Pass to reach central Colorado and Utah in order to trade with the Utes. The two routes met at the Green River, then headed generally southwest through Utah, including today's Cedar City, to the modern border corner of Arizona, Utah, and Nevada.

In the northwest corner of Arizona, the two northern Colorado-Utah routes joined the old Armijo route—then, shortly, the trail split again as parties made different decisions regarding how to traverse the difficult dry terrain of Nevada and eastern California between the Mojave Desert and Death Valley. Finally, near today's Barstow, California, the trails once again converged to follow the Mojave River up to Cajon Pass (near today's I-15) and cross between the San Jacinto and San Gabriel Mountains—the last major mountain obstacles before reaching Los Angeles.

Old Spanish Trail heading toward
Blue Diamond, Nevada

PREVIOUS SPREAD: Dry Mesa from the Old Spanish Trail, Utah (left); La Virgin Maria near Cebolla, New Mexico (top right); Wilson Arch, Utah (middle right); Colorado River near Moab, Utah (bottom right)

LEFT: Veyo Volcano, Old Spanish Trail, Utah (top); Resting Springs, Old Spanish Trail through Mojave Desert, California (bottom)

OPPOSITE: Joshua trees and camouflaged communications tower, Mojave Valley, California

LIVING THE HISTORY

On the official national historic trail, more than 50 National Park Service Passport to Your National Parks sites are available at historic sites and visitor centers. The trail runs through such iconic destinations as Grand Junction, Colorado (hiking, mountain biking, horseback riding); Moab, Utah (mountain biking, rock scrambling); Abiquiú, New Mexico (Georgia O'Keeffe's famed home in the red-rock country near New Mexico's Continental Divide); Arches National Park and Mojave National Preserve; and the Pacific Crest National Scenic Trail near Cajon Pass and the Continental Divide National Scenic Trail at Cochetopa Pass in Colorado. As a result, today's visitors following the route have almost unlimited opportunities to hike, bicycle, and drive through mountains and plateaus that look very much the same as the landscapes the traders from the 1800s would have seen.

Ghost Ranch, Abiquiú, New Mexico

Armijo began his journey from Abiquiú in November 1829. Today, Abiquiú is better known for Ghost Ranch, about 13 miles north, where Georgia O'Keeffe painted the landscape of cliffs and mesas as well as the bleached skulls and bones she found in the high drylands. Owned by the Presbyterian Church, the ranch today is a multipurpose retreat center with museums of anthropology and paleontology, a 12,000-volume library, and a network of trails that lets visitors experience the land on horse or on foot. The Continental Divide National Scenic Trail crosses the ranch and heads north to Colorado, where it will intersect again with the Old Spanish Trail's Northern Route at Cochetopa Pass.

Navajo National Monument, Arizona

The land surrounding the Navajo National Monument is part of the Navajo Nation, which makes this site home to two different eras and cultures. The Navajo, or Diné, have lived in this region for several hundred years, and would have been the American Indians who interacted with the 19th-century traders on the Old Spanish Trail. Before them, the region was inhabited first by hunter-gatherers who lived in the Tsegi and Nitsin Canyons, then, around 2,000 years ago, by agriculturalists who grew maize and other crops and began to live in more settled villages. The Navajo National Monument thus represents a cultural history that goes centuries farther back in time to the ancestral Pueblo culture that emerged as early farmers began to depend on farming for most of their food and to build masonry houses. Then, sometime in the 1300s, they disappeared and moved on. Visitors can experience the land on three short self-guided trails, on two longer ranger-guided cliff-dwellings tours, or on a rugged 17-mile backcountry round-trip hike.

Cochetopa Pass, Colorado

From Taos, New Mexico, traders on the Northern Route of the Old Spanish Trail headed north, intending to trade with indigenous tribes in what would later be the states of Colorado and Utah. But that meant they would have to cross the formidable Continental Divide in the high mountains of Colorado. Cochetopa Pass—"Pass of the Buffalos" in the Ute language—was a navigable if difficult route. Its success as a pack trail route made it a target for exploration for the transcontinental railroad, but to no avail. An 1848 expedition led by John Charles Frémont ended in failure. In mid-December, mules and men began freezing to death, with men resorting to cannibalism before being rescued. An 1853 expedition was no more successful. Captain John W. Gunnison surveyed the area for a railroad route, but was later killed in a Paiute raid. Today, Cochetopa Pass is on the Continental Divide National Scenic Trail, and walkers can experience for themselves the challenges of passing through this terrain.

Arches National Park, Moab, Utah

In 1988, a section of the Old Spanish Trail in Arches National Park was placed on the National Register of Historic Places, and a section of the trail is visible next to the visitor center. Two thousand stone arches have given this park some of the most distinctive and iconic vistas in the National Park System. Ancient tools and petroglyphs tell us that hunter-gatherers lived in the region thousands of years ago, followed by Pueblo people who later moved elsewhere. Ute and Paiute tribes were living here when the first Spanish explorers came through in the late 1700s. The Old Spanish Trail's Northern Route enabled trade with American Indians. By the 1800s, traders and settlers had established a small settlement that

later became Moab. When hiking through the park, imagine trying to move pack animals laden with goods for trade through a landscape of rock and sand and mesas.

Las Vegas, Nevada

Yes, really. Before it was alight with neon, Las Vegas was "the Meadows," named by the Armijo Expedition for the greenery that surrounds its artesian wells. For the next two decades, Las Vegas was a watering hole on the Old Spanish Trail. The Old Las Vegas Mormon Fort State Historic Park tells the story of Mormons who built the first nonnative settlement in the Las Vegas Valley in 1855. (They abandoned it two years later at the beginning of the Utah War to go to Salt Lake City; the fort then passed through a series of owners and occupiers before becoming a state park in 1991.) More local history—Paiutes, mining history, the coming of the railroads, gaming, and a re-created ghost town—is found nearby at Clark County Museum in Henderson and at Red Rock Canyon National Conservation Area, where visitors can see what the region looked like before it became the capital of kitsch.

Mojave National Preserve Headquarters, Barstow, California

Located between Las Vegas and Los Angeles, the 1.6 million-acre Mojave National Preserve is a fierce landscape where sand dunes, canyons, volcanic cinder cones, mesas, the largest Joshua tree forest in the world, and the superbloom compete for attention. The Mojave Road shared part of its route with the Old Spanish Trail, crossing today's preserve from east to west. The route was first used by various indigenous tribes to transport goods from the Southwest to the coast. Later, it was used by Spanish explorers and Mexican and European American traders. The desiccated remains of abandoned mines, homesteads, and military outposts that had been established to protect the water sources and the travelers who relied on them are hidden in the mountains. Today, the Mojave Road is a popular four-wheel-drive route that gives travelers a sense of the vastness of the land and the vulnerability of traveling through it—though to get the true 19th-century experience requires leaving the safety and air-conditioning of the vehicle to get out and walk. The park headquarters are an hour and a half (by car) west in Barstow, where several other sites interpret aspects of the desert landscape and the history of transportation through the region: the Barstow Main Street Mural honors the Old Spanish Trail in Santa Fe; the Mojave River Valley Museum examines the scientific, cultural, and historical heritage of the region; the Desert Discovery Center focuses on the desert environment; and, for a modern take on interstate trade and travel routes, the Route 66 Mother Road Museum tells the story of one of America's first major highways.

Above, left: Stone arch, Ghost Ranch, New Mexico;
Above, right: Old Las Vegas Mormon Fort, Nevada

PART TWO

EAST COAST

★

The path of American history and settlement is multi-directional. It began with a southward migration after Asian peoples crossed the Bering Sea many thousands of years ago. Later, the Polynesians traveled northeast to Hawai'i, the Spaniards came north from Mexico City, and the French sent southbound forays from their trading posts in Canada. • But it is the westward movement of the English, across the Atlantic and onto the eastern American shores, that dominates our history books. Our national mythology is full of Pilgrims and Puritans, Jamestown settlers, Redcoats and Patriots, and the eventual revolution that gave us our government structure and constitution. • So we know about Paul Revere (one if by land, two if by sea), Patrick Henry (liberty or death), George Washington (cherry tree, wooden

teeth, Valley Forge), and Nathan Hale (whose one life was given for his country). We know about Thomas Jefferson penning the Declaration of Independence, and John Hancock signing it in letters so big that most of us remember him today for that, if for nothing else.

Four of America's national historic trails are dedicated to the East Coast. They commemorate the settlement of the East (by the English) and subsequent wars (also with the English). In chronological order, these trails begin with the first comprehensive English exploration and mapping of the Chesapeake Bay. They then follow two important military campaigns of the Revolutionary War, one in the South and one covering most of the mid-Atlantic and New England states. The last trail in this section commemorates the naval battle that led to the defeat of the English in the War of 1812 and the writing of America's national anthem.

What is unique about the East Coast trails is that three of them—the Captain John Smith Chesapeake, the Washington-Rochambeau Revolutionary Route,

and the Star-Spangled Banner National Historic Trails—have an important waterways component, all centered around the Chesapeake Bay. Visitors can explore the region via parks, beaches, and wild-life refuges around the bay, and also at historic sites, interpretive centers, and museums. But many of the historic events commemorated by these trails took place on the bay itself. Contemporary visitors who explore the bay—and especially its more remote tributaries—can paddle or sail their way into an experience that transcends the hundreds of years that separate us from the Chesapeake of Captain John Smith or Francis Scott Key.

Chesapeake Bay is America's largest estuary. Two hundred miles long with an average depth of only 21 feet, it is fed by tributaries that bring water from six states and Washington, DC. The three trails cover the length of the bay from its southern outlet to the Atlantic Ocean (near Norfolk and Yorktown, Virginia) north of Baltimore, as well as some of its tributaries. Some parts of the trails on land overlap with each other as well.

Initially conceived as a water trail, the Captain John Smith Chesapeake National Historic Trail traces the voyages taken by John Smith to explore and map the Chesapeake Bay from 1607 to 1609. The trail was later reenvisioned to include sites on land that pertained to the exploration of the bay and to the cultures of its indigenous people.

The Washington-Rochambeau Revolutionary Route National Historic Trail commemorates the Franco-American alliance that contributed to the Continental Army's victory at Yorktown. The French and the Americans moved on both land and water, so this trail is a network of land and water routes. By winning the Battle of the Chesapeake on September 5, 1781, French naval forces blocked the British from escaping into the Atlantic Ocean. Charles Cornwallis was effectively besieged at Yorktown, unable to access reinforcements or evacuate to the sea. The British surrender on October 19, 1781, was the de facto end of the war, although the Treaty of Paris was not signed until 1783.

Last, the Star-Spangled Banner National Historic Trail commemorates the naval battles that took place in 1814 clear on the other side of the Chesapeake Bay.

PREVIOUS SPREAD: Black Point and Jamestown Island, from Back River, Captain John Smith Chesapeake Trail, Virginia

BELOW: Fort McHenry National Monument, Star-Spangled Banner Trail, Maryland

OPPOSITE: Stone wall in the woods, Washington-Rochambeau Revolutionary Route Trail, Connecticut

The trail follows the path of the British, who invaded the bay, occupied Washington, DC, and burned the White House and the Capitol; it also commemorates the events that led to the writing of America's national anthem. The British were stopped at Fort McHenry, in Baltimore, where a decisive naval victory for the Americans led to the end of the war, though the final battles and peace treaty were not concluded until 1815.

The sole all-terrestrial trail in the East is the Overmountain Victory National Historic Trail, which takes place culturally and environmentally about as far away as it is possible to get from the Eastern Seaboard and still be in the American colonies. Here, we experience the story of revolution as it sometimes occurred, one spontaneously formed ragtag group at a time. The Overmountain Victory Trail commemorates a two-week march by Appalachian settlers who had been goaded into action by a combination of British insults and heavy-handed threats. The march culminated in a surprise victory for the colonials over the British on Kings Mountain in South Carolina. Thomas Jefferson called it one of the most important victories of the entire war.

In combination, the four eastern trails paint a picture of the British colonial era and early American nationhood. By following the paths of explorers and soldiers, they take us through parts of the East, some of which still look very much as they might have in our colonial past, and some of which would be unrecognizable. Whether paddling a canoe, walking alongside a New England stone wall, crossing a stile over an Appalachian wooden fence, wandering on a dirt road through forests and fields on the path taken by Washington's soldiers, contemplating the capital from the shores of the Potomac River, or touring a living history exhibit at Colonial Williamsburg, a visitor to the eastern national historic trails has the opportunity to experience pockets of America that connect us to the past.

Wolf Creek, Abingdon Muster
Grounds, Overmountain Victory
Trail, Virginia

Captain John Smith
Chesapeake Trail

John Smith may be an ordinary Anglo-American name, but there was nothing ordinary about one particular John Smith who sailed to America in 1607. Even a CliffsNotes version of his résumé would make an unbelievable Hollywood saga. An Englishman, Smith fought for Dutch independence from Spain, sailed and pirated on a merchant ship in the Mediterranean, fought on behalf of Austrians in Hungary, acquired the title of "gentleman" by beheading a trio of Turkish generals, was sold as a Turkish slave, and was knighted by a Transylvanian prince. All by the time he was 24.

When Smith returned to England—the long way, having killed his Turkish captor somewhere on the Black Sea, escaped through Russia and Poland, and then traveled through western Europe and North Africa—he found that his native country was ablaze with colonization fever. Previous attempts to establish an English colony at Roanoke had been unsuccessful—the settlement had been mysteriously abandoned, and only rumors and conjecture remained as to the fate of the settlers. But what was known as a fact was that Spain and England had signed a peace treaty, and that Spain, with its head start in trans-Atlantic trade (and pillaging), was now returning from the New World, its ships laden with gold and silver. Inspired by the promise of riches and more adventure, Smith invested in and joined the Virginia Company's three-ship expedition. Their assignment: to cross the Atlantic Ocean and establish a colony somewhere on North American shores between latitudes 34 and 41.

Specifically, the 104 settlers were expected to build their homes, become self-supporting, and, while they were at it, find a westward passage to the Pacific Ocean and to the stores of gold the English knew were hidden in the American wilderness. It was an assignment that would have been the equivalent of asking Neil Armstrong in 1969 to land on the moon, and, while he was at it, build a house, plant a garden, find a route to the dark side, and bring back some uranium.

It was not a happy journey. The Atlantic Ocean was surly and uncooperative, extending what might have been a monthlong crossing into a five-month ordeal. Smith had long since lost his taste for deference and class hierarchies, and his adventure-hardened personality did not smoothly coexist with some of the leaders, who already viewed him and his claim to being a "gentleman" with some disdain. Having irritated one of the leaders and chief investors during the long, slow, uncomfortable trip, Smith was charged with mutiny and spent the last 13 weeks of the journey in chains. But when the ships reached land in April 1607, the leaders opened their secret sealed orders and discovered that Smith had been named to the governing council of the new colony. Like a cat surviving to live yet another of its nine lives, he was released to take on the new role. And as it turned out, Smith's leadership might have been the key ingredient that saved the colony.

The settlers as a group represented a cross section of British society. Gentry, as usual, were installed at the top of the pecking order; beside them were military men, because it was expected that the colonists would need to defend themselves against the Spaniards and the American Indians. But the majority were lower-class city people, many of them unemployed urbanites with few skills that could be

Sunset over Chesapeake Bay, Elk Neck State Park, Maryland

CANADA

NEW YORK

90

ALBANY ⭐

88

86

Binghamton

81

87

PENNSYLVANIA

Scranton

84

80

84

Fort Montgomery

79

80

76

State College

78

Allentown

78

New York

OHIO

476

Reading

Princeton

Pittsburgh

HARRISBURG ⭐

76

TRENTON ⭐

70

Philadelphia

295

81

NEW JERSEY

68

Wilmington

95

MARYLAND

Baltimore

DOVER ⭐

ANNAPOLIS ⭐

79

WASHINGTON, DC ⭐

DELAWARE

WEST VIRGINIA

81

⭐ CHARLESTON

Fredericksburg

VIRGINIA

95

64

64

RICHMOND ⭐

77

Yorktown

81

Hampton

85

N

CAPTAIN JOHN SMITH
CHESAPEAKE
NATIONAL HISTORIC TRAIL

0   50 Miles

95

applied to the demands of the new and strange environment. Occupations included minister (of course), blacksmith, mason, tailor, barber, bricklayer, carpenter, surgeon, unskilled laborer, and seaman. Few were farmers, and none were knowledgeable about how to adapt to and live off an unfamiliar land. Many were disinclined to work. The results were immediate and devastating: the colony struggled to feed itself almost from the start. A combination of challenges—unclean water, lack of food, American Indian attacks, and disease—killed more than half of the original 104, and new groups of colonists who arrived in the early years suffered equally horrendous, and sometimes greater, death rates.

Smith exhibited leadership in three important ways. First, he was able to trade with the indigenous people for badly needed food. His journals describe his famous first meeting with Chief Powhatan during which he claimed that Pocahontas saved his life by throwing herself between Smith and a would-be executioner. Later, relations would sour, and he and the chief would plot to kill each other. But in the early months, help from Powhatan and his people may have saved the settlement from starvation.

Second, Smith led the first European explorations of Chesapeake Bay—America's largest estuary and the third-largest estuary in the world. He journeyed between 2,500 and 3,000 miles on the bay and its tributaries in a barge that was 32 feet long, eight feet wide, and open to the weather. His two most extensive expeditions, beginning in June and ending in September of 1608, were among the most important European explorations in colonial North America. While Smith's adventures from Istanbul to Powhatan villages may have been the stuff of legends, his explorations, the cultural information he returned with, his written records, and the maps he drew were the stuff of history. He must have been an extraordinary notetaker and draftsman, with a keen grasp of the navigational tools of the day. Using little more than a compass, a crude sextant, an hourglass, and a notebook, Smith's map of Virginia and the Chesapeake Bay contained not only geographic features, but also the locations of more than 200 American Indian towns and information about the different tribes he encoun-

tered. Published in 1612, it was used as a practical guide to the Chesapeake for more than 70 years. Even looking at it today, more than 400 years after the fact, the geographical accuracy is remarkable and some of the place names are unchanged.

Third, in September 1609, Smith took over as the colony's leader. Quoting 2nd Thessalonians 3:10 in the Bible's New Testament, he announced that "he that will not work shall not eat." With that mandate, the fort was repaired and expanded, defenses were reinforced, trees were harvested and cut into clapboard for building, crops were planted, and a well was dug. (However, gold—one of the hoped-for bounties from the New World—was not found. Nor was a route to the Pacific.)

Smith's determined leadership was controversial. It may have saved the colony, but his relationships with both the local population and his own people were volatile and frequently ended in accusations, death threats, and violence. A suspicious explosion injured him while he was sleeping on a boat in 1609, forcing his return to England. In 1614, he returned to the New World to conduct another American expedition, this time on the coast of New England, where he made maps that were used by the Mayflower Pilgrims. Smith died in England in 1631 at age 51, having added to his already impressive résumé of Old World achievements—sailor, mercenary, pirate, soldier, slave to a Turk, and knight to the prince of Transylvania—his New World achievements of explorer, mutineer, colonial governor, admiral, author, navigator, mapmaker, and one of the founders of the first permanent English settlement in America.

The original core mandate of the Captain John Smith Chesapeake National Historic Trail was to follow Smith's settlement of Jamestown (from 1607 to 1609) and his voyages on the Chesapeake Bay and its tributaries (most notably, the two major expeditions in the summer of 1608). That mandate was later expanded to include the natural environment and the role of American Indians, both as original inhabitants of the region, and as contemporary residents and stewards. Thus, in addition to the tributaries Smith explored, today's trail includes other tributaries that acted as transportation arteries for the indigenous people who lived in the region long before Smith set sail for a new world that was already old.

Par for the course in the Europeanization of America, the colonists moved in, displacing the original inhabitants of the Chesapeake and forcing them to move again and again throughout the 1600s and 1700s. As the region became more and more English, American Indians continued to live in the area, subjected to a series of assaults both physical and cultural: skirmishes, enslavement, broken treaties, cultural eradication, forced assimilation, historic revisionism, migration (both voluntary and involuntary), and racist legislation. But in the 2000s, reorganization and reaffirmation of tribal governments ultimately led to federal recognition of them as sovereign nations. Today, 16 federally or state-recognized tribes inhabit their ancestral lands in the Chesapeake. Despite the typical story of displacement and broken treaties, two tribes live on reservations that were set aside for them in the 1600s; the cultural center of the Pamunkey people is on land secured via a treaty with the British. Several Chesapeake-area tribes invite the public to powwows, which take place from May through September, including the Nanticoke in Delaware and the Mattaponi, Nansemond, Chickahominy, and Monacan in Virginia.

One of the newest national historic trails (established in 2006), the Captain John Smith Chesapeake Trail is in development, balancing multicultural stories of past and present. Under study is Werowocomoco, a sacred site to seven tribes: Chickahominy, Eastern Chickahominy, Mattaponi, Nansemond, Pamunkey, Rappahannock, and Upper Mattaponi. When it opens, it will contain interpretive information about its importance to American Indians, as well as its role in the first interactions between them and the British. This is where Smith was brought when he was, according to the story, saved by Pocahontas. Until the site opens, nearby Gloucester County Visitor Center has a good exhibit about it.

THE ROUTE

Chesapeake Bay is the largest estuary in the United States. The Captain John Smith Chesapeake National Historic Trail stretches up and down the length of the bay and into its major tributaries in Virginia, Maryland,

Delaware, Pennsylvania, New York, and Washington, DC. Smith ventured up many of the Chesapeake's major rivers, including the York, James, Potomac, Rappahannock, Patuxent, Patapsco, Pocomoke, and Nanticoke. The trail follows his explorations. It also ventures into other tributaries of the riparian network that feeds into the bay, extending all the way north across Pennsylvania on the Susquehanna River to just south of Cooperstown, New York, although Smith only sailed a short distance upstream on the river.

The Captain John Smith Chesapeake Trail is America's first water-based national historic trail. The popular *Boater's Guide to the Captain John Smith Chesapeake National Historic Trail* (available online) gives all levels of paddlers, sailors, and motorboaters the information needed to explore the bay and its tributary rivers and see the natural beauty and wildlife. For an even closer view, the Chesapeake Conservancy offers an enormously popular series of webcams, which allow viewers at home to watch peregrine, osprey, and great blue herons in their natural settings.

Two other national historic trails also include water elements: the Washington-Rochambeau Revolutionary Route National Historic Trail follows the land and water routes that led to the American victory at Yorktown, and the Star-Spangled Banner National Historic Trail commemorates the decisive Chesapeake Bay battles of the War of 1812. Like the Captain John Smith Chesapeake Trail, both of these trails focus on the Chesapeake Bay—and both deal with historic events that happened during or immediately after the British colonial period and America's Revolutionary War. As a result, there is some overlap, and visitors to the Chesapeake may often see historic markers from all three of these trails at some of the same sites.

In addition to its water component, the Captain John Smith Chesapeake Trail's land components include numerous historic sites, interpretive sites, museums, and living history centers, including several sites focusing on American Indian culture. For example, at the head of Maryland's Patuxent River, the Patuxent River Park, Jug Bay Wetlands Sanctuary, Merkle Wildlife Sanctuary, and Mount Calvert combine colonial history, American Indian culture, and pristine landscapes.

Captain John Smith Statue, Colonial National Historical Park, Virginia

PREVIOUS SPREAD: Patuxent River from Merkle Wildlife Sanctuary, Maryland (left); Wye Island Natural Resources Management Area, Maryland (top right); Calvert Cliffs on shore of Chesapeake Bay, Calvert Cliffs State Park, Maryland (middle right); Battle Creek Cypress Swamp, Maryland (bottom right)

LEFT: Rock Run, Susquehanna State Park, Maryland (top); Boardwalk to Potomac River, Caledon State Park, Virginia (bottom)

OPPOSITE: First Landing State Park, Cape Henry, Virginia

LIVING THE HISTORY

Sailing the bay, paddling its rivers, exploring the shoreline, hiking in state parks, visiting wildlife refuges, or experiencing historic Jamestown: all explore and interpret different aspects of the Chesapeake Bay. While modern cities like Baltimore and Wilmington are part of today's Chesapeake, sites that focus on John Smith and his explorations of the bay, or the American Indian presence in and use of its riparian corridors, offer opportunities to walk or paddle into quieter, less-developed parts of the bay and its tributaries the way Smith might have seen them.

Jamestown National Historic Site, Jamestown, Virginia

Along with Williamsburg and Yorktown, Jamestown is one of three locations included in Virginia's Historic Triangle. At Historic Jamestowne, visitors can watch artisans use techniques from the 1600s at the glasshouse and see remains of the original 1607 James Fort being uncovered at an archaeological dig. At nearby Jamestown Settlement, the living history museum highlights include a re-created Powhatan village, where visitors are guided through the daily life of the American Indians that Smith would have encountered; reproductions of the first three ships that sailed from England to Jamestown; and a replica of James Fort, where visitors can see the details of shipboard life, from how meals were prepared to how arms and armor were worn and used.

Captain John Smith GeoTour, Virginia, Maryland, and Delaware

The Captain John Smith GeoTour is a geocaching challenge that leads participants on a treasure hunt to find more than 50 caches hidden in places associated with Smith and his crew. Clues and GPS data lead geocachers from refuges to parks to museums to towns in Virginia, Maryland, and Delaware, following the Chesapeake Bay and the rivers and creeks that Smith explored. This project starts online (visit Geocaching.com/play/geotours/ captainjohnsmith), but quickly takes visitors into the field to sites that represent stories and scenes from Smith's adventures on the bay.

Havre de Grace Maritime Museum, Havre de Grace, Maryland

The Havre de Grace Maritime Museum is located where the Susquehanna River flows into the Chesapeake Bay. Smith sailed only a short way up this estuarian river, where fresh water, wetlands, a tidal cove, and a forested area all come together. As an ecological edge, where different ecosystems intersect, the region is rich with flora and fauna. That, and a navigable river, made it a rich environment for generations of American Indian tribes. Permanent exhibits include "Beyond Jamestown," focusing on Smith's second exploratory voyage, which brought him to the upper bay, and exhibits on various aspects of work and play on the bay, including fishing, shipbuilding, the Coast Guard, and water safety.

Point Comfort (Fort Monroe), Hampton, Virginia

In 1619, "twenty and odd" Africans arrived at Point Comfort (today's Fort Monroe in Hampton, Virginia). They were the first Africans known to be forcibly settled in the North American British colonies. The Africans had been on a Spanish slave ship that was attacked by an English privateer in the southern Gulf of Mexico; they were taken on board the English ship and off-loaded in Virginia in trade for provisions needed by their captors to return home. In 2011, President Barack Obama declared Fort Monroe a national monument in recognition of what is now considered the beginning of slavery in the United States. The fort includes a museum and a walking tour. Interestingly, since it is the site where slavery began, it was known as "Freedom's Fortress" during the Civil War. The Union Army held the fort in 1861, and three escaped slaves took refuge at the fort with the army, where they were declared "contraband of war," not to be returned. Thousands more slaves followed suit and also found freedom at this first place of American slavery.

James River, Virginia

The southernmost major tributary of the Chesapeake Bay, the James River passes through Richmond, Virginia, and joins the bay near Norfolk, near its outlet to the Atlantic Ocean. The Upper James River Water Trail is popular for canoeing and kayaking. Visitors not only experience the river as Smith might have—in an open, human-powered boat—but also see a relatively unspoiled stretch of a Chesapeake Bay tributary. (Paddlers should check that water levels are safe for their level of experience—according to local outfitters, optimum conditions are when the Buchanan River gauge shows water levels between two and four feet.) Kayaking and river rafting are popular on the lower James River, especially near Richmond, where typical rapids range from Class II to

Class IV. Intermediate boaters unfamiliar with the lines and rapids should take advantage of the many guide services available.

Zimmerman Center for Heritage, Wrightsville, Pennsylvania

The Zimmerman Center for Heritage covers the history of the Susquehanna River and the Susquehannock people who lived there. It serves as Pennsylvania's official center for the Captain John Smith Chesapeake Trail. Next door is Native Lands County Park, believed to be the site of the last-known town of the Susquehannock. Until sometime in the late 17th century, a log stockade wall would have enclosed about 16 longhouses, each building serving as a home to extended family groups of up to 50 people. Today, these adjacent locations offer hiking trails, guided interpretive walks, an art collection, exhibits of American Indian artifacts, and opportunities to kayak and canoe.

National Museum of the American Indian, Washington, DC

The National Museum of the American Indian has permanent, traveling, and temporary exhibits exploring multiple facets of American Indian life and culture. The ongoing exhibition *Return to a Native Place: Algonquian Peoples of the Chesapeake* presents photographs, maps, ceremonial artifacts, everyday objects, and interactive displays to interpret indigenous culture in the region. It covers history from the 1600s to the present, as well as the presence and lives of American Indians living in the Chesapeake today.

Rappahannock River Valley National Wildlife Refuge, Tappahannock, Virginia

The Rappahannock River Valley National Wildlife Refuge was founded in 1996 largely to help protect critical habitat for bald eagles and other migratory species. A nature center and interpretive trail provide information about the large numbers of eagles that are seen year-round, as well as information about other resident and migrating birds: great blue herons, turkey vultures, red-tailed hawks, woodpeckers,

and a host of songbirds. Hiking trails and a kayak launch take visitors through the ancestral home of the Rappahannock people, whose tribal center is nearby.

Top: Werowocomoco wetlands; *Above, left:* Great blue heron, Jug Bay Wetlands Sanctuary, Maryland; *Above, right:* Great egret along Chickahominy River, Chickahominy Wildlife Management Area, Virginia

Overmountain Victory Trail

330 MILES ➤ VIRGINIA · TENNESSEE · NORTH CAROLINA · SOUTH CAROLINA

Reenactor at gravesite of William Campbell, Aspenvale Cemetery, Virginia

OPPOSITE: Overmountain Victory Trail crossing Wolf Creek, Abingdon Muster Grounds, Virginia

In 1780, a British officer annoyed a handful of settlers living west of the Blue Ridge Mountains near the border of what is now Virginia, Tennessee, and North Carolina.

The Overmountain Men weren't supposed to be there. A royal edict, intended to smooth tensions between the American Indians and colonists, had ordered white settlers to stay on the eastern side of the Appalachians. The western side was reserved for American Indians. But here on the far western frontier, settlers weren't overly concerned with edicts, or the English king, or even the Revolutionary War, most of which was being fought in faraway coastal cities and in places like Pennsylvania and New England, which had nothing to do with them.

But now the war had been dragging on for five fraught years. British Major General Charles Cornwallis had decided to solicit support from colonists in the southern states; he assumed a friendly reception because the South had previously thrived on a healthy trade with England. By 1780, the British had notched a string of southern victories, including the capture of Savannah and Charleston. To seal the deal, Cornwallis sent Major Patrick Ferguson west to the Appalachian frontier to recruit southern supporters and put down any signs of uprising.

Instead of suppressing an insurrection, Ferguson promptly incited one by insultingly referring to the Appalachian settlers as "backwater men." After some protracted mountain skirmishing, Ferguson followed up by ordering settlers to lay down their arms and support the king or he "would march his army over the mountains, hang their leaders, and lay their country waste with fire and sword."

Appalachian Mountain clichés are well worn—hot tempers, cold whiskey, and long-burning feuds—but they have their origins in reality. This is not a place where bluster and threats from outsiders are likely to have the desired result. The ultimatum was a catastrophic misjudgment.

The Overmountain Men reacted spontaneously: farmers, artisans, hunters, and trappers put down

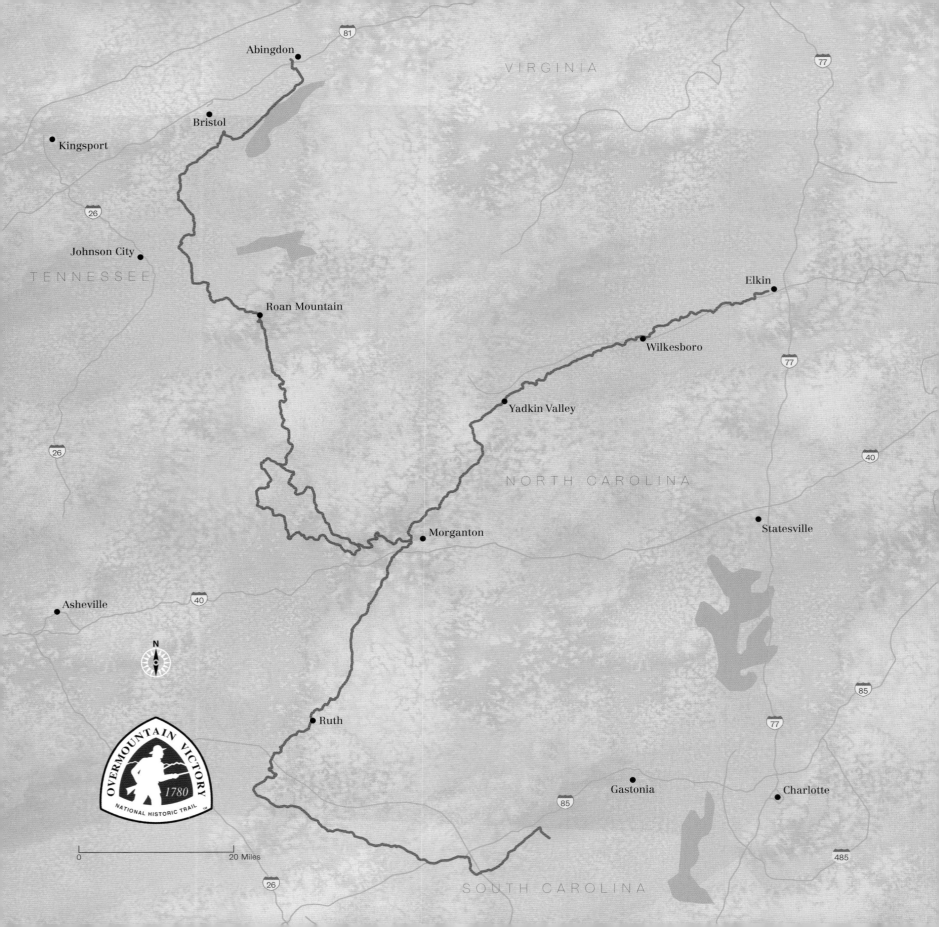

the tools of their daily lives, picked up their muskets, and mustered to form an expedition that would put a stop to the British threat. The main group of western Appalachian settlers—from over the mountains—gathered west of the Blue Ridge, near the present border of southwestern Virginia, western North Carolina, and eastern Tennessee. A second group drew settlers from the region just east of today's Blue Ridge Parkway. The two parties met in Morganton, North Carolina, then proceeded together on a dogleg path that went first southwest, then turned southeast to Kings Mountain on the South Carolina-North Carolina border. There, the British had established what they thought was a secure defensive position. It was the king's mountain, said Ferguson, and, for now, he was the king of it.

For the Patriots' part, a simple plan simply worked: surround the mountain, confine the enemy to the summit, and keep firing from the cover of the mountain's trees and rocks until the job was done. The 65-minute battle was a rout. The English suffered 290 killed, 163 wounded, and 668 taken prisoner. The Patriots' casualties were 28 killed and 60 wounded.

Coming after a sequence of recent loyalist victories—the fall of Charleston, the rout of the American army at the Battle of Camden, and the Waxhaws Massacre—the American victory at Kings Mountain was a turning point in the war in the South. Both a strategic victory and a psychological one, the surprising success raised morale on the part of the Patriots while forcing Cornwallis to reevaluate his assumption that he could count on southern support. With the loss of Ferguson, the disbandment of his militia, and the threat of riled Patriots in the mountains, Cornwallis abandoned plans for further action in North Carolina and retreated to South Carolina.

The Battle of Kings Mountain may be one of the most-ignored major battles of the Revolutionary War. Often omitted on lists of crucial battles, it has nonetheless been remembered in a national historic trail and in annual reenactments where participants re-create the entire two-week march to the mountain. And it has been remembered by presidents as well. In *The Winning of the West,* Theodore Roosevelt wrote, "This brilliant victory marked the turning point of the American Revolution." Thomas Jefferson described it as "the turn of the tide of success, which terminated the Revolutionary War, with the seal of our independence." And, speaking at Kings Mountain, Herbert Hoover said, "It was a little army and a little battle, but it was of mighty portent. History has done scant justice to its significance, which rightly should place it beside Lexington and Bunker Hill, Trenton, and Yorktown, as one of the crucial engagements in our long struggle for independence."

THE ROUTE

The 330-mile Overmountain Victory National Historic Trail commemorates the Battle of Kings Mountain by following the route the Overmountain Men took from the two mustering points in Virginia and North Carolina.

The main trail leads from the western ("overmountain") side of the Appalachians in Abingdon, Virginia. From the Abingdon mustering point, the main route runs generally southwest to Bluff City, then continues south to present-day Elizabethton, Tennessee. From there, it heads southeast to cross the main ridge of the Appalachians over Roan Mountain, the highest point on the trail. After the mountain, the group split into two for a short while, then reassembled before zigzagging east to Morganton.

The second group assembled in Elkin, North Carolina, east of the Blue Ridge, and followed a generally southwest line for 70 miles through Rutherford County, North Carolina, to Morganton, where the two paths converged and continued east together to Kings Mountain on the South Carolina-North Carolina border.

Today's Overmountain Victory Trail is a Y-shaped trail with two northern termini. The original route taken by the Patriots is known to history, but parts of it are inaccessible today. A commemorative motor route follows the general trajectory of the historic trail on state highways and roads; some of this route is contiguous with the original trail, and some of it parallels the old trail on nearby modern roads. In its annual reenactment march, the Overmountain Victory Trail Association uses a combination of back roads, dirt roads, and hiking trails to stay as close as possible to the original route.

FOLLOWING SPREAD: Fife and Drum Corps (top left) and Fort Watauga (bottom left), Sycamore Shoals State Historic Park, Tennessee; Shelving Rock, where the Overmountain Men stored their gunpowder to keep it dry, Tennessee (right)

North Toe River, North Carolina

FOLLOWING SPREAD: Yadkin River Valley, North Carolina (left); Robert Scruggs House, Cowpens National Battlefield, South Carolina (top right); Gravesite of Major Patrick Ferguson, Kings Mountain National Military Park, South Carolina (bottom right)

LIVING THE HISTORY

The Overmountain Victory Trail comprises a marked autoroute, 87 miles of hikeable trail segments ranging from half a mile to 11 miles in length, interpretive centers, and a national military park. Sections of trail that are appropriate for hiking are marked with the trail logo, which is the profile of an Overmountain Man on a brown-and-white triangle.

Annual Overmountain Victory Trail Reenactment March, Entire Route

The highlight event on the Overmountain Victory National Historic Trail is the annual reenactment march. In the South, reenactment usually refers to Civil War history, with Yankees and Rebels in perennial battle. But here, in the tristate area where Virginia, Tennessee, and North Carolina meet, it is all about Patriots and Redcoats. Held in late September and early October each year, the reenactment march stays as close as possible to the dates, route, and campsites of the original Overmountain Men. Some participants walk the entire route wearing Revolutionary-period clothing. Others tag along in cars or join the walkers for short stretches.

One aspect that completely breaks with history is the food: supporters of the march bring modern-day treats and feasts so today's marchers don't have to rely on the cornmeal slop that sustained the Overmountain Men. During the rest of the year, the organization sponsors other interpretive and reenactment events, including programs that teach 18th-century skills such as camping (without Gore-Tex, fleece, and synthetic insulators), cooking (with cast-iron pots, not titanium), and marksmanship (using muskets).

Keller Interpretive Center, Abingdon Muster Grounds, Virginia

At the trail's northern terminus in Virginia, the Abingdon Muster Grounds consists of a nine-acre park where the main company of Overmountain Men who lived west of the Blue Ridge assembled to start their pursuit of the British. The on-site Keller Interpretive Center exhibits artifacts associated with Virginia's Appalachian frontier, the Battle of Kings Mountain, and the Revolutionary War period in southwestern Virginia. The schedule of interpretive activities includes musket and rifle demonstrations, children's games from the colonial era, textile demonstrations, and performances of colonial music.

Sycamore Shoals State Historic Park, Tennessee

Sycamore Shoals already had a long history before being used as the mustering point for

an additional 600-man contingent of North Carolina militiamen. An important frontier settlement, the town claims a place in history because it instituted the first recognized majority-rule system of government in America in 1772. Later, disagreements, failed negotiations, and skirmishes with the Cherokee led to the building of Fort Watauga, which was connected to other tristate settlements by a series of trails. The state historic park today contains a reconstruction of Fort Watauga, a visitor center, trails, and picnic facilities. Exhibits, videos, and reenactments bring the Appalachian colonial period and the Revolutionary War to life.

Roan Mountain, North Carolina

Coming from west of the Blue Ridge, the Overmountain Men had to climb over some of the highest mountains in the East. Their route took them across Roan Mountain, which is now on the Appalachian National Scenic Trail. To experience what it would have been like to cross these mountains in the days before roads and automobiles, hikers can follow the Appalachian Trail 11 miles from Roan Mountain to the Overmountain Shelter (currently closed to hikers), where the Overmountain Men crossed 4,682-foot Yellow Mountain Gap. Roan Mountain has one of the largest natural displays of rhododendron in the world. The Overmountain Men would not have experienced that pleasure—at least not on the occasion of their autumn march across the mountains—but hikers today can enjoy the wildflower bloom if they visit in late June and early July. The Overmountain Men would have seen the area at the beginning of fall foliage, which peaks in October, starting at the higher elevations.

Kings Mountain National Military Park, South Carolina

The Kings Mountain National Military Park has a visitor center with exhibits and information interpreting the battle. From the visitor center, a 1.5-mile paved trail leads around the base of the mountain, starting at the lower Patriot lines and then climbing to

the crest where the redcoats were trapped. Several monuments commemorate the battle, and Patrick Ferguson, the British commander, is buried here. Next door to the national military park, the Kings Mountain State Park includes a living history farm, which contains exhibits of an early 19th-century farm, including the barn, the blacksmith and carpenter shops, and a cotton gin. Crowders Mountain State Park, next door but on the North Carolina side of the border, is a popular destination for rock climbers. A strenuous

6.2-mile Ridgeline Trail runs from the park to the 16-mile Kings Mountain National Recreation Trail, which passes through Kings Mountain State Park and leads back to Kings Mountain National Military Park.

Opposite: Annual Overmountain Victory Trail March, South Carolina; *Above:* Walking the original trace of the Overmountain Victory Trail as part of the annual march, Hampton Creek Cove State Natural Area, Tennessee

Washington-Rochambeau Revolutionary Route Trail

600 MILES ➤ MASSACHUSETTS • RHODE ISLAND • CONNECTICUT • NEW YORK • NEW JERSEY
PENNSYLVANIA • DELAWARE • MARYLAND • WASHINGTON, DC • VIRGINIA

"George Washington slept here." True or not, it is one of the most common claims to history at colonial-era inns in the eastern United States.

The name Jean-Baptiste Donatien de Vimeur, comte de Rochambeau, is not nearly as well known. Signs honoring the Frenchman in villages dating from the colonial era are few and far between. But Rochambeau's role in the American War of Independence was a pivotal one: it is possible that without this French general, and the army and navy support France provided, Americans might today be singing "God Save the Queen" rather than "My Country 'Tis of Thee."

The Washington-Rochambeau Revolutionary Route National Historic Trail commemorates the Franco-American alliance that led to victory at the Siege of Yorktown and the end of the American War of Independence. The French—seemingly at perpetual war with the English—had unofficially been aiding breakaway American colonists even before the Declaration of Independence. In 1778, they made their partisanship official and entered the war on the side of the Americans. The Expédition Particulière (in English, the "Special Expedition") was their code name for a plan to sail French troops to North America to support the American rebel forces.

Some 5,400 French officers and men arrived in Narragansett Bay off Newport, Rhode Island, on July 11, 1780. Having arrived late in the campaign season and ravaged by scurvy after three months on the ocean, Rochambeau's forces needed time to recuperate. Washington wanted to capture New York City, but

he needed the cooperation and support of the French Navy for a successful siege operation. Those plans changed in August 1781, when news arrived that Admiral François Joseph Paul de Grasse was sailing his fleet to the Chesapeake rather than New York City. With the French fleet heading for the Chesapeake, Washington and Rochambeau realized that if they deployed their troops to the Chesapeake, they could create a land-and-sea siege circle around Britain's last operational field army, led by Lord Charles Cornwallis. But it was late in the season; in September 1780, they decided to delay the siege until the summer of 1781.

So French troops remained in their winter quarters for nearly a year while Patriots and Redcoats remained mired in stalemate and Washington and Rochambeau fine-tuned their plans. In June 1781, Rochambeau marched his troops across Connecticut to rendezvous with Washington's Continental Army in New York's Hudson River Valley.

All that was now required was to move 6,500 men some 400 miles from New York to Virginia in a hot and humid mid-Atlantic summer. The movement of the combined French and American armies, some marching on land, some sailing on the Chesapeake Bay, would be one of the largest movement of troops in the American War of Independence. The French Army alone involved 239 hired wagoneers, 15 cooks (most of them women), and 210 wagons drawn by some 1,200 oxen. Along the way, the French were greeted with more than a little war-weary suspicion of foreigners, especially among those who remembered fighting them during the French and Indian War.

Rochambeau Statue and Monument, King Park, Rhode Island

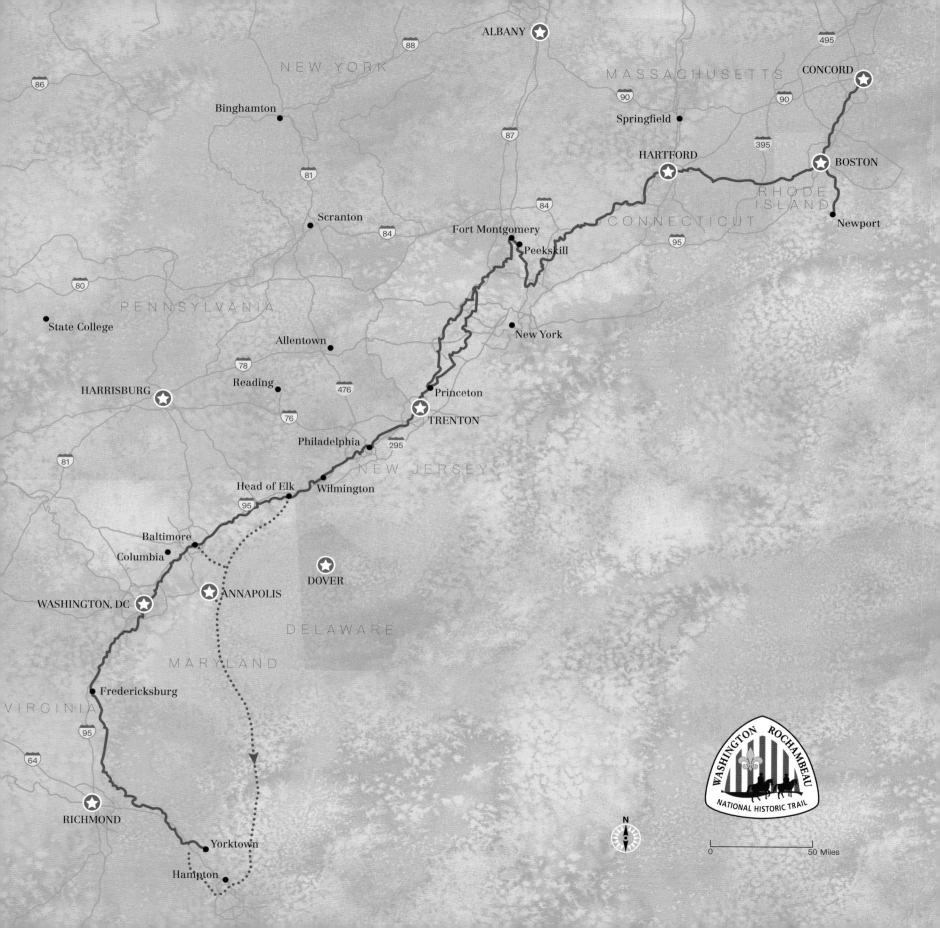

ALBANY

NEW YORK

MASSACHUSETTS

CONCORD

Binghamton

Springfield

HARTFORD

BOSTON

RHODE
ISLAND

Scranton

Newport

CONNECTICUT

Fort Montgomery

Peekskill

PENNSYLVANIA

State College

New York

Allentown

HARRISBURG

Reading

Princeton

TRENTON

Philadelphia

NEW JERSEY

Head of Elk

Wilmington

Baltimore

Columbia

DOVER

WASHINGTON, DC

ANNAPOLIS

DELAWARE

MARYLAND

Fredericksburg

VIRGINIA

RICHMOND

Yorktown

Hampton

WASHINGTON ROCHAMBEAU

NATIONAL HISTORIC TRAIL

N

0   50 Miles

Anyone who has hiked a fair distance in a mid-Atlantic heat wave knows the stench of sweat-soaked gear and debilitating heat-induced exhaustion. The War of Independence soldiers would have made for serious competition in the bedraggled and filthy department. The French started out impressively attired in wool uniforms, which quickly became oppressively hot. The Americans were a mismatched and ragtag lot, wearing lightweight linens, which at this point in the war had disintegrated into rags. Each man carried his own weapons, tools for making bullets, utensils, and personal items; a typical load was 60 pounds, carried eight hours a day over 12 to 15 miles.

The thousands of men marching represented all factions of American society—and French society too, with both armies adhering to the tradition of military rank aligning with social rank. Most of the American troops were of English descent, some were Germans, and some were French Canadians. African American slaves and freemen—described by a French officer as "merry, confident, and sturdy"—fought on both sides of the war. Some thought their chances for improved status lay with the British; others wagered on the Americans.

On September 5, with both Washington's and Rochambeau's armies still on the march, the French Navy defeated a British fleet at the outlet of the Chesapeake Bay to the Atlantic. After this Battle of the Capes, the French Navy controlled access to the bay. British ships carrying reinforcements and supplies from New York could not enter the bay from the Atlantic Ocean. And Cornwallis was trapped inside, unable to evacuate his troops to safety in the Atlantic. On September 28, the combined French and American forces began the Siege of Yorktown. This decisive major battle of the American War of Independence ended on October 19 with the surrender of Cornwallis.

The path to peace was underway: the defeat at Yorktown led to the resignation of the British prime minister in March 1782. But the end of the war was almost as protracted as the war itself had been, slowed by the speed of communications, negotiation details, and lingering skirmishes all over the world. It took almost another year and a half before the Treaty of Paris was signed, then two more months before the

British withdrew their remaining troops. In January 1783, the Continental Congress ratified the treaty. The House of Commons ratified it in London on April 9. Finally, the war was over—on the ground, on paper, and in the eyes of the world.

In the meantime, Washington's and Rochambeau's forces had to walk back, the same way they had come—the Americans to points north; the French to Boston, where, on Christmas Day 1782, they boarded ships bound for the West Indies. This time, the French soldiers received a hero's welcome. More than two years after arriving in America, the Expédition Particulière was finally over.

THE ROUTE

The Washington-Rochambeau Revolutionary Route National Historic Trail commemorates more than 600 miles of land and water routes and sites used by the French and American armies as they marched, sailed, camped, and rested from New England to Virginia—and then back again. The route has three northern termini: Rhode Island's Narragansett Bay, where the French landed in 1780; New York's Hudson River Valley, where Washington's Continental Army was stationed; and Boston, where, after the victory at Yorktown, the French departed American shores. The southern terminus is at Yorktown, Virginia.

After spending the winter in Newport, Rhode Island, and Lebanon, Connecticut, Rochambeau's men marched across Connecticut to New York's Hudson River Valley in June 1781. Having joined together with Washington's men, the two armies then headed south, circling clear of New York to avoid detection, and passing through New Jersey, Pennsylvania, and Delaware. At Elkton, Maryland, some of the men sailed south to Yorktown. The land forces continued to Baltimore, where the remainder of the Continental Army boarded ships, and to Annapolis, where the French forces boarded vessels to College Landing near Williamsburg, Virginia. After the siege, Rochambeau's forces wintered in Williamsburg and marched back north the next summer. Their return journey followed the same basic path, except this time the northern terminus was in Boston, where they boarded their ships for the West Indies.

FOLLOWING SPREAD: Granite post along Washington-Rochambeau Revolutionary Route Trail, Connecticut (left); Stone walls dating to Rochambeau's time along Plainfield Pike, Rhode Island (top right); Original segment of the Washington-Rochambeau Revolutionary Route Trail along Old Canterbury Road, Connecticut (bottom right)

PREVIOUS SPREAD: Joseph Webb House, Connecticut (top left); Tower of Victory, Washington's Headquarters State Historic Site, New York (bottom left); Replica of soldier's hut, Morristown National Historical Park, New Jersey (right)

OPPOSITE: Cannon overlooking York River, Yorktown Battlefield, Colonial National Historical Park, Virginia

RIGHT: Victory Monument, Virginia (top); Surrender Field, Yorktown Battlefield, Colonial National Historical Park, Virginia (bottom)

LIVING THE HISTORY

Dozens of historic sites along the Washington-Rochambeau Revolutionary Route Trail are on the National Register of Historic Places or have been recognized and preserved by local or regional historical commissions and governments. Though the East Coast's many urban centers have put a coat of glass, steel, cement, pavement, and lighting over the world of colonial wagons and dirt paths, some of the rural back roads still give visitors a sense of the landscape through which Rochambeau's army marched.

Colony House, Newport, Rhode Island

On July 10, 1780, Admiral Charles-Henri-Louis d'Arsac de Ternay sailed the French fleet into Narragansett Bay in Newport, carrying some 450 officers and 5,300 men under Rochambeau. The French remained wintered in Newport through 1781, until joining forces with Washington's troops on the Yorktown Campaign. Today, Newport visitors can experience the New England coastline along with classic colonial architecture and historic sites, many associated with the French presence. The Colony House is a center feature in the town; during the Revolution, it served as a hospital for British and later French forces quartered in Newport. In 1781, when Washington came to Newport to visit the French Army, a banquet was held in the great hall on the first floor.

March Routes and Historic Sites, Connecticut

Many sections of the route in Connecticut have been placed on the National Register of Historic Places. Some certified sections of the route have preserved structures from the colonial period, and, with limited modern housing development, many of the farms, pastures, woods, streams, winding roads, steep hills, stone walls, and even the occasional tavern look very much like they might have in 1781. While much of the Washington-Rochambeau Revolutionary Route Trail today is surrounded by modern

development, driving, bicycling, or walking along some of these segments gives visitors a chance to peer into the past. The register lists each certified section of the march route, along with GPS coordinates and around 20 historic buildings, taverns, and town squares.

Millstone Valley National Scenic Byway, New Jersey

One of the most scenic and historically evocative sections of the Washington-Rochambeau Revolutionary Route Trail is the 27-mile-long Millstone Valley National Scenic Byway, located just northeast of Princeton, New Jersey, along both sides of the Millstone River. The byway's 18th-century architecture and historic sites evoke the multiple times the Continental Army passed through this valley, beginning on January 3, 1777, after victory in the Battle of Princeton. Three lines of troops first converged on the Route to Yorktown in 1781 in the village of Rocky Hill. Two years later, George Washington made his headquarters at the Rockingham Historic Site, also on the byway. Of further interest to walkers and cyclists who enjoy history are the well-preserved features of the 19th-century Delaware and Raritan Canal State Park, which includes canal houses, locks, spillways, and a maintained towpath. Just south of the byway, in Trenton, the Old Barracks Museum is the only military structure left in New Jersey that is associated with the

American Revolution. It was used by both the British and the Americans, depending on who controlled the region, for purposes ranging from quartering troops to giving smallpox inoculations.

Independence National Historical Park, Philadelphia, Pennsylvania

On September 3–4, 1781, the Continental Congress watched the French Army march in front of the Pennsylvania State House, now known as Independence Hall, as they moved to their camp just west of Philadelphia. Today, the Museum of the American Revolution tells the story of the entire American Revolution, including the march to Yorktown. Iconic Independence Hall is a five-minute walk away, at the center of Independence National Historical Park. The park encompasses a collection of Philadelphia historic sites, including the Liberty Bell Center, the Independence Square buildings, the Franklin Court sites, the Declaration House (where Thomas Jefferson lived while drafting the Declaration of Independence), the New Hall Military Museum (which focuses on the history of the Continental Army), and the President's House site (originally home to both Washington and Adams, it now contains a display about liberty and slavery). Visitors experiencing museum overload can unwind in the Schuylkill River Greenways National Heritage Area, the so-called

Revolutionary River, which connects such iconic sites as Philadelphia and Valley Forge and offers hiking trailheads and boating access points.

Mount Vernon, Virginia

As the French and American armies moved toward Yorktown in September 1781, Washington veered aside to visit his Virginia home for the first time in six years. He entertained Rochambeau and his staff there before continuing on to Yorktown. His home is now open to the public—something he approved of during his lifetime, writing, "I have no objection to any sober or orderly person's gratifying their curiosity in viewing the buildings." The current property contains about 500 acres and some 30 buildings near the riverfront, many of which—barns, slave quarters, a pioneer farm, an operational blacksmith shop, and a working whiskey distillery—can be toured. From here, the 18-mile-long Mount Vernon bicycle trail follows the Potomac to Alexandria and Arlington, Virginia, and, on the other side of the river, Washington, DC. It then joins with the C&O Canal, a project that Washington was involved in planning and developing; the canal towpath is now the heart of the Potomac Heritage National Scenic Trail.

Yorktown Battlefield, Colonial National Historical Park, Virginia

The Yorktown Battlefield is part of the Colonial National Historical Park—administered by the National Park Service—which includes several sites in the historic triangle of Jamestown, Yorktown, and the historic district of Colonial Williamsburg. The 23-mile Colonial Parkway links the sites. In Yorktown, the park operates the Yorktown Battlefield. The visitor center offers an introductory film and museum exhibits, including the tents used by Washington during the siege. Ranger-led walking tours explore fortifications, cannons, and the site of the final surrender. Historic sites in the town and park include a victory monument; the Nelson House, where surrender negotiations took place; the Moore House, which was home to one of the signers of the Declaration of Independence and may have served as Cornwallis's headquarters during the Siege of Yorktown; and the American Revolution Museum at Yorktown.

Colonial Williamsburg, Virginia

In late September 1781, the French and American armies converged at the town of Williamsburg, then the capital of colonial Virginia, to make the last final march to Yorktown. After the victory, the French Army spent the winter in and around Williamsburg before marching north to Boston. Today, Colonial Williamsburg is one of the world's premier living history museums, presenting and interpreting colonial history through interpretive displays and interactive programs with costumed employees playing the roles of colonial gentlemen, workers, slaves, housewives, and artisans. The 300-acre historic area includes several hundred restored or re-created buildings from the 18th century, along with other buildings from the 17th and 19th centuries.

Above, left: Museum of the American Revolution, Pennsylvania; *Above, right:* Cannon at Grand French Battery, Yorktown Battlefield Colonial National Historical Park, Virginia

Star-Spangled Banner Trail

290 MILES ➤ MARYLAND · WASHINGTON, DC · VIRGINIA

Fireworks over Fort McHenry National Monument and Historic Shrine, Maryland

OPPOSITE: Fort McHenry National Monument and Historic Shrine, Maryland

On a September evening in 1814, an American lawyer, who also happened to be an amateur poet, visited a British warship to negotiate a prisoner exchange. Dinner turned into detention when his hosts realized that the visitor had observed the number and positions of British ships that were preparing for an assault on American forces. Francis Scott Key was politely but firmly kept on board for an unplanned stay as the British bombarded Fort McHenry and the Americans fought back. So it was that he spent the early dawn hours of the morning of September 14—watching the "rockets' red glare, the bombs bursting in air," and staring into the dawning light to see if the flag was still there.

The poem he wrote, originally titled "Defence [*sic*] of Fort M'Henry" had four verses, one of which we now know as the words to the American national anthem. The tune, it should be noted, was not composed by Key; it belonged to a popular drinking song titled "To Anacreon in Heaven." An *English* drinking song. Despite the tune's enemy origins and the fact that it is often considered unsingable, the combination of tune and words proved irresistible. The song we now know as "The Star-Spangled Banner" became increasingly popular and, in 1931, more than 100 years after Key penned his lines, a congressional resolution signed by President Herbert Hoover granted it official status as America's national anthem.

The Star-Spangled Banner National Historic Trail is named after the anthem, but it follows the events of the entire Chesapeake Campaign of the War of 1812, which took place from 1813 to 1814. While much of the War of 1812 took place in the Great Lakes and the last battle was fought in New Orleans, the Chesapeake Campaign was directed at America's morale.

The bay itself was important on several levels. America's largest estuary was a waterway to the interior of Virginia and the mid-Atlantic states. To the west, the Potomac River led to the American center of government in Washington, DC. To the south, the bay was an important byway to the agricultural slave-and-tobacco economy of Virginia. And to the

New Castle

NEW
JERSEY

95

Aberdeen

MARYLAND

70

83

70

Baltimore

Columbia

270

95

DOVER ⭐

Germantown

95

97

DELAWARE

Silver Spring

ANNAPOLIS
⭐

Bowie

WASHINGTON, DC ⭐

Easton

Arlington

66

Centreville

Alexandria

VIRGINIA

Salisbury

Fredericksburg

Spotsylvania

STAR-SPANGLED
BANNER
NATIONAL HISTORIC TRAIL

N

0   20 Miles

95

Accomac

north, it led to Baltimore, a hub of maritime trade and shipbuilding. Baltimore, in particular, was of keen interest to the British because it had developed a reputation as a harbor for privateers, which were the vessels licensed to attack enemy ships. The British viewed these ships as pirates, and the city of Baltimore as their home base.

In August and September of 1814, the English made their move. On August 24 and 25, they captured Washington, DC, where they burned the Capitol, the Treasury, the White House, and 3,000 volumes of the Library of Congress. In early September, they launched the pivotal attack on Baltimore: 25 hours of rockets, bombs, and cannonballs flying into the air, across the water, and at enemy ships. But after a rainy night of bombardment, the Americans still held their positions. As the British retreated, the enormous flag that had been commissioned by Major George Armistead, commander of Fort McHenry, was raised—and seen by Francis Scott Key, still imprisoned on a British ship 8 miles away.

How big would a flag have to be in order to be visible from 8 miles away? The flag Key saw was a 30-by-42-foot behemoth—a flag so large it had been sewn together in the loft of a brewery because that was the only space big enough for the job. The flag took up about as much space as the footprint of a house that has a 1,200-square-foot main floor. Today, however, what is left of the original flag measures only 30 by 34 feet; the missing 8 feet of length (and 240 square feet of flag) have been lost to memento seekers. In private hands for several decades after the war, the flag was owned by a family that sometimes agreed to requests for a fragment from veterans, government officials, and other prominent citizens. Many of those fragments were framed, donated to museums, and even donated to the Smithsonian, where the main flag resides—today under lock and key in a climate-controlled protective museum case.

The Star-Spangled Banner may have survived the bombardment, but the flag Key saw by the dawn's early light did not look like the one we salute today. The flag waving above Fort McHenry had 15 stars—which we would expect, because there were only 15 states in 1814—but it also had 15 stripes. In 1795, when Vermont and Kentucky joined the Union, the number of stars and stripes was changed to reflect the number of states. In 1818, that decision was revisited, and Congress decided that the number of stripes would stay stable at 13 for the original 13 colonies, while the stars would reflect the number of states.

With 15 stripes and 14 stars (it should have 15, but one was snipped off for a souvenir hunter), with or without all of its original length, the flag that survived the Battle of Baltimore is and always will be the Star-Spangled Banner. Sewn in a brewery and celebrated by a poem set to the tune of a British drinking song, it is the flag that became a symbol of the will of a young country to survive against overwhelming odds.

THE ROUTE

Wandering around and through the parks and waterways of Maryland, Virginia, and Washington, DC, the Star-Spangled Banner National Historic Trail follows the Chesapeake Bay and several of its tributaries to trace the path of American and British troops and naval ships during the final decisive battles of the War of 1812, and also incorporates the Star-Spangled Banner Byway, a driving route. The trail commemorates the Battle of Baltimore at Fort McHenry; the invasion and burning of Washington, DC; and the birth of America's national anthem.

The trail extends from Tangier Island, Virginia, through Washington, DC; Annapolis and Baltimore, Maryland; and into parts of Maryland's Eastern Shore. Although part of the trail is a water route, sites on land include museums, forts, historic homes, and interpretive exhibits that relate to various aspects of the role the Chesapeake Bay played in 1814 to bring an end to the war. It also highlights some of the distinctive landscapes and waterways of the Chesapeake region. In wildlife refuges and parks on the Potomac, Patuxent, and Patapsco Rivers, and on the shores and islands of the Chesapeake Bay, visitors can stand in places that look much as the British and Americans might have seen them more than 200 years ago.

FOLLOWING SPREAD: Battle of Bladensburg Monument near Bladensburg Waterfront Park, Maryland (top left); Reenactors at Fort Howard Park, Maryland (middle left); Historic Sotterley Plantation, Hollywood, Maryland (bottom left); Boardwalk through Battle Creek Cypress Swamp, Maryland (right)

LEFT: Fort McHenry National Monument and Historic Shrine, Maryland (top); Deer at North Point State Park, Maryland (bottom left); First Division Monument, Eisenhower Executive Office Building, Washington, DC (bottom right)

OPPOSITE: Potomac River from George Washington Birthplace National Monument, Virginia

LIVING THE HISTORY

The Star-Spangled Banner Trail offers water-based opportunities such as sailing, paddling, and boat tours. Land-based activities include hiking, biking, and geocaching. Some of the museums, visitor centers, and markers on the trail are contiguous with the Captain John Smith Chesapeake and Washington-Rochambeau Revolutionary Route National Historic Trails. The trail connects five national historic landmarks, four National Park Service sites, 37 National Register properties, two national natural landmarks, and 39 Chesapeake Bay Gateways.

Star-Spangled Banner Geotrail, Entire Route

Launched in 2010, the Star-Spangled Banner Geotrail is a geocaching challenge that takes visitors to more than 30 forts, museums, battlefields, ships, parks, and preserves associated with the national historic trail. This multistate project is a partnership between the Maryland Geocaching Society and the National Park Service. Participants use GPSes to locate a hidden cache. The GPS coordinates give the location, but the precise hiding place may be revealed through riddles and clues that lead searchers from one cache to the next. In addition to exploring the seascape of the War of 1812 in the Chesapeake, many of the caches also relate to the geography of the bay and its rivers.

Kenneth E. Behring Center, National Museum of American History, Washington, DC

The National Museum of American History in Washington, DC, is the home of *the* Star-Spangled Banner, the flag that inspired Francis Scott Key to write his immortal poem. The flag is displayed in an environmentally controlled chamber that protects it from damaging light and corrosion. An interactive table allows visitors to examine details of the flag. The exhibit describes how the flag was kept as a family keepsake in the 19th century, during which snippets were given as mementos to some of the people who requested them. It also explains the Smithsonian Institution's preservation efforts, and describes how the Star-Spangled Banner has been used to express different ideas about what it means to be an American.

Star-Spangled Banner Flag House, Baltimore, Maryland

A flag maker (yes, that was a job) named Mary Pickersgill sewed the flag that inspired the poem. Pickersgill was commissioned by the commander of Fort McHenry. She worked on the flag, along with her daughters, her niece, and an African American servant named Grace Wisher, in her brick home—although the final assembly was done in the loft of a brewery because the flag was so big. In addition to owning her own business, Pickersgill also owned her own home (unusual for a colonial woman). In the colonial version of Airbnb, she even added a boarder's room. The house is now a museum run by a nonprofit.

Pride of Baltimore II, Baltimore Harbor, Maryland

The best way to experience the Chesapeake, of course, is on the water. When the *Pride of Baltimore II* is in her home harbor, a deck tour or day sail is a way to step back into history and experience the bay the way the seamen of 1812 might have. The *Pride of Baltimore II* is actually the third *Pride of Baltimore.* The first was officially named the *Chasseur*, a legendary Baltimore-built topsail schooner that was active in the War of 1812; it was nicknamed the "Pride of Baltimore." The first reproduction *Pride of Baltimore* was built in 1977 in Baltimore's Inner Harbor. She copied the sleek maneuverable design of the 19th-century Baltimore clippers that privateers used to attack British merchant ships during the War of 1812. After sailing more than 150,000 nautical miles, she sank in a storm near Puerto Rico in 1986. The current *Pride of Baltimore II* was built in 1986–1988 and is nicknamed "America's Star-Spangled Ambassador." She has sailed more than 275,000 nautical miles to 200 ports in 40 countries.

Fort McHenry National Monument and Historic Shrine, Baltimore, Maryland

The War of 1812 was a confusing mess of old rivalries and new politics, extending from lingering ill will left over from the Revolutionary War to Napoleonic conflicts in Europe to the possibility of America chasing the British out of southern Canada (and perhaps taking over) to arguments over Atlantic blockades and impressed seamen. A film at Fort McHenry tries to untangle the web of causes and rivalries that caused the young America to go to war again and the British to burn the Capitol. Exhibits include officers' quarters, bunk rooms, storage areas, and the ramparts and cannons overlooking the bay. The fort also hosts living history interpretations and firing demonstrations complete with a waving flag (if the winds cooperate).

Maryland Historical Society, Baltimore, Maryland

The prize artifact at the Maryland Historical Society is the piece of yellowed paper that contains the handwritten lyrics to "The Star-Spangled Banner"—then called "Defence [*sic*] of Fort M'Henry." If you ever want to learn the other three verses, that's where you will find them. The oldest continuously operating cultural institution in the state, the society houses the most significant collection of Maryland cultural artifacts. The museum's collection includes portraits and miniatures of Maryland heroes from the War of 1812, including one of Francis Scott Key himself, and paintings of schooners used by American privateers against British merchant ships. Also featured are furniture, textiles, quilts, samplers, clothing, accessories, bed and table linens, flags, porcelain, pottery, stoneware, glass, baskets, sketchbooks, architectural drawings, agricultural equipment, toys, dolls, and archaeological objects.

Francis Scott Key Memorial Park, Washington, DC

Washington, DC, is full of enormous memorials. This is not one of them. The small, formal park and memorial dedicated to Francis Scott Key is located in the heart of Georgetown. The site includes a bronze bust of Key, exhibits that tell his story, and a historically correct 1814 American flag with 15 stars and 15 stripes. Key and his family lived in a house (since torn down) close to the present-day memorial for 25 years. Note that only seven minutes away (if there's no traffic), but accessed from the other side of the Potomac River, is Theodore Roosevelt Island, which has hiking trails that give a good idea of what the Potomac would have looked like before development.

Top: Exterior of the room housing the Star-Spangled Banner, Smithsonian National Museum of American History, Washington, DC; *Middle left:* Desk of Mary Pickersgill, maker of the flag that inspired Francis Scott Key's famous poem, Star-Spangled Banner Flag House, Baltimore, Maryland; *Middle right:* Francis Scott Key Memorial, Washington, DC; *Bottom:* Living history at Fort McHenry National Monument and Historic Shrine, Baltimore, Maryland

PART THREE

WESTWARD EXPANSION

★

In 1803, Thomas Jefferson made the biggest real estate deal in American history. The American president paid the French emperor $15 million for about 828,000 square miles of land. Far away in France, Napoleon Bonaparte signed away not only French Louisiana, but also all the land France had formerly claimed between the Gulf of Mexico and the northern border of what would become Montana. For about three cents an acre, Jefferson acquired all or parts of 14 future states (and, for a time, bits of two future Canadian provinces). • Like any good real estate buyer, Jefferson wanted to know the details of his purchase. He appointed Meriwether Lewis and William Clark to explore the Missouri River, learn about and trade with the American Indians, find a continuous water route from the East to the

Pacific Ocean, and gain knowledge about "other objects worthy of notice":

> the soil & face of the country, it's [sic] growth & vegetable productions, especially those not of the U.S.; the animals of the country generally, & especially those not known in the U.S.; the remains & accounts of any which may be deemed rare or extinct; the mineral productions of every kind, but more particularly metals, limestone, pit coal, & saltpetre; salines & mineral waters, noting the temperature of the last & such circumstances as may indicate their character; volcanic appearances; climate as characterized by the thermometer, by the proportion of rainy, cloudy, & clear days, by lightening [sic], hail, snow, ice, by the access & recess of frost, by the winds, prevailing at different seasons, the dates at which particular plants put forth or lose their flowers, or leaf, times of appearance of particular birds, reptiles, or insects.

The route of the journey taken to fulfill this impossibly enormous assignment is the Lewis and Clark National Historic Trail. It passes nearly 5,000 miles through 16 states, following the route of the Corps of Discovery as the group traveled on foot, on horseback, and by boat to explore not only the Louisiana Purchase, but also lands to its west, including what would become Idaho, Oregon, and Washington, all the way to the Pacific coast. Lewis and Clark returned with the most detailed and copious notes in the history of exploration, although their expedition only scratched the surface of the enormous region: a partial list of places they did not visit includes the Wind River Mountains, the region that is now Yellowstone and Glacier National Parks, and the critically important South Pass on the Continental Divide.

Their journey is the linchpin for American western discovery, emigration, and settlement, all of which are commemorated by the seven trails in this section.

In the years that followed the Corps of Discovery Expedition, other explorers, fur trappers, traders, and mountain men filled in some of the blank spots on the map. While Lewis and Clark had successfully crossed the Continental Divide, they had not found a route suitable for wagons (let alone the nonexistent continuous water route Jefferson had hoped for). But by 1812, South Pass had been identified as a passable wagon route across the Continental Divide, and idle curiosity about the West turned into active interest as more and more reports drifted back. A few years later, a young Jim Bridger became the first Anglo-American to see the Salt Lake Valley. By 1821, the US flag had 24 stars on it, and the country now extended clear to the Mississippi River. To the southwest, Mexico achieved independence from Spain and instituted more relaxed trade regulations.

The Santa Fe National Historic Trail celebrates a trade route that sprang into use almost overnight, after Mexico indicated a willingness to trade with the United States. The route connected Santa Fe and St. Louis—and, when linked with other trails, created a trail network that extended to the Pacific Ocean, Mexico City, and points east in the United States. It was a vital part of the Southwest's transition from Spanish to Mexican to American control.

To the north, another, much larger migration exploded as Americans began looking toward Oregon, California, and Utah. The idea of Manifest Destiny told Americans that their expansion across the country was necessary, desirable, and inevitable. The emigrant paths commemorated by the next four trails were ground into the earth by oxen, mules, cattle, horses, and wagons as more than 400,000 settlers, adventurers, and pilgrims heeded that call and made their way west between 1843 and 1869.

The Oregon National Historic Trail follows settlers bound for the Willamette Valley, starting with the first large-scale wagon trains of 1843. The Mormon Pioneer National Historic Trail follows the members of the Church of Jesus Christ of Latter-day Saints as they embarked on an exodus to Utah in 1847. The California National Historic Trail celebrates the gold rush, which began in 1848 and established the economic foundation of the American West. Finally, the Pony Express National Historic Trail commemorates the mail service that opened communications between the West and the rest of the American continent.

These four trails are closely interwoven. Emigrants started from various points along the Missouri

PREVIOUS SPREAD: Jefferson River through Sheep Gulch, Lewis and Clark Trail, Lewis and Clark Caverns State Park, Montana

Burial site of Isaac Allen, Santa Fe Trail, Point of Rocks, New Mexico

Platte River, Mormon Pioneer
Trail, Nebraska

River, but the trails converged 200 miles away near Fort Kearny in central Nebraska and shared the same basic route for about the next 800 miles. Sometimes variations emerged—high water might require a different route to cross the Platte River; the Mormons elected to separate themselves from the other groups by traveling on the north bank while everyone else followed the south bank—but many of the historic sites east of the Continental Divide apply to all four of the trails.

Fort Kearny is the gateway to the emigrant trails. It was established in 1848 because the location had become the convergence point for various wagon trains. Those first 200 miles were the shakedown part of the trip: time to learn to manage a wagon, to establish the routines of travel, to schedule daily chores, to realize that a family needed more of this and less of that, and what had they been thinking when they decided to take along an accordion and a violin instead of a frying pan and an extra pair of shoes? Fort Kearny was what long-distance hikers

today would call a trail town: a place where settlers could repair or buy gear and emergency supplies, get medical attention, or post a letter. It was also the point of no return—the place where emigrants cut the proverbial umbilical cord. From here forward, chances to buy or repair supplies would be few and far between.

Today, Kearney is the modest county seat of Nebraska's Buffalo County right off I-80, just about halfway across the state. (The "e" in the name of the town was added, reputedly as a result of postmen routinely misspelling the name of the fort.) Kearney has perhaps 30,000 inhabitants, a rather good art museum, a visitor center that commemorates all four of the emigrant trails, and an annual sandhill crane migration that animal behaviorist Jane Goodall has called "one of the most impressive wildlife migrations in the world."

That crane migration is worth noting because, as so often happens, wildlife knows the best travel routes—and, as with so many paths, people follow in the footsteps, or, in this case, the wingbeats, of wildlife.

Cranes have been migrating along the Platte River for millennia. Heading north and west from Fort Kearny, the annual travel ways of 500,000 birds converged with the once-in-a-lifetime journey of thousands—and in some years tens of thousands—of settlers on all four of the trails that shared the same path heading west.

For the cranes, the Platte—"a mile wide, an inch deep"—offered safe roosting and nighttime protection from predators in its braided shallows. For the settlers, the river—described as "too thin to plow, too thick to drink"—offered the safety of an assured water source through what would come to be known, quite erroneously, as the Great American Desert. (And, not unimportantly, the settlers made use of the "ribeye in the sky" as a food source for their journey, severely depleting the crane population.) When the paths diverged, the cranes continued north, one wingbeat at a time, to Alaska and even Siberia, while the settlers forged their way west, one step at a time, to South Pass on the Continental Divide.

The four trails continued contiguously through western Nebraska, where vertical landforms began to loom, and bluffs, pinnacles, and towers gave the landscape a decidedly western accent. Landmarks could now be seen from miles away: Courthouse and Jail Rocks, Chimney Rock poking into the sky, and Scotts Bluff, where Oregon-bound travelers could tell themselves they had completed one-third of the journey. Continuing up the North Platte into what is now Wyoming, the four trails reached Fort Laramie. Built as a post for trade with the regional American Indians, Fort Laramie became a major resupply post and military fort. Some spots in Wyoming still carry the names of the past into the future: at Register Cliff and Independence Rock, 170-year-old graffiti is still visible. Nearby, wagon ruts—some five feet deep—are etched into the land. The final stretch to the Continental Divide was a trek along the Sweetwater River, which leads around the north side of the Great Divide Basin. The Sweetwater made travel possible in a region known for alkaline ponds and hard, desert-like terrain, part of Wyoming's Red Desert. But even with the river, this high, dry plateau could still pack a punch, with howling winds and early winter storms that sometimes ended in tragedy.

Past what is now called Atlantic City, the settlers climbed up and over the anticlimactic high plateau of South Pass to Pacific Springs (the place names describing the job of the Continental Divide). The emigrants were hardened now, and the Continental Divide was behind them. Once on the western slope, the four trails split from each other like the ends of a badly frayed rope, breaking into tributaries and alternate routes, depending on trail conditions, season, and destination. The Oregon Trail continued west along the Snake and Columbia Rivers to Oregon and the Willamette Valley. The California Trail used two or three alternate routes to turn southwest, cross Nevada, and enter California, where it broke up even more to lead to goldfields and settlements all over the state. The Mormon Pioneer Trail headed south to Salt Lake City, and the Pony Express Trail followed an arrow-straight path to connect St. Joseph, Missouri, and Sacramento, California. In all, some 400,000 people migrated west using the route from the Platte River to

View of Jail Rock from Courthouse Rock, Mormon Pioneer Trail, Nebraska

South Pass—70,000 Mormons went to the Salt Lake Valley; 250,000 emigrants headed to California and its goldfields; and 80,000 settlers headed to Oregon.

Together, these four trails form a network that allows visitors to experience the Old West through scores of national parks, forests, Bureau of Land Management lands, and state and local parks; hundreds of certified historic sites, museums, interpretive sites, and markers; and thousands of miles of roadways and trails.

The final trail in this section is a bit of an anomaly because it takes place even farther west and north, and it tells several stories spread across hundreds of years in time. The Iditarod National Historic Trail is a 2,300-mile network of dogsled trails that were first used to connect Native Alaskan settlements during the arctic and subarctic winters, and later used by gold miners and settlers to reach the Alaskan interior. Today, the Iditarod network is Alaska's only national historic trail, and the only winter trail on the national historic trails roster—most of it is only usable when marshes and swamps are frozen and snow covers the ground. It is also unique because it reaches across centuries and cultures—commemorating Native Alaskan culture, dogsledding, the role of winter trails in the gold rush, the Mercy Run of 1925, and the famed Iditarod endurance race—while offering the opportunity to experience Alaska's winter interior on dogsleds, snowshoes, cross-country skis, and snowmobiles.

The Wild West is no longer as wild as it once was, and the frontier has long since been declared closed. But, even if it is no longer as wild, the West remains as big, and, in the open expanses between cities and airports, wild lands still look very much as they once did. Visitors to the seven national historic trails in this section can experience a little of what it must have been like to strike into the unknown and face the enormity of the western landscape.

Dogsled team passing the rocks along the Yukon River, Iditarod Trail, Alaska

Lewis and Clark Trail

4,900 MILES PENNSYLVANIA • OHIO • WEST VIRGINIA • KENTUCKY • INDIANA • ILLINOIS
MISSOURI • KANSAS • NEBRASKA • IOWA • SOUTH DAKOTA • NORTH DAKOTA
MONTANA • IDAHO • OREGON • WASHINGTON

When Thomas Jefferson charged Meriwether Lewis and William Clark with the task of finding a route across the 828,000 square miles of the newly purchased Louisiana Territory, he could hardly have anticipated that he would become the proud owner of a presidential prairie dog.

The prairie dog in question was the lucky survivor of an attempted drowning. Encountering the unfamiliar animals for the first time, a member of the Corps of Discovery did what any self-respecting explorer would do: he killed one and cooked it for the captains' dinner. Intrigued by the little creatures, Clark decided to catch some using the made-up-on-the-spot hunting method of pouring barrels of water into the burrows. It was a less-than-impressive success: after several hours, a single prairie dog was caught. But this specimen was not destined for the stew pot. Taken on board, it rode on the expedition keelboat and spent the winter of 1804–1805 in the camp at Fort Mandan, now in North Dakota.

The following April, Lewis and Clark sent a shipment of specimens and artifacts back east to Jefferson; they decided the prairie dog had another purpose. Along with animal skins, skeletons, soil samples, rocks, plants, seeds, American Indian buffalo robes, pottery, pipes, bows and arrows, and antelope, deer, and elk antlers, they included four live magpies, a prairie hen, and the prairie dog with this shipment. Only one of the magpies and the prairie dog survived. It spent a brief time amusing the president before living out its life in a Philadelphia museum.

The Corps of Discovery was charged with much more than collecting samples, artifacts, and unusual animals. The group was assigned to discover, evaluate, and describe travel routes, take notes, make maps, and establish trade relations with myriad American Indian tribes from the Missouri River to the Pacific Northwest coast. Think of all the things American citizens—other than a few isolated traders and trappers—had never seen in 1803: the Rocky Mountains of Wyoming and Montana; the Continental Divide; the volcanoes of the Cascades; the great westward-flowing Snake and Columbia Rivers; sagebrush, tumbleweed, and Douglas firs; and grizzly bears, miles-long herds of buffalo, mountain goats, bighorn sheep—and prairie dogs.

And then consider the assignment: to explore a linear distance to the Pacific Ocean and back of some 4,000 miles. (The actual distance was longer, as the expedition did not take an as-the-crow-flies line.) An extremely fit walker might have covered 20 to 25 miles a day—if they knew where they were going and didn't have to take time out to hunt, fish, or gather their food, not to mention dine, trade, negotiate with various tribes they met along the way, or haul all their gear upstream or downstream. Even when using horses and boats, the expedition would not have traveled much faster than it did under human power, and when towing boats upstream or portaging around obstacles, progress was much slower. Winter stopped them entirely, forcing the expedition to camp in one place for months on end.

Marker designating campsite of the Lewis and Clark Expedition, McGarry Bar Primitive Boat Camp, Upper Missouri River Breaks National Monument, Montana

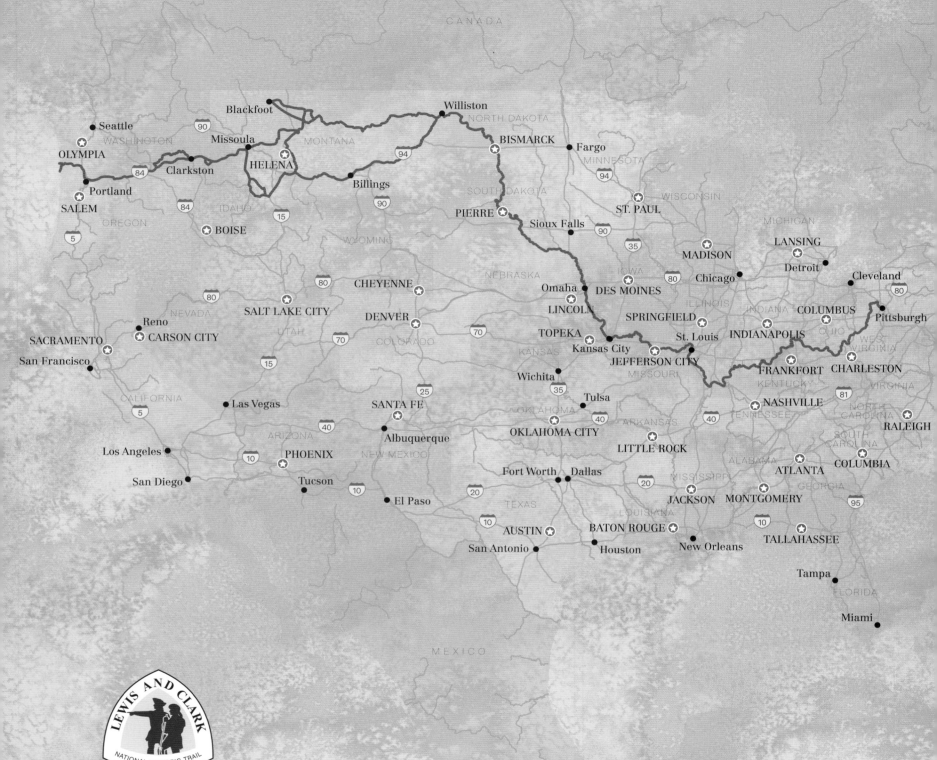

Seattle

OLYMPIA

Portland

SALEM

Clarkston

Blackfoot

Missoula

HELENA

Billings

BOISE

OLYMPIA

WASHINGTON

OREGON

IDAHO

MONTANA

Williston

NORTH DAKOTA

BISMARCK

Fargo

MINNESOTA

SOUTH DAKOTA

PIERRE

Sioux Falls

ST. PAUL

WISCONSIN

MICHIGAN

MADISON

LANSING

Detroit

Cleveland

Pittsburgh

CHEYENNE

DENVER

SALT LAKE CITY

Reno

CARSON CITY

SACRAMENTO

San Francisco

NEVADA

UTAH

WYOMING

COLORADO

NEBRASKA

IOWA

Chicago

DES MOINES

Omaha

LINCOLN

SPRINGFIELD

St. Louis

INDIANAPOLIS

COLUMBUS

ILLINOIS

INDIANA

OHIO

WEST VIRGINIA

CHARLESTON

FRANKFORT

KENTUCKY

VIRGINIA

RALEIGH

NORTH CAROLINA

TOPEKA

Kansas City

JEFFERSON CITY

KANSAS

MISSOURI

Wichita

Tulsa

NASHVILLE

TENNESSEE

SOUTH CAROLINA

COLUMBIA

Las Vegas

SANTA FE

Albuquerque

CALIFORNIA

ARIZONA

NEW MEXICO

OKLAHOMA CITY

OKLAHOMA

ARKANSAS

LITTLE ROCK

ATLANTA

GEORGIA

ALABAMA

Los Angeles

PHOENIX

Tucson

El Paso

Fort Worth

Dallas

MISSISSIPPI

JACKSON

MONTGOMERY

San Diego

AUSTIN

TEXAS

San Antonio

Houston

BATON ROUGE

LOUISIANA

New Orleans

TALLAHASSEE

MEXICO

Tampa

FLORIDA

Miami

CANADA

LEWIS AND CLARK

NATIONAL HISTORIC TRAIL

0   500 Miles

N

Equipment, too, would have been a challenge. There were no fiberglass boats, no ultralight tents, no Gore-Tex rain gear, no freeze-dried foods, no GPS coordinates or cell phones or Google maps. Gear in 1803 was heavy and cumbersome, never mind the lack of lifetime warranties and overnight-expressed replacement gear that is available to modern explorers. Most of all, without proper maps, the journey was full of surprises: too much water, lack of water, navigable rivers, impassable rapids, steep-walled canyons, endless prairies that looked like deserts but supported millions of bison, snow-clad mountain ranges with passes that may or may not be passable, and bears, mountain lions, and rattlesnakes.

Lewis and Clark did exactly as charged. Over the nearly three years they spent west of the Mississippi, the expedition not only shipped back enough artifacts to fill a museum, but also took some of the most copious notes in the history of exploration. Here are a few random highlights and oddities:

> The expedition allocated an enormous amount of its budget and packing space for bales of gifts to give to American Indians they met along the way. Gifts had several important purposes: to display American technology and tools (corn mills, needles and thread, sheet metal, pocket looking glasses, butcher knives); to encourage American Indian consumerism and a desire to trade (combs, flannel, handkerchiefs, lockets, earrings); and to establish good relations, without which the expedition would not have succeeded (pipe tomahawks, beads, and peace medals showing the face of Jefferson, the new "great father").

> The Corps of Discovery mapped its route and named features. Some of the names came from American Indians; other names commemorated aspects of the expedition, prominent characteristics of a landform or waterway, or incidents. For example, Camp Fortunate marked the place where Sacagawea (sometimes spelled Sacajawea) found her long-separated brother. Some were named for some of the men, as well as for Sacagawea's son, Lewis's dog, prominent political leaders, and a few special women back home.

> The slowest part of the trip was an 18-mile portage around the Great Falls of the Missouri River. It took about three weeks to haul the heavy wooden boats (called pirogues) over slopes, gullies, rocks, roots, prickly pear cacti, and dust around the five cascades, whose torrents could be heard from 7 miles away. Going upstream in the keelboat, the expedition covered about 10 to 20 miles per day. In contrast, on the return journey, while canoeing down the Missouri River with the current behind them, they were able to cover 70 miles in a single day.

> The expedition held the first American court-martials in the Louisiana Territory. The charges included theft of alcohol and ensuing drunkenness, sleeping on guard duty, desertion, and "mutinous expression," among others. Lashes (or, in the last case, expulsion from the expedition) were the punishment. This treatment was seen as barbaric by the Arikara, who were present at the event and pleaded for leniency for the convicted.

William Clark's signature (behind protective glass) carved into a sandstone bluff along the Yellowstone River, Pompeys Pillar National Monument, Montana

- Sacagawea, the Shoshone woman who became famous for accompanying the expedition up the headwaters of the Missouri and facilitating interactions with American Indian tribes, had her own storied history: she was kidnapped by the Hidatsas and sold to a French trapper named Charbonneau, who took her as his wife. When she accompanied the expedition, she had just given birth to her son and carried him with her. Near the Missouri headwaters, she found her home country and her long-separated brother, who was now a Shoshone chief.

- The corps encountered and depended on the generosity of many tribes, but Lewis described the Nez Perce as "the most hospitable, honest, and sincere people that we have met with in our voyage" and noted, about their gift of horses (which may have saved the expedition from starvation in the Bitterroot Mountains), that "this is a much greater act of hospitality than we have witnessed from any nation or tribe since we have passed the Rocky Mountains"—a not-so-small irony as explained in a later chapter about the national historic trail devoted to the history of that tribe.

- The expedition lost only one member, who died of illness. Members of the Corps of Discovery killed two young Blackfeet boys, who, Lewis charged, were attempting to steal guns and horses.

- The expedition did indeed find a way to the Pacific Ocean—although it was several more years before a route was found that could accommodate wagon traffic.

- While the Charbonneau family returned to the Knife River villages, Lewis and Clark and their men returned home to a hero's welcome and a hero's reward: each man received double pay and 320 acres of land. The captains got 1,600 acres apiece. (Sacagawea was never paid for her services to the expedition.) Lewis was named governor of the Louisiana Territory, and Clark became superintendent of Indian Affairs for the West and governor of the Missouri Territory.

- Lewis died only a few years later, at the age of 35, on the Natchez Trace in Tennessee. History does not know whether he was the victim of murder or suicide; competing theories include political skullduggery, bandits, the debilitating effects of malaria, and insanity due to syphilis.

- William Clark died in 1838, at age 68. In 2001, President Bill Clinton promoted Clark to the posthumous rank of captain in the US Army. He also presented the title of honorary sergeant, regular army, to Sacagawea and to York, Clark's personal slave, who was the first African American to cross the continent and was instrumental in the expedition's success (though, like Sacagawea, he was never paid for his services).

THE ROUTE

When certified in 1978, the Lewis and Clark National Historic Trail started at the expedition's jumping-off point at Wood River, Illinois, near where the Missouri River meets the Mississippi River 20 miles upstream from St. Louis. In 2019, the John D. Dingell Jr. Conservation, Management, and Recreation Act extended the trail an additional 1,200 miles to include the expedition's preparatory route along the Ohio and Mississippi Rivers.

Today's Lewis and Clark Trail therefore begins in Pittsburgh, where, over the summer of 1803, Lewis supervised the construction of the expedition keelboat. The route follows his boat trip down the Ohio River to St. Louis, and then to the winter quarters at Camp Wood (also known as Camp River Dubois), where the expedition did its final organization of men and gear—counting up supplies, arms, scientific equipment, items for trade, and gifts for American Indians—and then outfitting and packing the boats.

The expedition was largely an exploration of the river systems of the American interior and Northwest. Jefferson wrote, "The object of your mission is to explore the Missouri river, & such principal stream of it, as, by it's [sic] course & communication with the waters of the Pacific Ocean, may offer the most direct & practicable water communication across this continent, for the purposes of commerce."

Some of the regions through which the expedition passed are protected as wilderness and might be recognizable if the Corps of Discovery could visit them today. Other landscapes and river segments have

Camas blooms, Weippe Prairie, Idaho (top); Sergeant Floyd Monument, commemorating the only member of the Corps of Discovery to die on the journey, Sioux City, Iowa (bottom left); Monument to Sacagawea and her son, Three Forks, Montana (bottom right)

been altered—by nature, development, industry, river management, damming, flooding, and pavement.

From Camp Wood (long since destroyed by changing courses of the Mississippi, Missouri, and Wood Rivers), the expedition moved upstream on the Missouri River, which forms the border of what is now Missouri and Kansas, then Iowa and Nebraska (with a little bit of overlap). The members of the corps crossed South Dakota and then, in North Dakota, halted at the earthen lodge villages of the Mandan and Hidatsa tribes, where they built Fort Mandan for their winter quarters and moved in (with the prairie dog). But Fort Mandan is notable for a much more important reason: it is here that Lewis and Clark met Sacagawea, who would accompany the expedition up the Missouri and beyond.

The trail then follows the route the Corps of Discovery members took the next spring as they continued upriver to the Great Falls of the Missouri River in Montana, and then on to the headwaters of the Missouri at Three Forks. There, they took the westernmost tributary until they reached Camp Fortunate, where they found Sacagawea's homeland. Continuing west and up into the region of the Continental Divide, they were forced to leave the river for an overland route, as the rivers were unnavigable. They crossed the rugged Continental Divide three times in the Bitterroot Mountains (once over a pass whose name—Lost Trail Pass—tells us something about their experiences there), got caught in early winter snow, and were almost starving when they were helped onward by the Nez Perce.

Now on the Pacific side of the Continental Divide, the trail continues west, following the route the corps members traversed down the Clearwater, Snake, and Columbia Rivers using dugout canoes they had built themselves, with methods learned from the Nez Perce. Surviving dangerous rapids, they wintered near the mouth of the Columbia River at Fort Clatsop.

Then, in the spring of 1806, they set out eastward to do it all over again—but backward this time (and with a few extra exploratory loops in Montana).

Clark Canyon Reservoir, which inundated
the site of Camp Fortunate, Montana

PREVIOUS SPREAD: General location where the Lewis and Clark Expedition set off from Wood River, Lewis and Clark State Historic Site, Illinois (top left); Replica of Lewis and Clark's keelboat, Lewis and Clark State Park, Iowa (middle left); Earth lodges at On-A-Slant Indian Village, Fort Abraham Lincoln State Park, North Dakota (bottom left); Moon over the Missouri River, Upper Missouri River Breaks National Monument, Montana (right)

OPPOSITE: Grand Natural Wall along the Missouri River, Upper Missouri River Breaks National Monument, Montana

RIGHT: Balanced rock formations and eroded hoodoos above the Missouri River (top and bottom right) and Rocky Mountain sheep (bottom left), Upper Missouri River Breaks National Monument, Montana

PREVIOUS SPREAD: Black Eagle Falls along the Missouri River, Montana (top left); Tepees on the shore of Jefferson River, Montana (bottom left); Madison and Jefferson Rivers converging to create the Missouri River, Missouri Headwaters State Park, Montana (right)

OPPOSITE: Lolo Motorway near Green Swoard Camp, Bitterroot Mountains, Idaho

RIGHT: Monument atop Lemhi Pass designating where Lewis realized it would not be an easy descent to the Pacific Ocean, Idaho (top); Cape Disappointment State Park, Washington (bottom)

LIVING THE HISTORY

About 80 percent of the expedition's journey was accomplished by boat: canoes, keelboats, and pirogues (flat-bottomed canoes) traveling on the Ohio, Mississippi, Missouri, Jefferson, Clearwater, Snake, and Columbia Rivers. Long stretches of the Columbia and Missouri are hardworking rivers today—managed, dammed, and developed for industry and agriculture. But some sections still evoke the wild and scenic past. Sightseeing boats take visitors on the Upper Missouri (a designated wild and scenic river) and the Gates of the Mountains segment (both in Montana). Auto and RV touring also bring visitors close to the original route. Lewis and Clark route markers are found along back roads, interstates, and scenic byways; maps make it possible to parallel the expedition's river travel, as well as follow some of its land-based segments. In addition, this trail is especially rich in interpretive sites located at expedition campsites, forts, and on American Indian lands, and has several large interpretive centers with state-of-the-art exhibits and replica artifacts focusing on different aspects of the expedition.

Gateway Arch National Park, St. Louis, Missouri

Gateway Arch National Park includes the Gateway Arch, the Museum at the Gateway Arch, and the Old Courthouse (one of the oldest buildings in St. Louis). The 630-foot-tall stainless-steel arch is the tallest monument in the United States. Designed to withstand high winds and earthquakes, it is a monument to the spirit of western pioneers. The Museum at the Gateway Arch is below the arch. Its exhibits include an overview of the Lewis and Clark Expedition and an extensive collection of artifacts about the westward migration movements of the 1800s.

Katy Trail State Park Rail Trail, Missouri

Nearly 240 miles long, the Katy Trail spans almost the full width of Missouri following the former corridor of the Missouri-Kansas-Texas Railroad. It is the country's longest continuous rail trail. About 125 miles between Cooper County and St. Charles County are designated as an official segment of the Lewis and Clark Trail. The trail takes bicyclists, walkers, runners, equestrians, nature lovers, and history buffs through rural farmland and small towns along the Missouri River. The Katy Trail is a millennium legacy trail and was included in the Rails-to-Trails Conservancy Hall of Fame in 2008; it is also part of the American Discovery Trail.

Missouri River Basin Lewis and Clark Visitor Center, Nebraska City, Nebraska

The unique focus of this interpretive center is the scientific documentation of the flora and fauna recorded by the Lewis and Clark Expedition (178 species of plants and 122 species of animals new to European and European American science). Located on a 79-acre wooded bluff, the center offers a view that gives visitors a sense of what Lewis and Clark might have seen as they made their way up the Missouri River. Inside the center, visitors can view each of the 122 new animal species that Lewis and Clark recorded in their journals. Mounts of buffalo, black bears, bobcats, mule deer, wolves, elk, mountain goats, pronghorn antelope, and beavers bring the animal ecology of the plains and bluffs to life. Many of the mounts are realistic action poses—including a grizzly bear that growls at visitors from behind some trees. Outdoors, trails around the property offer a chance to spot wildlife such as deer, turkeys, raccoons, and more.

North Dakota Lewis and Clark Interpretive Center and Fort Mandan, Washburn, North Dakota

Fort Mandan was one of the most important sites of the Lewis and Clark Expedition. The fort no longer exists, but a full-scale replica is found at the Lewis and Clark Interpretive Center approximately 10 miles downriver. As the first winter encampment among the American Indians, Fort Mandan was where expedition leaders engaged in diplomacy with regional tribes, prepared for the next part of the journey, and consolidated the records and specimens they would send downriver to Jefferson in the spring. It is also where Lewis and Clark met some of the people who became central to the success of the expedition: Sacagawea, who accompanied them and facilitated trade and councils as well as good relations with American Indians like the Shoshone along the way; her French husband, the trapper and trader Toussaint Charbonneau; and Sheheke-shote, a chief who traveled with Lewis and Clark on the 1806 return journey to meet Jefferson. The museum features state-of-the-art exhibits and hundreds of artifacts about the expedition and the Mandan and Hidatsa people.

Upper Missouri River Breaks National Monument, James Kipp State Park to Fort Benton, Montana

The 150-mile journey on the Missouri River through the Upper Missouri Breaks National Monument in Montana is one of the great multiday canoe or kayak journeys in the United States. The river rarely exceeds Class 1 as it meanders through fantastic badlands of sandstone riverbanks containing a spectacular array of ecological, geological, and historical sites. The national monument extends from Fort Benton to the Charles M. Russell National Wildlife Refuge and includes six wilderness study areas, segments of the Lewis and Clark Trail and the Nez Perce Trail, the Cow Creek Area of Critical Environmental Concern, and the Fort Benton National Historic Landmark. Designated as a wild and scenic river by Congress, many parts of this corridor have remained largely unchanged in the 200 years since Lewis and Clark passed through.

Lewis and Clark National Historic Trail Interpretive Center, Great Falls, Montana

The Great Falls of the Missouri River were an important navigational landmark for the Corps of Discovery, but the portage was one of the most time-consuming and difficult parts of the expedition. The interpretive center communicates the sense of challenge, discovery, and awe members of the corps would have felt as they explored farther and farther into the unknown. Exhibits focus on the daily life of the expedition, the environment, and the American Indians. The center also houses the Lewis and Clark Trail Heritage Foundation's office and the William P. Sherman Library, which is open to the public. A network of hiking trails leads along the Missouri River and its cliffs and bluffs.

Top: Katy Trail, Missouri; *Middle left:* Replica of Fort Mandan, Lewis and Clark Interpretive Center, North Dakota; *Middle right:* Life-size diorama of the Corps of Discovery portaging dugout canoes around Great Falls, Missouri River, Lewis and Clark Interpretive Center, Montana; *Bottom:* Cliffs above the Missouri River, Upper Missouri River Breaks National Monument, Montana

Lolo Trail, Bitterroot Mountains, Idaho

The Lewis and Clark Expedition was charged with exploring the riverways of the American interior to find a way to the Pacific. But by definition, the crossing of the Continental Divide, which separates the Atlantic and Pacific drainages, was a land crossing. It proved to be one of the most difficult sections of the entire trip. Early winter snowstorms, frigid temperatures, a shortage of food, steep mountains, and impassible canyons delayed the travelers as they trekked over the Continental Divide, then followed the Bitterroot River down the other side. At Lolo Pass, they picked up the Lolo Trail, an ancient indigenous trade and hunting route that followed the ridgetops to north of today's Highway 12. The Lolo Pass Visitor Center displays information on the journey across the Bitterroot Mountains, as well as the 1877 flight of the Nez Perce. In addition to being part of both national historic trails, the Lolo Trail is itself a national historic landmark, with interconnecting routes that offer opportunities for backcountry auto touring, mountain biking, and hiking. The Lolo Motorway—also called Forest Road 500—was built by the Civilian Conservation Corps in the 1930s. It takes summertime travelers with four-wheel-drive vehicles through some of Lewis and Clark's actual land route through green meadows, forests of lodgepole and ponderosa pine, and ridgelines with mountain views.

Sacajawea Interpretive, Cultural, and Educational Center, Salmon, Idaho

Exhibits and education programs at the center focus on the Agaidika and Shoshone-Bannock tribes, the Lewis and Clark Expedition, western frontier life, and the natural environment. The center contains displays about Sacajawea and her role in the expedition. The center is open Memorial Day through Labor Day; the walking trails (which sometimes become groomed cross-country ski trails in winter) are open year-round.

Columbia Gorge Discovery Center and Museum, The Dalles, Oregon

One unique exhibit at the center is the result of 16 years of research about the 30-ton cargo the Corps of Discovery carried across the continent. The exhibits show how Lewis and Clark decided on and acquired their cargo—not only supplies

for themselves, but also tons of trade goods and gifts for American Indians they met. And once they acquired their supplies, they had to pack them—and then transport them upriver. An interactive exhibit lets visitors figure it out for themselves as they step into a canvas tent, heft a load that a corps member would have hauled, aim a flintlock rifle, and check out medicine that would have been used for almost any ailment suffered by anyone in the expedition over the course of more than two years.

Lewis and Clark National Historical Park, Oregon and Washington

Lewis and Clark spent their final winter at Fort Clatsop on the mouth of the Columbia River. A replica at the Lewis and Clark National Historical Park gives visitors a sense of the expedition's daily life with demonstrations (in season) of such early 19th-century skills as shooting a flintlock gun, tanning hides, and making candles. The park encompasses sites along the Columbia River and the Pacific coast that were visited and explored by members of the Corps of Discovery, and a rich assortment of museums tells segments of the story, including the nearby Lewis and Clark Interpretive Center at Cape Disappointment. Trails lead to

majestic vistas, coastal rain forests, and beaches, where surf fishing, clam digging, charter fishing, and wildlife viewing are favorite activities.

Lewis and Clark Bicycle Trail, Illinois to Washington

The Lewis and Clark Bicycle Trail begins in Hartford, Illinois, close to where the expedition began its journey up the Missouri River. The trail currently has 4,589 mapped miles, including spurs, detours, and Lewis's looping return path, which split off from Clark's route in order to explore more of Montana and the Marias River. However, a cyclist going from end to end would cover closer to 3,200 miles, depending on the choice of routes. The bicycle route parallels the expedition's river journeys on the Missouri and Columbia Rivers as closely as possible, using a combination of paved roads, bike paths, rail trails, and gravel roads. The terrain includes plains, river corridors, and, of course, steep mountains.

Opposite: Fresh summer snowfall along the Lolo Motorway, Bitterroot Mountains, Idaho; *Above:* Replica of Fort Clatsop near the mouth of the Columbia River, Lewis and Clark National Historical Park, Oregon

Santa Fe Trail

New Spain was already an established territory by the time the English and French made landfall in America. Spanish citizens in Santa Fe, on New Spain's northern frontier, had never had much of an association with points east: their orientation was traditionally south-facing, toward Mexico City, the Spanish capital at the heart of Spanish North America. And they did not welcome outsiders. When upstart American adventurers began to venture across the border in the early 1800s to try to trade with Spanish citizens, they were met very much like today's immigrants who attempt to cross the other way: with suspicion, expulsion, or even arrest.

Attitudes changed in 1821, when Mexico achieved independence from Spain and its new government reversed Spain's closed-door policy. Americans were now looking west, inspired by reports from traders, explorers, and trappers. And Santa Feans, after generations of material deprivation, were equally eager to buy American goods. An American trader named William Becknell, who was familiar with American Indian trails and Spanish and French trading routes, made quick work of identifying an improved trail from Missouri to Santa Fe that later accommodated wagon trains. A trade route—and a business—was born.

From 1821 to 1848, the 1,200-mile Santa Fe Trail served as a key spoke in an international hub of trade routes from the American heartland through American Indian territories to Santa Fe, and from there either south on El Camino Real de Tierra Adentro to Mexico City, or, starting in 1829, west on the Old Spanish Trail to Los Angeles and the Pacific Ocean. It was one of the most important trade routes in American history.

As with all of the early trade and emigrant routes, the Santa Fe Trail had many of the same challenges as any other trail where humans and livestock plodded through difficult terrain: dust, mud, river crossings, punishing rocks, gnats, mosquitoes, cold, and heat. But some of the challenges were uniquely its own.

Unlike the Old Spanish Trail, the Santa Fe Trail was navigable by wagon. Until the very end of the trail on the approach to Santa Fe, the hills, passes, and canyons were not the wagon-eating behemoths that would challenge travelers on the Oregon Trail, or force traders on the Old Spanish Trail to use pack mules instead of wagons. But the landscape of high, arid, treeless plains was fierce in its own way. The forests of Missouri provided shade and shelter, but as the wagon trains moved west, forests gave way to shadeless tallgrass prairie. Often, the plains looked like undulating oceanic waves of grass, interrupted only occasionally by the thin strips of water-loving cottonwoods that lined the drainages.

The farther west the travelers went, the drier the terrain. In western Kansas, shortgrass prairies dominated, followed by the semiarid, semidesert exposed plains and the rain-challenged lands beyond the 100th meridian. Here, raging storms swept across the wide western sky, and lightning threatened travelers and livestock alike (although only one of those two reacted by stampeding). Streams swelled into torrents with stormwater, while wildfires, strong winds, hailstorms, migrating buffalo, and blizzards could stop a wagon train in an exposed open landscape where there was no possibility of shelter in any direction. Even when the weather was calm, the climate was

Remnants of a wagon, Santa Fe Trail Center, Kansas

challenging: hot, dry summers alternated with bitter, frigid winters. Meanwhile, potable water was scarce and unpredictable: the amount of water in drainages that travelers relied on could vary by as much as 90 percent depending on rainfall and the season.

Changing politics—Spanish, Mexican, French, Osage, Comanche, Apache, Texan, and Anglo-American—also created uncertainties for travelers and traders. With a few exceptions, Santa Fe's remoteness and the Spanish empire's unfriendly policies deterred most foreign traders; thus, colonists' only alternatives to the overpriced (but legal) goods coming northward from Chihuahua along the camino came from trade with neighboring American Indian communities. After Mexican independence, however, the new regime opened its borders to American wagon trains bringing in needed consumer goods. But the trail connected more nations than just Mexico and the United States. As dictated in the Osage Treaty of 1825, the Osage permitted the wagon trains to pass, and traded with them as they came through their territory. The Comanche demanded compensation for granting passage through their lands, and they also traded for—and sometimes raided for—items they wanted. Neighboring Apaches attacked some of the wagon trains, and allowed others to pass.

From one year to the next, the wagon trains responded to shifting alliances and relations by adjusting their routes and travel strategies. Caravan sizes increased because larger parties were safer. The wagon trains switched to using oxen to pull the wagons; traders believed that American Indians were less likely to raid a wagon train led by oxen because they valued horses and mules more. The balance of power and the nature of tensions ebbed and flowed. By the 1840s, heavy wagon train traffic in the Arkansas Valley prevented bison herds from migrating to important seasonal grazing land. Traffic along the trail changed native homelands forever, creating conflict over essential resources like bison and grass and prompting the US Army to take an increasingly larger role in protecting traders and travelers.

The politics of the trail continued to change: after 1836, there was another player in town. Texas had gained its lone-star liberation from Mexico. Now an independent republic, Texas claimed territory between the Rio Grande and Arkansas Rivers extending all the way to present-day Wyoming. Conflicts between Mexicans and Texan militias spread to the trail and threatened the wagon trains. Because of the high value of trade along the Santa Fe Trail, American troops were sent to protect the wagon trains, even though Santa Fe—and much of the trail—wasn't on American territory.

The Santa Feans might have appreciated the American military's protection of their trade goods from the east, but they would soon have reason to regret having been quite so welcoming. From the earliest days of the Santa Fe Trail, Becknell had worked with government surveyors to map the trail for military use. Now, a generation later, war was brewing, and the trail would soon be an invasion conduit for the American army.

The conflict between the United States and Mexico began with a border dispute precipitated by Texas statehood. But the leaders of the United States had a much larger motive to escalate the conflict and gain control of Mexican lands in what is now the American Southwest. The newly elected President James K. Polk wanted to fulfill the nation's self-proclaimed Manifest Destiny by expanding westward to the Pacific Ocean. So in 1846, when armed conflict began over the Texas border issue, it quickly exploded into all-out war, with Americans using the Santa Fe Trail to occupy New Mexico and the Southwest. When the dust settled two years later, the Americans had won the Mexican-American War (known in Mexico as the *Intervención estadounidense en México*—the United States Intervention in Mexico). Signed in 1848, the Treaty of Guadalupe Hidalgo gave about one-third of what had been Mexico to the United States, including lands that would become the states of New Mexico and Arizona, along with Mexican claims in Colorado, Utah, Nevada, California, and parts of Oklahoma, Kansas, and Wyoming.

The last period of armed conflict along the trail took place in 1862, when the Civil War arrived in the Southwest. Texan Confederates moved north up the Rio Grande Valley, following the general route of El Camino Real de Tierra Adentro to take Albuquerque and Santa Fe—and eventually the goldfields of Colorado too. But they were stopped along the Santa Fe Trail at Glorieta Pass (just southeast of Santa Fe) in one of the most decisive western battles of the war, which kept the vital trail supply line in Union hands.

In its nearly 60-year heyday, the Santa Fe Trail served as an international trade route between Mexico and America, bringing consumer goods from the American heartland to Mexico's northern frontier. It served as a military supply line to support forts with troops, supplies, and munitions. After the Mexican-American War, it served as a national road and commercial highway, connecting the United States to its new territories in the Southwest. As a transport and communications highway, its traffic boomed to previously unknown levels, serving stagecoach lines, gold seekers taking a southern route to the California and Colorado goldfields, adventurers, missionaries, New Mexican families, and emigrants.

The trail slowly shortened as railroads reached increasingly farther westward. In 1880, the Atchison, Topeka, and Santa Fe Railroad arrived in Santa Fe, and in the seeming blink of an eye, trade on the Santa Fe Trail was eliminated, replaced by more efficient railway lines that could carry more goods faster and cheaper across the country. But while the wagon trains faded into history, the route remained alive. As is so often seen, functioning travel routes are too valuable to sink into the landscape. Today, modern highways and interstate systems bring people and commercial goods from one end of the country to the other. Some of the main highways across Missouri, Kansas, and Oklahoma follow the line of the wagons that preceded them.

THE ROUTE

William Becknell's successful 1821 expedition began in Franklin, Missouri, now an abandoned site between New Franklin and Boonville on the Missouri River just west of Columbia. Becknell followed the Missouri River west to Independence and Kansas City, then continued due west, roughly following what is today's Route 56. (More accurately, Highway 56 follows the general contours of the old Santa Fe Trail.)

At Great Bend in central Kansas, the Santa Fe National Historic Trail picked up the Arkansas River and followed it to Larned, where the trail split into a web of alternates. Travelers needed to choose between so-called wet routes (which had water, but sometimes too much of it in the form of dangerous river crossings) and dry routes (which were shortcuts with safer crossings, but long stretches with no water at all).

Between Fort Dodge and Cimarron, still in central Kansas, parties began to sort themselves into two main groups. The first continued west on the Mountain Route first taken by Becknell. It followed the Arkansas River into Colorado, then swung southwest into New Mexico, staying east of the Sangre de Cristo Mountains. This route was longer and generally considered more difficult, with potentially dangerous river crossings and a steep and rigorous climb over Raton Pass near Santa Fe.

The southern, more popular Cimarron Route headed southwest, ultimately joining with the Cimarron River on a trail that anticipated today's Highway 56. Running through southwest Kansas and western Oklahoma's panhandle, it was about 100 miles shorter than the Mountain Route, but had long waterless stretches, including a 60-mile dry passage between Cimarron and the Cimarron River.

The two routes converged at Watrous in northern New Mexico, and then doglegged to go around the southern end of the Sangre de Cristo Mountains. The last stretch headed southwest through Las Vegas and Starvation Peak, and then turned northwest for the final push to Santa Fe.

Big Springs, Arrow Rock State Historic Site, Missouri

FOLLOWING SPREAD: Fort Osage National Historic Landmark, Missouri (top left); Cave Spring, Cave Spring Historic Site, Missouri (bottom left); Pawnee Rock, Kansas (right)

PREVIOUS SPREAD: Boggsville Historic Site, Colorado (top left); Inscriptions on Autograph Rock, Oklahoma (middle left); Mule deer in front of the Rabbit Ears, New Mexico (bottom left); Moonrise over Santa Fe Trail ruts, Kiowa National Grassland, New Mexico (right)

LEFT: Round Mound, New Mexico (top); Fort Union National Monument, New Mexico (bottom)

OPPOSITE: Pecos National Historical Park, New Mexico

LIVING THE HISTORY

The easiest way to experience the trail is to follow the Santa Fe Trail National Scenic Byway, a highway route that follows the trail's path through Colorado and New Mexico. Along the way are dozens of local museums and interpretive sites, many of them with artifacts from the Santa Fe Trail. The National Park Service website contains information about sites where visitors can see swales still dug into the land from the wagon trains. A few national grasslands preserve the wavelike oceans of shortgrass and tallgrass prairies the settlers and traders would have driven across.

National Frontier Trails Museum, Independence, Missouri

The National Frontier Trails Museum focuses on three great western routes—the Santa Fe, Oregon, and California Trails—and also has exhibits about the Lewis and Clark Expedition and the early fur trappers and traders who brought back information about the selection and routing of viable emigrant wagon trails. Displays—including authentic covered wagons, trail artifacts, and original diaries and letters—demonstrate the similarities and differences among the trails and the impact the 19th-century emigrants had on American history.

Tallgrass Prairie National Preserve, Strong City, Kansas

Managed as a partnership between the National Park Service and The Nature Conservancy, this preserve contains some of the last remaining tallgrass prairie in North America. Note that "tallgrass" is not always tall. In autumn in a well-watered year, grasses can grow as high as a buffalo's back, but in spring, grasses may be as short as six inches. It takes all season, and plenty of rain, to reach maximum height—which could be eight feet or more. The Santa Fe Trail went through many miles of this type of grassland, which once covered 170 million acres of midwestern America. Exhibits at the visitor center discuss the Santa Fe Trail and the ecology of the

grasslands, which are accessible via walking trails. The trail itself passes about 15 miles north of the preserve, through the Council Grove area, considered one of the most important cities in Kansas because of its role in Santa Fe Trail history. In 1825, a treaty negotiated there between the Osage and American representatives allowed the Santa Fe Trail to pass through Osage lands without fear of travelers being raided. In 1860, Seth Hays, the founder and first white settler in Council Grove, recorded the passage of 5,405 Mexican and European American traders, 1,532 wagons, and 17,282 mules, oxen, and horses.

Barton County Historical Society Museum, Great Bend, Kansas

Exhibits begin with the Paleoindian Period and continue through European settlement, including the Santa Fe Trail, trading posts, and Fort Zarah. The museum also has a reconstructed historical village that contains a church, one-room schoolhouse, windmill, post office building, railroad depot, barn, and residences.

Coronado Quivira Museum, Lyons, Kansas

This museum is noted by the National Park Service as "one of the best small museums in Kansas." It has four major displays: the Quivira, or early American Indians who lived here; Coronado, who passed through here searching for fabled Cibola and its rumored stores of

gold; the Santa Fe Trail; and the homesteaders and permanent settlers.

Cimarron and Comanche National Grasslands, Colorado and Kansas

West of the 100th meridian, rainfall drops below 20 inches a year, too little to support the tallgrass prairies farther east. So the next leg of the journey was through shortgrass prairie. The Cimarron National Grassland (southwestern Kansas) and the Comanche National Grassland (southeastern Colorado) are the two easternmost units of the Pike and San Isabel National Forests. The Santa Fe Trail once cut diagonally through what is now the Cimarron National Grassland; today, a trail parallels the historic route through the 100,000-acre preserve. Across the border, in Colorado, the Comanche National Grassland contains more than 440,000 acres in two separate sites, one near Springfield and one near La Junta. Several alternates of the Santa Fe Trail, including the Mountain Route, the Granada-Fort Union Wagon Road, and the Aubry Cutoff, also passed through these grasslands.

Bent's Old Fort National Historic Site, near La Junta, Colorado

Located on the Santa Fe Trail's Mountain Route, Bent's Old Fort is a reconstructed 1840s adobe fur-trading post. Originally built in 1833, it

was used by trappers and travelers to trade with one another and with the Cheyenne and Arapaho people. The fort was abandoned in 1849. Today's interpretive program and a schedule of ever-changing living history demonstrations and special events focus on the fort's history, American Indian heritage, Hispanic heritage, the Santa Fe Trail, and frontier skills and life. A short hiking trail with interpretive signs winds its way through the cottonwood trees alongside the Arkansas River past a marsh that is rich with endemic bird species.

Philmont Scout Ranch, near Cimarron, New Mexico

Two sites owned by the famed Philmont Scout Ranch near Cimarron, New Mexico, have close historic associations with the Santa Fe Trail: the Kit Carson Home and Museum and the historic Lucien Maxwell House. The house dates from the mid-1800s, when Lucien Maxwell invited Kit Carson to his ranch on the Rayado River. At the time, Comanche and Apache raids were common; Carson, and later a detachment of US Army dragoons, helped provide security for the settlement, which became a stop on the Santa Fe Trail. Abandoned soon after Maxwell moved away, the house was later restored. The Kit Carson Museum is a separate structure that opened in 1950 with furniture and artifacts that show how life on the Santa Fe Trail was lived in the 1850s. In the living history program, guides in period clothing demonstrate frontier skills such as blacksmithing, cooking, shooting, and farming. Tours of the Lucien Maxwell House can be arranged ahead of time by contacting the museum.

Top: Aerial view of Point of Rocks, Cimarron National Grassland, Kansas; *Middle left:* Tree stump where George Sibley signed a treaty with the Osage to allow travelers safe passage along the Santa Fe Trail, Kansas; *Middle right*: Wagon wheel monument, Kansas; *Bottom*: Bent's Old Fort National Historic Site, Colorado

Oregon Trail

2,200 MILES ➤ MISSOURI · KANSAS · NEBRASKA · WYOMING · IDAHO · OREGON · WASHINGTON

Consider the longest family trip you ever took in a car. Toys, devices, the license game, snacks, pit stops, spilled drinks, food debris, endless squabbling, and the ubiquitous refrain of "Are we there yet?"

Now imagine doing it in 1843—for 2,000 miles, on foot (without a cell phone!). You would have oxen pulling your supplies; your family would be pulling at your patience. And only your optimism and hope would carry you through territory no one knew much about: mountains, canyons, river crossings, and plains with grass so high it would tickle your nose even if you were sitting atop a horse.

You'd have to have a very, very good reason to do it. Like all emigrants, you would either be running from something—persecution, religious strife, war— or toward something—the promise of land, gold, or opportunity. In 1843, you might have been doing both. You'd be getting away from a sticky recession that had begun six years earlier and showed no signs of abating. And you'd be moving toward a beacon— land! opportunity! wealth!—that shone from the West.

In the almost 40 years since the Lewis and Clark Expedition, an ever-increasing number of explorers, adventurers, traders, trappers, and surveyors had ventured into the great expanse of the Louisiana Purchase and points west. The reports they sent back fueled the hopes of the unemployed, the landless, the adventurous, and the entrepreneurial. Each year, a trickle of adventurous parties headed out into the Great American Desert, across the Continental Divide, and into the Pacific Northwest.

Now, with jobs scarce and profits stagnant in the East, that trickle had grown into a steady stream.

In 1843, the first large-scale wagon train migration departed from Independence, Missouri. On the Oregon Trail alone, the estimated number of migrants increased from 875 in 1843 to 2,500 in 1845 to 4,000 in 1847 to 10,000 in 1852. In all, between 1843 and 1868, more than 80,000 people made the 2,000-mile journey to the Willamette Valley in Oregon. And 320,000 more settlers used the eastern section of the Oregon Trail to start their journeys to California and Utah.

So: You would pack your essentials. You'd buy a sturdy wagon or two, a team of at least six oxen, and maybe some cattle. You'd get your family to the Missouri River, and then ferry across it. And you'd start to walk. Yes, walk. Children's book illustrations and Hollywood movies aside, the livestock that pulled the wagons were sometimes overburdened under the weight of supplies, the primitive wagons had no shock-absorbing springs to protect passengers, and the trail was so rough that a bucket of milk could be churned into butter just by hanging it off the wagon. Pregnant women and small children might take an occasional turn bouncing around the wagon, perhaps lying on a sleeping platform improvised by laying a feather bed mattress atop some storage boxes. Some settlers rode horses. But for the most part, the emigrants walked.

Some of the daily challenges would be recognizable to a 21st-century walker. Although the technology of outdoor equipment has advanced light-years between then and now, the stubbornly pedestrian concerns that fill a walker's mind remain the same as they ever were. Issues such as wild animals, rattlesnakes, rain and mud, potable water, sore muscles, and broken gear transcend time. True, no one exploring the

Covered wagon, Rock Creek Station State Historical Park, Nebraska

CANADA

Everett
Seattle
Tacoma
Spokane
OLYMPIA
WASHINGTON
MONTANA
Yakima
NORTH DAKOTA
Fargo
HELENA
BISMARCK
Portland
84
The Dalles
Billings
SALEM
Eugene
IDAHO
SOUTH DAKOTA
OREGON
BOISE
PIERRE
Sioux Falls
5
Twin Falls
WYOMING
Casper
NEBRASKA
Omaha
Reno
CHEYENNE
SALT LAKE CITY
Fort Collins
LINCOLN
CARSON CITY
NEVADA
Provo
Kansas
City
SACRAMENTO
DENVER
Oakland
UTAH
TOPEKA
San Francisco
COLORADO
KANSAS
70
Colorado Springs
Fresno
Pueblo
Wichita
CALIFORNIA
15
Las Vegas
Tulsa
Bakersfield
25
SANTA FE
OKLAHOMA
40
Los Angeles
ARIZONA
Amarillo
Anaheim
NEW MEXICO
OKLAHOMA CITY
40
San Diego
Yuma
PHOENIX
10
Dallas
Tucson
Las Cruces
Fort Worth
10
El Paso
20
TEXAS
10
AUSTIN
Houston
MEXICO
San Antonio

OREGON TRAIL
NATIONAL HISTORIC TRAIL

0   100   200 Miles

N

Oregon National Historic Trail today—whether in a car or on foot—worries about Indian attacks, but in fact, most of the Oregon settlers didn't have to worry about that either—attacks were far more common in the imagination than on the ground. (According to the National Oregon/California Trail Center in Idaho, historical studies indicate that between 1840 and 1860 American Indians killed 362 emigrants, but emigrants killed 426 American Indians.) Settlers did, however, have to worry about accidents such as being run over by a wagon, drowning in a river crossing, or dying of any number of diseases—dysentery, smallpox, whooping cough, mumps, measles, typhoid, and cholera—that stalked the wagon trains, the fetid camps, and the polluted water supplies. It is estimated that about 10 percent—somewhere between 20,000 and 30,000 people—of the emigrants who set out on the journey are buried somewhere along the trail, many of them underneath the trail itself, where the earth would be compacted by the passage of livestock and the bodies would be safe from scavenging animals.

How on earth would you even begin to equip yourself for a trip like this? Sorting out the logistics of what to take and what to leave at home is common to all travelers across time and space, but packing for the Oregon Trail involved a whole other order of triage. With no towns and few forts, opportunities to resupply and repair broken equipment were few and far between. You'd need to pack enough food to survive for five months—and have enough left over to get started in a new home. From a 21st-century mindset, it sounds like a survivalist planning to outlast the fallout of a nuclear attack. By comparison, a modern car trip across the country is a walk in the park.

But travelers never truly stride into the unknown: there is (almost) always someone who has gone before, so there is almost always at least a trace of a trail. You would follow the route taken by the trickle of earlier settlers, who would have followed the trappers and explorers, who would have followed the American Indians, who might have followed the wildlife—including the hundreds of thousands of cranes annually migrating overhead along the Platte River.

You would also have the wisdom passed back from those ahead. Travel blogs are an ancient idea

wrapped in shiny new digital packaging; the idea of a travel guide dates to at least the first century, when *The Periplus of the Erythraean Sea* told Indian Ocean traders what to expect on the coasts of India, Arabia, and East Africa. The 19th-century version of a first-century periplus consisted of pamphlets, circulars, or books filled with hard-won advice. And, like 21st-century bloggers, diarists shared everything from their day-to-day routines to descriptions of the landscape to equipment lists and packing tips. As a practical matter, traders in Independence, Missouri, sprang into business seemingly overnight to help would-be emigrants cross items off their shopping lists.

To start, you'd need a wagon, usually pulled by two or more yokes of oxen. It would be a sturdy farm wagon—the Conestoga wagons used by the eastern settlers who crossed the Appalachians were too heavy and bulky for the demands of western trails. The so-called prairie schooners could carry perhaps

Tombstone of Oregon Trail traveler near Scott Spring, Kansas (left); Common items carried along the Oregon Trail, Scotts Bluff National Monument, Nebraska (right)

2,400 pounds each, most of which would be allocated to food. If you had a large family, you might need two wagons to haul the recommended amounts: a family of four might need 600 pounds of flour, 400 pounds of salted pork, 200 pounds of lard, plus maybe 400 more pounds of other supplies: coffee, tea, sugar, rice, biscuits, beans, cheese, dried pumpkins, cornmeal, and dried fruits and meats. Some families trailed a few cattle to butcher along the way (though cattle were hard to manage and drive). Some brought a milk cow. Others hoped to hunt buffalo, deer, and antelope.

As for equipment, let's take it by function: for sleeping, you'd need a canvas tent, foldable mattresses, and wool blankets; for travel, two changes of clothes (per person), a belt, and several pairs of boots; for cleaning up, a washboard and tub, plus soap; for eating, cookpots, dishes, and eating utensils; for the animals and wagons, saddles, harnesses, bridles, ropes, and hobbles, plus veterinary supplies for horses and oxen and shoeing and cuing equipment to protect their feet (yes, oxen were shod; an ox shoe is called a cue); and for defense, hunting, and butchering, knives, pistols, and rifles. And then there were the extras: books, Bibles, writing quills, ink, and paper; scissors, pins, needles, and thread; and, maybe most important, whether you smoked or not, tobacco. Just as good as currency, you could use it to trade with American Indians and with your fellow travelers.

Finally, you'd need tools. Anything practical would do if it could be used to build a house, start a farm, make furniture, repair a wagon, clear brush that blocked the trail, build a raft or a bridge, or shore up an embankment. Hatchets, awls, picks, saws, plows, axes, shovels, hoes, and a dozen other kinds of tools were packed into wagons and brought out for the job at hand, whether they were intended for it or not. When settlers didn't have what they needed, they traded among themselves, or they found abandoned equipment—sometimes because a settler had died, and sometimes because a traveler decided the hassle of carrying something outweighed its value.

Days on the trail settled into the rhythms of a regular routine: there was breaking camp and breakfast, then walking and lunch (which they called nooning), then walking some more. At night, the settlers circled the wagons and took care of the animals, made camp, cooked, and ate. Evenings were spent in exhausted slumber, or perhaps relaxing with storytelling, writing letters or journals, games, or music. The trains slogged along, covering 15 to 20 miles more or less every day, regardless of rain or snow or beating-down sunshine; across prairies, over mountains, and down canyons. Sometimes the routine was interrupted by runaway animals, by a herd of bison, or by challenges such as high water or flooding, wet weather, steep climbs and descents, and long, dry stretches. Does it sound like fun? Like an adventure? Like an ordeal? Or perhaps like the stuff of a 1990s video game? Diaries from Oregon Trail travelers run the gamut. It was the trip of a lifetime, say some. Others just wanted to get it over with. Like so much of history, it depends on whose book you read.

THE ROUTE

The jumping-off point for the Oregon National Historic Trail is generally considered to be Independence, Missouri, on the east bank of the Missouri River near today's Kansas City. But as time went on, more towns grew up along the Missouri, and new ferry services enabled settlers to cross the river at different places. So the Oregon Trail is often described as a rope with frayed ends, as emigrants began their treks from whichever river town was most convenient to them. Once on the western side of the river, they would cut through the northeastern corner of Kansas and start out across Nebraska.

The frayed ends of the rope came together at the Platte River near what is today Kearney, Nebraska. From there, only one wagon route led across the Continental Divide. From Fort Kearny to South Pass in Wyoming, all the emigrant routes followed the same general course up the Platte and North Platte Rivers, then along the Sweetwater River as it led around the north side of the Great Divide Basin, and, finally, up and over the Continental Divide at South Pass.

On the Pacific side of the Continental Divide, the rules were different. Nearly halfway into the journey, the settlers were trail hardened, but the landscape had new challenges. Land on the Pacific side of the watershed was mountainous, with steep pitches, close

Lightning storm over the
Platte River, Nebraska

canyons, and fast-running streams and rivers that were sometimes difficult to cross. A series of alternate trails and cutoffs developed depending on the season, the flow of water, the availability of assistance from regional American Indians, and the confidence a party had in its ability to drive stock or wagons one way versus another.

So now the rope began to fray again as emigrants made different decisions, and as those headed for different destinations began to peel off the main route. At Fort Bridger, the Mormons (and many California-bound settlers too), whose routes had thus far been roughly contiguous with the Oregon Trail, turned southwest for Utah. The Oregon Trail settlers continued northwest. After reaching the Snake River at Fort Hall, they loosely followed the river across Idaho, then crossed the Blue Mountains of northeastern Oregon, and at last met up with the Columbia River. This was the last challenge, and a major one, as yesteryear's untamed, undammed Columbia was a very different and much wilder river than it is today. Ultimately, two choices emerged, neither of them easy. The first was to build rafts and use them to attempt to float wagons down the treacherous Columbia—a process that reduced many a family's possessions to splinters. The second was to take the mountainous Barlow Road, which opened in 1846 and offered an escape from the river at the price of a steep and difficult climb around Mount Hood.

Which would you have taken? Today's outdoors lovers see both the Columbia River Gorge and Mount Hood as treasures to be cherished, not obstacles to be avoided. The settlers had a different perspective as they lugged a wagon, a few oxen, an exhausted family, and whatever was left of the ton or more of possessions they had so carefully counted and packed five months ago. But now, with these last challenges, the emigrants got their first glimpse of Mount Hood. Success—and the trail's end in Oregon City—was finally in sight.

Iskuulpa Creek Drainage, Blue
Mountains, Oregon

Erected by the people of Lincoln County in the year 1980 to perpetuate the site of Old Fort McPherson and the Oregon Trail

PREVIOUS SPREAD: Wagon wheels sculpture, O'Fallon's Bluff, Nebraska (top left); Statue of frontier soldier at site of Fort McPherson, Nebraska (bottom left); Chimney Rock, Nebraska (middle); Oregon Trail from Mitchell Pass, Scotts Bluff National Monument, Nebraska (right)

OPPOSITE: View south along the Avenue of Rocks, Wyoming

RIGHT: Stone memorial at South Pass, Wyoming (top); Cow carcass along the Oregon Trail (bottom)

PREVIOUS SPREAD: Storm clouds over Church Buttes, Wyoming (left); Moonrise over the Big Sandy River near Big Timber Station, Wyoming (top right); Reconstructed wagon ferry beside the Green River, Wyoming (middle right); Twin Falls Cataract, Snake River (bottom right)

LEFT: Walking through a remote region of Eastern Oregon (top); View of Blue Mountains from the Oregon Trail, Oregon (bottom)

OPPOSITE: Replica of the West Barlow Road Tollgate, Oregon

LIVING THE HISTORY

Many of the sites described here, especially those on the eastern side of the Continental Divide, apply not only to the Oregon Trail, but also to the Mormon Pioneer, California, and Pony Express Trails, which share many hundreds of miles of the same route. The National Park Service app, NPS Oregon Trail, can also be used to locate more than 80 sites to visit along the trail.

The Archway, Kearney, Nebraska

The Archway is a museum in an indoor bridge that was built over I-80. The museum commemorates all the national historic trails that passed through Fort Kearny with permanent exhibits that give an overview of the history of the various movements and show how life was lived on the emigrant trails. Just a few minutes away is Fort Kearny State Historical Park. Its modest offerings—a museum and some reconstructed fort buildings—belie its importance as the convergence point for all the emigrant trails and the last opportunity for settlers to adjust supplies, repair gear, or send a letter home before striking out into the unknown. If you visit this region in March, be sure to stop in Kearney to see the annual crane migration.

Scotts Bluff National Monument, Western Nebraska

For Oregon Trail travelers, the Midwest became the West near Cozad, Nebraska. Courthouse and Jail Rocks came into view, followed by Chimney Rock (now a national historic site), and then Scotts Bluff (now a national monument). Mitchell Pass, at the base of Scotts Bluff, was seen as the gateway to the West. This new vertical landscape announced that the emigrants had completed about a third of the journey—and that the remaining miles were going to involve a lot more in the way of bluffs, mountains, mesas, and plateaus. Scotts Bluff National Monument contains more than 3,000 acres, including historic trail remnants. Long a travel, trade, and hunt route for American Indians, the area is also unique for its combination of geology, paleontology, and a distinctive environment of mixed-grass prairie, rugged badlands, towering bluffs, and riparian areas. Visitors can hike up to (or down from) the bluff, where an overlook gives a view of the landscape the emigrants crossed.

National Historic Trails Interpretive Center, Casper, Wyoming

This interpretive center offers a commanding view of the North Platte River. The museum focuses on the four emigrant national historic trails, with interpretive programs, exhibits, multimedia presentations, special events, and interactive exhibits. Visitors can climb into a prairie schooner for a simulation that shows just how difficult and dangerous it was for pioneer wagons to cross the river. Other hands-on exhibits include trying to pull a Mormon handcart (and then imagine trying to pull it across the continent, or in the snow). The museum's *Footsteps to the Past* video reenacts the history as related in pioneer diaries.

South Pass City, South Pass, Wyoming

Looking more like a high plateau than a mountain pass, South Pass was the easiest and most wagon-friendly place to cross the Continental Divide. It was also the site of its own gold rush in the 1860s. Today, South Pass City is a living history interpretive site where visitors can see elements of western pioneer life, complete with hands-on tours into some of the gold-mine tunnels. Hiking is also available—the Continental Divide National Scenic Trail passes through South Pass, as do all of the emigrant national historic trails and other variants and offshoots. The historic site is open from mid-May through September.

National Oregon/California Trail Center, Montpelier, Idaho

Located on the path of the Oregon Trail, this center uses actors working in historically accurate interpretive settings to tell the story of the Oregon and California pioneers. A re-creation of the wagon train experience includes buying provisions (at the gun and mercantile shops), being guided along the trail by actors, riding in a computer-simulated wagon, and singing around a pioneer encampment fire. Related exhibits include the Oregon Trail paintings of Idaho artist Gary Stone and the Rails and Trails Museum, which highlights the history of the Bear Lake Valley.

Three Island Crossing State Park, near Glenns Ferry, Idaho

For Oregon Trail pioneers, crossing the Snake River was always dangerous. The Three Island Crossing was one of the most important and difficult river fords in Idaho. Arriving here prompted a critical decision: whether to take the safer route along the south side of the Snake River, which would add time (and dry, desolate conditions) to the journey, or whether to cross the river at this point, which was notoriously dangerous but gave those who were successful a better route to Fort Boise. Visitors can see interpretive trail re-creations and museum exhibits about the Oregon Trail.

Columbia River Gorge National Scenic Area, Oregon and Washington

The Columbia River Gorge National Scenic Area stretches 85 miles on both sides of the Columbia River along the border between Oregon and Washington. Today's Columbia River is nothing like the wild and free river that challenged the settlers to the point that many emigrants elected to haul their wagons around Mount Hood rather than face the churning rapids. Today, the river has been tamed by dams, but it has also become one of Oregon's powerhouse recreation sites for river sports such as windsurfing, sailing, and kayaking. Hikers can also explore a wide network of trails in the gorge—including a circumambulation of Mount Hood and a section of the Pacific Crest National Scenic Trail—which continue south to cross Barlow Pass, where emigrants avoiding the river would have taken their wagons. The History Museum of Hood River County in Hood River contains exhibits about American Indian culture; Oregon Trail pioneers; the role of timber, logging, and agriculture; the story of the region's Japanese Americans; and the development of outdoor recreation. The Columbia Gorge Discovery Center is located in The Dalles, Oregon, just about where the settlers would have had their first real taste of the power of the river—and where many of them elected to fight the mountains instead. The center introduces visitors to the geology, flora, fauna, history, and development of the gorge.

Top: Sculpture at National Historic Trails Interpretive Center, Wyoming; *Bottom:* National Oregon/California Trail Center, Idaho

Mormon Pioneer Trail

1,300 MILES ➤ ILLINOIS • IOWA • NEBRASKA • WYOMING • UTAH

A chosen people on an exodus. Hardship in an endless, arid landscape. Multiple crossings of multiple rivers. A holy city and a lake filled with salt. A commitment to make the desert bloom.

We could be talking about ancient Israel. And indeed, 170 years ago, when the Mormon pioneers crossed to the American West, they would have framed their experiences in the images and language of the Old Testament. Two completely different historic events, separated by geography and several thousand years, shared the same iconography. As stories so often do, one gave hope to the other. The stories of ancient Jewish endurance, survival, and triumph motivated and sustained the Mormons traveling across the plains and mountains of the frontier, trying to find and establish their own Zion in their own promised land.

Between 1846, when the first Mormon exploratory expedition left Nauvoo, Illinois, to survey the land west of the Continental Divide, and 1868, when news of the soon-to-be-completed transcontinental railroad made overland wagon travel obsolete, approximately 70,000 Mormon religious refugees left the eastern and midwestern United States to establish their City of God in Utah. It is a movement unique in American history: an exodus away from what was then the United States to find religious independence elsewhere.

Freedom of religion has been an inalienable part of the American fabric since the dawn of European migration to the New World. It is inscribed in the very first amendment to the Constitution, and it is inscribed in our stories too. Sometimes new arrivals fled religious persecution, such as the 17th-century Puritans who arrived in New England, Bibles in hand,

to found their city on a hill. Sometimes religious differences morphed into economic persecution, as when 19th-century Irish Catholics fled starvation brought on by the politics and policies of Protestant English overlords, and then faced discrimination in their new American homes where "Irish need not apply." And sometimes religion was recast as race, as with Jews fleeing Nazi Germany in the 20th century—when, that is, they could gain admittance to America.

So the Mormon story is an anomaly: an American-born religion that sought to find its independence elsewhere, rather than a religion born elsewhere that sought freedom on American shores. While Mormonism accounts for only 1.7 percent of the American population, it seems somehow fitting that the only national historic trail that commemorates a religious movement focuses on this unique American story.

The Mormon Pioneer National Historic Trail passes in or through five states—Illinois, Iowa, Nebraska, Wyoming, and Utah. But the story begins in western New York, where, in 1827, 21-year-old Joseph Smith announced that an angel named Moroni had directed him to a set of golden plates inscribed with the tenets of God's true church. Moroni was a practical sort of angel: he happened to have a set of tools Smith could use to translate God's language into English. Smith transcribed the scripture into what became the Book of Mormon; then, in 1830, he incorporated the Church of Jesus Christ of Latter-day Saints.

The nascent church rattled around the Midwest for a few years, gaining converts in America. It also sent missionaries back to Europe, particularly the British Isles and Scandinavia, and many of the

Courthouse and Jail Rocks, Scotts Bluff National Monument, Nebraska

CANADA
MONTANA
NORTH DAKOTA
MINNESOTA
SOUTH DAKOTA
IDAHO
WYOMING
IOWA
NEBRASKA
UTAH
COLORADO
KANSAS
MISSOURI
OKLAHOMA
ARIZONA
NEW MEXICO
ARKANSAS
TEXAS
HELENA
Billings
BISMARCK
Fargo
Minneapolis
PIERRE
Sioux Falls
Casper
Scottsbluff
Cedar Rapids
CHEYENNE
Omaha
SALT LAKE CITY
LINCOLN
Nauvoo
Fort Collins
Provo
DENVER
TOPEKA
Kansas City
Columbia
Colorado Springs
JEFFERSON CITY
Pueblo
Wichita
Tulsa
SANTA FE
OKLAHOMA CITY
Albuquerque
LITTLE ROCK
PHOENIX
Dallas
29
94
90
15
35
80
70
25
40
MORMON PIONEER
NATIONAL HISTORIC TRAIL
0
100
200 Miles
N

ensuing converts immigrated to America. Congregating here, being driven out there, the Latter-day Saints moved around until, in 1838, they finally settled on the Mississippi River in Illinois. The community of Nauvoo, a Hebrew word meaning "beautiful place," attracted thousands of Mormons and became the largest town in Illinois.

As with new college roommates trying to coexist despite disparate backgrounds, for a time relations between the newcomer Mormons and their neighbors were polite and mutually tolerant. Mormons were seen to be orderly and hardworking—qualities that were valued in these newly settled midwestern states. One could gloss over a few differences in religious beliefs if the folks next door tended to their affairs and could help a neighbor out once in a while.

But, as with roommates, once-tolerable differences soon became rankling annoyances. Smith was considered a prophet by his followers, which was heresy to traditional Christians. And the Mormons were seen to be clannish, with political and business ambitions that were judged theocratic, exclusionary, threatening, and sometimes unethical.

And then there was polygamy—the match that set the pile of tinder afire. Smith had quietly broached the idea of what he called plural marriage to a select number of church members. But as the practice took hold, dissent grew not only with neighbors but also within the church itself. A local newspaper that opined on the subject was destroyed on Smith's orders; in response, Smith and his brother Hyrum were arrested and put in jail, where they were murdered by a mob of some 200 people. Tensions tightened between Latter-day Saints, Gentiles (the name the Latter-day Saints gave to non-Mormons), and former Mormons, leading to attacks on Mormons and their properties. Finally, Brigham Young, the new leader, plotted an exodus whereby the Mormons would leave the United States and cross into Mexican territory beyond the Continental Divide.

The 1846 exploratory party, charged with finding a route and a settlement site, wintered near Omaha, Nebraska, and reached Utah in 1847. Ironically, the region—though still officially part of Mexico—was already occupied by American forces fighting the Mexican-American War. (The Treaty of Guadalupe Hidalgo would permanently put it under American control in 1848.) Nonetheless, the Great Salt Lake was more than 1,000 miles away from the troubles in Nauvoo. The migration began, with each successive party improving the route and opening ferries to ease the way for future settlers. (Mormons crossed for free, but others—emigrants heading for Oregon and, after 1848, miners heading to California—were charged anywhere from $3 to $8.) Once in the valley of the Great Salt Lake, first-wave migrants established farms and settlements, grew crops, built fences, and husbanded herds so that the thousands of expected new migrants would have a toehold on their new life when they arrived. The Mormon migration and settlement was a community affair.

Community means family: with a larger percentage of women and children, the Mormons traveled slower than the California migrants, averaging a little more than 10 miles a day, as opposed to the 15 to 20 miles a day that was more common among the male-dominated miners-to-be. The Mormon emigrant trains were well organized with an almost military hierarchy. Families were assigned to traveling groups, each with its own leader; smaller groups made for more practical camping at sites where space and clean water were limited. The journey was arduous: as with all the emigrants on the western trails, the Mormons encountered accidents (being run over by a wagon, drowning, or falling), diseases (cholera and typhoid being common), and weather.

Historic reports, church sources, and general legends disagree on how many of the 70,000 or so Mormon pioneers died along the route, but one event has come to symbolize the difficulties of the journey. Starting in 1855, some of the poorer emigrants had begun to travel using handcarts, small wagons that were pushed and pulled by two to four people rather than by livestock. Carrying food, possessions, bedding, tents, and sometimes children, handcarts were cheaper because they reduced the number of larger wagons and oxen a party needed. But they came at a high cost in human energy: many of the handcarts were poorly made and, under constant battering from the rough trail, they started to malfunction only partway across the continent. It took enormous strength and endurance to manhandle them (literally) across 1,200 miles of plains, over the Continental Divide, and through the mesas and mountains of Wyoming and Idaho.

In 1856, nearly 3,000 Mormon pioneers from England, Wales, Scotland, and Scandinavia attempted to make the journey from the American Midwest to Utah. Without funds for full teams of oxen or horses, they were organized into 10 handcart companies.

Two of those companies, with a total of about 1,000 people, were led by James Willie and Edward Martin. Following bad advice (and ignoring warnings), they set out from the Missouri River in August, dangerously late in the traveling season. The story is an unfortunate and familiar one: inaccurate information, a late start, and an early winter set the stage for disaster.

In October, the Willie and Martin companies were struggling to push their poorly functioning handcarts along the Sweetwater River in Wyoming. In order to increase the speed of travel, leaders had reduced the amount of clothing and blankets allowed to each person, from 17 pounds to 10 pounds. Inadequately clothed and short on provisions, the two parties were completely exposed when heavy snow stopped them in their tracks near the Continental Divide. Two hundred and ten people died, and many of the rest barely survived, brought back from the brink of death by rescue parties that came back over the mountains for them. Today, a statue of Mormon pioneers pulling a handcart stands in Temple Square in downtown Salt Lake City, a testament to the challenges and travails the settlers had to overcome to reach their promised land.

THE ROUTE

The Mormon Pioneer National Historic Trail follows the settlers' route from Nauvoo, Illinois, on the banks of the Mississippi River, through Iowa, Nebraska, Wyoming, and Utah. After crossing Iowa, the Mormons headed west into central Nebraska, where they joined the paths of the other westbound emigrants near Fort Kearny. Like the Oregon Trail homesteaders and the California-bound miners, the Mormons followed the Platte River–North Platte–Sweetwater route to South Pass.

Following the Sweetwater River around the northeast rim of the Great Divide Basin, the route climbed over the Continental Divide at South Pass. From there, the emigrant trails continued together only for a few more days until, just south of the Wind River Mountains at a place called Parting of the Ways, the Mormons turned southwest for another three or four weeks of hard travel to their final destination at the Great Salt Lake.

Mormon handcart, Martin's Cove, Wyoming

OPPOSITE: Sweetwater River, Wyoming

LEFT: Mormon wagon on a ferry beside the Mississippi River, Nauvoo State Park, Illinois (top); Garden Grove camp location, Mormon Pioneer Historic Trailside Park, Iowa (bottom)

OPPOSITE: Devil's Gate along Sweetwater River, Wyoming

FOLLOWING SPREAD: Rocks forming an arrow along the west of Fort Bridger, Wyoming (top left); Mormon Pioneer Trek youth groups retracing the trail, Wyoming (middle left); Eroded hoodoos known as The Witches, Utah (bottom left); View from Big Mountain Pass, where the Mormons first glimpsed the Great Salt Lake Valley, Wasatch Mountains, Utah (right)

LIVING THE HISTORY

The Mormon Church runs a number of historic sites, museums, and exhibits, some of them with a historical focus, and others with a more evangelical bent. Markers are found along the route of the trail, and, in some places, wheel ruts are still visible. East of the Continental Divide at South Pass, the Mormon Pioneer Trail shared the same path as the other western emigrant trails; this section focuses on the sites and trails that are particular to the Mormon pioneers.

Nauvoo and the Carthage Jail, Illinois

Nauvoo can be toured by foot, by car, or in a horse- or oxen-drawn wagon. Missionaries act as guides at the visitor center and many of the sites. Restorations and reconstructions of historic buildings, homes, meeting halls, and workplaces—of blacksmiths, tinsmiths, shoemakers, gunsmiths, and printers—show how the settlers lived in the 1840s. Walking the Trail of Hope on a self-guided tour along Parley Street to the Mississippi River, visitors can read historical markers, many containing the words and thoughts of the emigrants themselves as they considered the journey ahead. Other sites include a reconstruction of the temple (only Mormons are permitted inside, but the grounds are open to the public); the Smith Family Cemetery, where church founder Joseph Smith, his brother, and others in his family are interred; and the Carthage Jail (about a half hour away by car), where Joseph and his brother Hyrum were killed.

Prairie Trails Museum of Wayne County, Corydon, Iowa

Exhibits in this museum depict the hardships and experiences of the pioneers as they traveled west. An exhibit dedicated to the Mormon pioneers includes maps, photos, illustrations, and a full-size replica of a family with a covered wagon and oxen. Notably, the hymn "Come, Come Ye Saints" was written by William Clayton on the banks of Locust Creek in southwestern Wayne County as the Mormon pioneers traveled across the area.

Mormon Trail Center at Historic Winter Quarters, Omaha, Nebraska

Winter Quarters was one of many Latter-day Saints encampments along the Missouri River on the Iowa-Nebraska border. The settlements were temporary homes on the way to the Salt Lake Valley, but they were sturdily built, with farms, businesses, and a newspaper—a solid place for a migrant community to stop, rest, and prepare for the journey ahead. The Mormon Trail Center at Historic Winter Quarters in Omaha, Nebraska, has interactive exhibits, artwork, reconstructed settings, and artifacts about the Latter-day Saints' westward migration from Nauvoo, the wintering-over at Omaha, and the trek to the Salt Lake Valley in Utah. Next to the trail center are the Winter Quarters Nebraska Temple and the Mormon Pioneer Cemetery, where a monument called Tragedy of Winter Quarters remembers the pioneers who died here.

Fort Laramie National Historic Site, Laramie, Wyoming

Up until this point, the Mormon pioneers had traveled on the north side of the Platte River, and most of the other emigrants had traveled on the south side. The Mormons had hoped to keep to themselves and avoid conflict during the journey. At Fort Laramie, however, the two routes converged and the Mormons traveled side by side with the 49ers and Oregon-bound settlers. Built in the 1830s to connect western fur traders with eastern markets, Fort Laramie served as one of the only trading posts on the entire route. Today, the park includes 12 restored buildings that date from 1849 to the 1880s, several unrestored ruins, a museum, a visitor center (located in the restored commissary storehouse), and hiking trails to the confluence of the Platte and Laramie Rivers. Nearby are two other important emigrant landmarks: Register Cliff, where thousands of emigrants scrawled their names into the soft sandstone, and Guernsey Ruts, where five-foot-deep ruts made by the tens of thousands of passing wagons are carved into the earth. Independence Rock, another landmark where emigrants left their names, is about an hour's drive away.

Fort Caspar, Casper, Wyoming

The North Platte River valley was the pathway for the Oregon, Mormon Pioneer, California, and Pony Express Trails, and, later, for the transcontinental telegraph line. As such, American Indians, trappers, traders, explorers, emigrants, and the US Army all passed through here. The site was also important because the Mormons who arrived here in the first exploratory expedition built a ferry consisting of dugout canoes made of cottonwood, a deck, oars, and a rudder. Brigham Young named nine men

to remain and operate the ferry while the rest of the party continued the journey west. Other emigrants began contracting with the Mormons to take them across the river, and a business was born. Through the 1852 season, Mormon men returned to the Casper area to operate the ferry. Eventually using a rope-and-pulley system with a floating deck, the Mormon ferry could get a loaded wagon from one side of the river to another in a mere five minutes. The Fort Caspar Museum features exhibits on regional and city history, including prehistoric peoples, Plains Indians, ranching, the energy industry, and the western emigrant trails and frontier army.

Mormon Handcart Historic Sites, near South Pass, Wyoming

The death of more than 200 Mormon pioneers during an early winter snowstorm at the crossing of the Continental Divide in Wyoming is one of the seminal events in the history of the Mormon pioneers. Nothing so clearly evokes the sacrifice and hardship of the transcontinental journey and the community spirit involved in rescuing those who could be rescued. The Mormon Church periodically holds reenactments where participants can experience the historic trek for themselves. Church-sponsored treks (some of which include pulling handcarts) are educational and evangelical about the Mormon faith. However, South Pass is accessible for anyone who wants to experience the landscape and imagine its history. The Continental Divide National Scenic Trail follows the emigrant routes up the Sweetwater River and across the pass. Today's hikers traverse the high, dry plateau where the Willie and Martin handcart companies were halted by snow. As you trek, don't forget to consider that you are not pushing or pulling a 100-pound wheeled vehicle with unpredictable hardware, and—given that you have access to 24-hour weather reporting—you have probably not ventured out in an early season blizzard. The Mormon Handcart Historic Sites include three separate locations where the stricken parties were aided by rescuers: Martin's Cove, Sixth Crossing, and Rock Creek Hollow.

Salt Lake City, Utah

"This is the place," said Mormon leader Brigham Young when he reached the foothills at Emigration Canyon near Salt Lake City, Utah. This Is The Place Heritage Park is a living history park on 450 acres, including a pioneer village, horseback riding trails, and interpretive demonstrations pertaining to the Mormon settlement of the Salt Lake Valley. Nearby, Ensign Peak looms over the Utah State Capitol Building and offers a more sweeping view of the city. From this height, Young and his advisers mapped plans for the settlement. Today, a hiking trail accessible from downtown has a small park with a memorial to the emigrants who died on the trek to Utah. The view extends to the southern end of the valley; interpretive signs at the top identify the mountains and other prominent features.

Above, left: Sculpture of Mormon family, Mormon Trail Center at Historic Winter Quarters, Nebraska; *Above, right:* Monument honoring Mormon pioneers, This Is The Place Heritage Park, Utah

California Trail

5,665 MILES ➤ MISSOURI · KANSAS · NEBRASKA · COLORADO · WYOMING
UTAH · IDAHO · NEVADA · CALIFORNIA · OREGON

Imagine the town you live in, and all the people you know. Now imagine that a rumor sweeps in, and then two out of every three men—your friends, neighbors, police officers, carpenters—simply leave.

In January 1848, a carpenter named James W. Marshall found gold along the American River while building a mill for his boss, John Sutter. Word spread faster and farther than the wildfires that alternately destroy and restore the western forests and, all of a sudden, Northern California's Sierra Nevada held out the next great promise of the American Dream. Lured by the glint of gold, men poured out of San Francisco while two-thirds of the male population of Oregon headed south to California, forging a wagon road that followed a decades-old trail through the Cascade Mountains. For many of the early arrivals, the promise paid off. When the Oregon miners returned home, the wealth they brought back with them helped jump-start the nascent economy of the newly settled territory.

The San Franciscans and Oregonians were the first responders, but they were only the tip of the iceberg. News of the discovery traveled east, first to Missouri and the Midwest, already the hub for westward migrations. And then it made its way into the New York newspapers and President James K. Polk's State of the Union address. The publishing business got into the action, putting out "how to pan for gold" booklets, while hardware stores sold sluicing pans and picks as fast as they could stock them. The 49ers, as they were called—many of them city boys who had never slept outside or harnessed a horse or stepped

in a river or dug for anything in the dirt—headed out in what became the biggest migration in American history. Also notable about this migration was its gender imbalance: unlike the settlers of the Oregon and Mormon Pioneer Trails, who often traveled with whole families, the California emigrants were overwhelmingly lone men out to seek their fortunes. The 1850 US census in California found a male-to-female ratio of almost 15 to 1.

The timing was uncanny. The Mexican-American War was just coming to an end, but even before the official end of Mexican rule in California, settlers, traders, and adventurers from the United States were pushing westward, trying to establish a trail to California. Just nine days after gold was discovered—but before word had spread—Mexico signed the Treaty of Guadalupe Hidalgo, giving up its land in California to the United States. With California in American control, the race was on.

On, but not easy. Like the Oregon-bound emigrants and the Mormons headed to Utah, the miners-to-be had to cross thousands of miles of rough road, sweltering prairies, and the Continental Divide. And even after, the dryland areas of Utah and Nevada and California's sky-piercing Sierra Nevada range presented yet more obstacles that were every bit as challenging.

The Bidwell-Bartleson Party made the first semi-successful attempt to forge a trail to California as early as 1841. The party was actually one of the pioneers of both the Oregon and California Trails—its members split after crossing the Continental Divide. The California-bound faction drove their livestock

California Trail near Carson Pass, California

CANADA

Everett
Seattle
Tacoma
OLYMPIA
WASHINGTON
Yakima
Spokane

MONTANA
HELENA
Billings

NORTH DAKOTA
BISMARCK
Fargo

Portland
SALEM
Eugene
OREGON

IDAHO
BOISE

SOUTH DAKOTA
PIERRE
Sioux Falls

Pocatello
WYOMING
Casper

Twin Falls

NEBRASKA
Omaha

Redding
Winnemucca
Elko
SALT LAKE CITY
Provo
UTAH

CHEYENNE
Fort Collins

LINCOLN
St. Joseph

Yuba City
Reno
CARSON CITY
NEVADA

DENVER
COLORADO

Kansas City
TOPEKA

SACRAMENTO
San Francisco
Stockton

Colorado Springs
Pueblo

KANSAS
Wichita

Fresno
CALIFORNIA

Las Vegas

SANTA FE
Albuquerque

Amarillo

OKLAHOMA
Tulsa

OKLAHOMA CITY

Bakersfield

Los Angeles
Anaheim
San Diego
Yuma
ARIZONA
PHOENIX
Tucson

NEW MEXICO

Las Cruces
El Paso

Fort Worth
Dallas

TEXAS

AUSTIN
Houston
San Antonio

MEXICO

CALIFORNIA TRAIL
NATIONAL HISTORIC TRAIL

N

0   100   200 Miles

and pack animals on a challenging route along the Humboldt River, and then dropped into the San Joaquin Valley of Central California after a difficult passage that no one wanted to repeat or recommend. In 1843, Joseph Walker found a safer, if circuitous, route that crossed the southern end of the Sierra over a pass that now bears his name. East of present-day Bakersfield, Walker Pass is the first of the Sierra Nevada passes that long-distance hikers cross on the Pacific Crest National Scenic Trail. The next half-dozen or so passes to the north are all above 10,000 feet; no settler with the intention of surviving would have used any of them as a route across the mountains.

The next navigable pass was far to the north. In 1844, a wagon party led by Elisha Stephens followed Walker's route to the Humboldt Sink, but then veered off to follow Chief Truckee of the Paiutes up what would become known as the Truckee River. That route led to a pass that is today a main thoroughfare through the Sierra Nevada. Unfortunately, the 1846 Donner Party did not have such an easy time of it. Late in starting and delayed on the way, they were caught off guard by an early winter storm that stranded them without enough food for a Sierra winter. Those who survived confessed to cannibalizing their dead companions. Today, the eponymous Donner Pass on I-80 commemorates the tragedy.

By the time news of the gold rush reached the East, the various spokes, spurs, and shortcuts of the California Trail had more or less been worked out by early arrivals, and the trail had become a constantly evolving network. More than 250,000 emigrants traveled to the glittering mountain streams and to the farmlands and towns that sprang up to support the miners, who were pulling out gold worth as much as $50 million a year.

Humboldt River through Carlin Canyon, Nevada

FOLLOWING SPREAD: Twin Sisters, City of Rocks National Reserve, Idaho

THE ROUTE

The first part of the California National Historic Trail follows the familiar route of the Oregon and Mormon Pioneer Trails. As time passed, more than a dozen alternate routes emerged from a string of towns that sprang up along the Missouri River from Omaha to Kansas City. But they all came together at Fort Kearny to follow the by-then mostly fixed route through central and western Nebraska; up the valleys of the Platte, North Platte, and Sweetwater Rivers; and over South Pass in Wyoming. Even so, different parties occasionally took slightly different routes, adjusting to variables such as time of year and how fast and high the rivers were running, which dictated whether it was safer to follow the north or south bank of the Platte, and where and how to cross the numerous tributaries.

On the western side of the Continental Divide, the trail again split into at least a dozen alternates, where different California-bound parties in different seasons chose different ways to cross the mountains and basins. One of the main routes remained contiguous with the Oregon Trail until about 50 miles southeast of Fort Hall, where the California-bound settlers turned to follow the Raft River to the City of Rocks in present-day Idaho (near the point where today's Nevada, Idaho, and Utah come together). Some settlers followed a route as far north as today's Pocatello, Idaho; others went due south to Utah and swung around the south shore of the Great Salt Lake.

The northern routes converged to follow Joseph Walker's Granite Pass Route to the Humboldt River; the southern routes converged to take the Hastings Cutoff just west of Salt Lake City. All the routes finally rejoined in eastern Nevada to follow the Humboldt River across the Great Basin, after which the California Trail again branched out, this time to a dozen named routes (and many more minor alternates) to hundreds of destinations in California's Sierra and north into the Cascades as far as Oregon. As a result, today's California Trail is a sprawling network of more than 5,000 miles of routes, trunk trails, variants, shortcuts, and alternates in 10 states, including about 1,000 miles where remnant wheel ruts and traces from travelers and their overland wagons are still visible.

PREVIOUS SPREAD: Parting of the Ways, California and Oregon Trails, Idaho (top left); Pronounced trace of the California Trail descending Granite Pass, Idaho (middle left); Flatiron Mountain along Goose Creek, Idaho (bottom left); Little Goose Creek Canyon, Nevada (right)

LEFT: Outcropping known as "Post Office Rock," where emigrants left messages for separated family members (top); Rock Springs, a popular water stop along the California Trail, Nevada (bottom)

OPPOSITE: Trace of the California Trail beside Wilkins-Montello Road, Thousand Springs Valley, Nevada

RAGTOWN CROSSING
DEDICATED
TO THOSE PIONEERS WHOSE
DETERMINATION BROUGHT THEM
ACROSS THE FORTY MILE DESERT
TO THIS SPOT AND SWEET WATER

PREVIOUS SPREAD: Forty Mile Desert, Nevada (left); Last water source from the Humboldt River before heading into the Forty Mile Desert, Humboldt Sink, Nevada (top right); Memorial to Ragtown Crossing, where emigrants reached the Carson River after crossing the Forty Mile Desert, Nevada (bottom right)

LEFT: Pickett Peak reflected in a pond in Hope Valley, California

FOLLOWING SPREAD: Trace of the California Trail ascending steep terrain out of Emigrant Valley, California (top left); Sign along Gold Rush Trail section of the California Trail (bottom left); California Trail descending from West Pass, California (right)

LIVING THE HISTORY

With more than 5,000 miles of travel routes included in the system, 10 states, 1,000 miles of wagon ruts, hundreds of historic sites and museums, and scores of national parks, forests, state parks, and preserves, it would take a lifetime to visit the entire California Trail. The sites described here showcase different aspects of the trail, from the gold mines that incited the mass migration to sites that interpret life and travel on the trail to parks where one can still experience the unspoiled western landscape that inspired and challenged the 49ers. There are even a few opportunities to pan for gold—some of which is still there, in "them thar hills."

Auto Touring, Entire Route

Much of the California Trail can be toured, sometimes exactly and sometimes approximately, by auto—especially four-wheel-drive vehicles. The National Park Service has published a series of extremely detailed *Auto Tour Route Interpretive Guides* that contain suggested touring routes in each state, as well as information about the history of western travel routes, museums, and interpretive sites. Back-road touring, especially in Nevada and California, introduces visitors to a landscape that in many places still looks very much like it might have 170 years ago.

Marshall Gold Discovery State Historic Park, Coloma, California

James W. Marshall discovered gold in 1848 at Sutter's Mill on the South Fork of the American River, and the American West was never the same. The valley the Nisenan tribe had once called the Cullumah—or "beautiful valley"—became the epicenter of a mass movement that dwarfed any emigration thus far seen in American history. Some 250,000 people seeking wealth ignited the dramatic population and economic growth of the West. Marshall Gold Discovery State Historic Park includes about 70 percent of the town of Coloma, buildings that date to the gold rush, the Gold Discovery Museum (with mining equipment, horse-drawn

vehicles, household implements, and other gold rush–related displays), and the gold discovery site itself, located in the still-visible channel of Sutter's Mill. Visitors can try their hand at panning for gold: mining by hand or with pans is permitted (bring your own or buy one at the mercantile).

City of Rocks National Reserve, Southern Idaho

The City of Rocks made an obvious impact on emigrants: the weathered granite rock formations were mentioned in virtually every account of the passage through Idaho. Like children seeing animals in the shapes of clouds, emigrants saw steeples, hotels, houses, temples, and palaces in the shapes of the rock formations. They left their mark as well: at Emigrant Canyon Spring, remnants of the Kelton to Boise stage station and wagon ruts can be seen; at Register Rock, emigrants used axle grease to scrawl their names or initials. In addition to its distinctive rock formations, the "silent city" (as the emigrants called it) contains an abundance of biological diversity, which adds a dramatic variety of natural textures, colors, and shapes to an already striking geological landscape. The national reserve and an adjacent state park offer a network of trails as well as more than 1,000 traditional and bolt-protected rock-climbing routes, some of which are among the most difficult in the United States.

Carson Emigrant Historic Trail, near Carson Pass, California

The Carson Emigrant Historic Trail is a certified national recreation trail that follows one of the original emigrant routes across the rugged Sierra Nevada. The trail was first discovered by the Mormon Battalion as they were attempting to find a wagon route over the Sierra. Place names like Carson Pass, Emigrant Creek, Tragedy Spring, Hope Valley, and Silver Lake give us thumbnail sketches of the emigrant experience. Physical evidence such as ruts from the wagons challenge visitors to imagine what it might have been like to make this crossing over the classical but formidable Sierra scenery while managing wagons and stock animals. West Pass is at the highest elevation of any of America's national historic trails. The Pacific Crest National Scenic Trail intersects the California Trail at Carson Pass. The trail is especially beautiful in early summer, when wildflowers carpet the newly snow-free alpine meadows.

Donner Memorial State Park Visitor Center and Pioneer Monument, Donner Pass, California

That an interstate can cross the Sierra belies the difficulty the early settlers had in crossing the range. Nowhere is this more true than at Donner Pass. Today, Donner Memorial

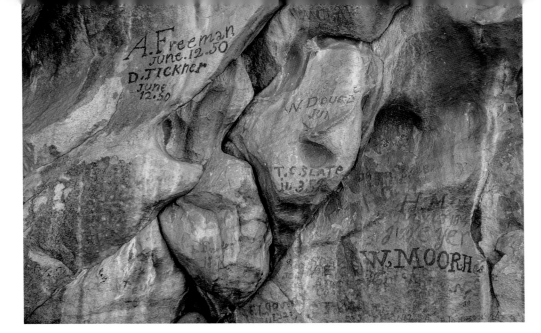

State Park is a bucolic retreat offering the summer vacationer opportunities for camping, picnicking, boating, fishing, waterskiing, and hiking. But exhibits at the visitor center and monument give visitors a different perspective of what the emigrants could, and did, face when crossing these mountains by wagon. The museum has exhibits about the Washoe people, the Chinese construction of the railroad, early motoring over the Sierra, the emigrant migration, and, of course, the tragically fated Donner Party, whose ordeal of cannibalism and survival over the course of a mountain winter is one of the best-known stories of the settlement of California. The Pacific Crest National Scenic Trail intersects this branch of the California Trail at the pass, and, for hikers, a detour into these high and wild mountains gives a clear picture of the challenges.

California Trail Interpretive Center, Elko, Nevada

Managed by the Bureau of Land Management, this state-of-the-art interpretive center tells the stories of the fur trappers, farmers, prospectors, merchants, and families who moved to California in the wake of the gold rush, hoping for a new start and new opportunities. Permanent and interactive exhibits give visitors a way to experience an encampment, sit in a pioneer wagon, listen to stories from emigrant journals, learn about the culture of the American Indian tribes, and discover why the trail was frequently called "The Elephant"—an image the emigrants used to convey that they had come face-to-face with something that, to them, crystallized the hardships, drama, and triumph of their journey.

Top: Emigrant names written in axle grease, Register Rock State Historic Site, Idaho; *Middle left:* Monument to James W. Marshall, the person who first found gold while working at Sutter's Mill, California; *Middle right:* Replica of Sutter's Mill, California; *Bottom left:* Wagon displayed at California Trail Interpretive Center, Nevada; *Bottom right (upper):* Painting depicting paddlewheelers arriving at Independence, Missouri; *Bottom right (lower):* Sign at entrance to California Trail Interpretive Center, Nevada

Pony Express Trail

1,966 MILES ➤ MISSOURI • KANSAS • NEBRASKA • COLORADO • WYOMING • UTAH • NEVADA • CALIFORNIA

If you were a young man in the winter of 1860, and if you were fit, skinny, adventurous, and able to handle a horse, opportunity beckoned. Interested parties were directed to report to the stables of the Pony Express in St. Joseph, Missouri.

The job was for the new Central Overland California and Pike's Peak Express Company, which had been founded in the early months of 1860. William H. Russell, Alexander Majors, and William B. Waddell proposed to use relay teams of horses and riders to deliver mail between St. Joseph, Missouri, and Sacramento, California.

Emigrant settlers, at their plodding pace of 15 miles a day, had taken more than 100 days to cover the distance. More recently, travelers using the newly formed stagecoach companies could cross the continent in a faster but still uncomfortable 25 days. The new company, better known to history as the Pony Express, announced that a letter could be delivered across the 1,900-mile distance in an almost unbelievable 10 days. The service was not cheap: initially, the cost to post a half-ounce letter was $5 (equivalent to about $140 in 2020). By the end of the Pony Express, 18 months later, the price had dropped to a more affordable but still pricey $1 per half-ounce letter (around $28 today).

Costly or not, the need for a timely mail service was compelling. By 1860, settlements in the Oregon and Utah Territory were thriving. California had entered the Union as a free state in 1850, and had dealt with slow and uncertain communications with the rest of the country for 10 years. Without a telegraph line or a transcontinental railroad, mail had to travel via a few private carriers or by the Butterfield Overland Mail service, which started in 1857 and crossed the southwestern territories of the United States. Neither met the need for a functional, reliable, and fast service. With tensions building before the Civil War, northern state politicians worried about the Butterfield Route running through Texas. They demanded a central route that the Union could control in the event of a war. Once southern states began seceding, northern politicians could set this new route.

Pony Express Monument, St. Joseph, Missouri

OPPOSITE: Pony Express re-rider, Wyoming

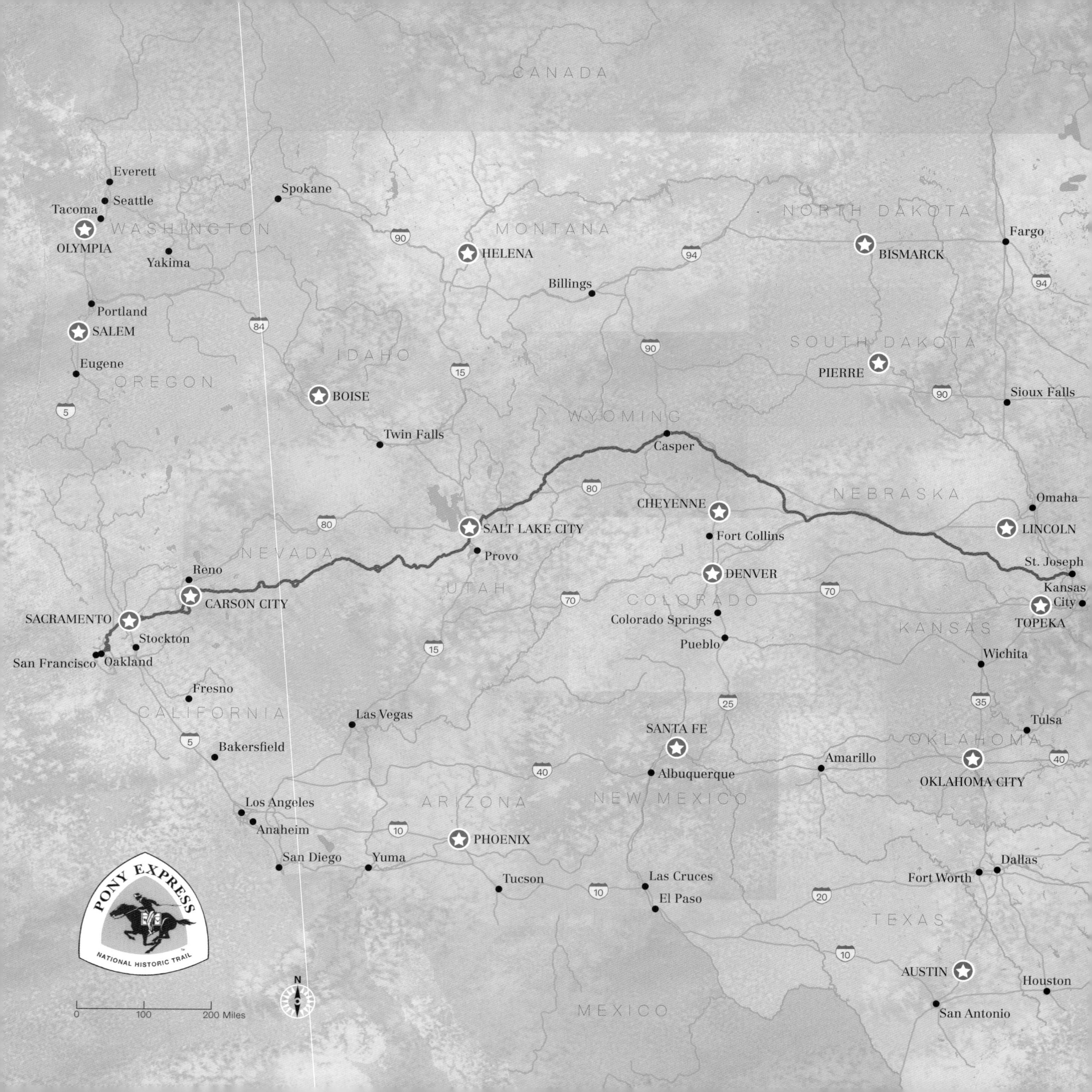

CANADA
WASHINGTON
Everett
Seattle
Tacoma
OLYMPIA
Yakima
Spokane
MONTANA
HELENA
Billings
NORTH DAKOTA
BISMARCK
Fargo
Portland
SALEM
Eugene
OREGON
IDAHO
BOISE
Twin Falls
SOUTH DAKOTA
PIERRE
Sioux Falls
WYOMING
Casper
CHEYENNE
Fort Collins
NEBRASKA
Omaha
LINCOLN
SALT LAKE CITY
Provo
NEVADA
Reno
CARSON CITY
UTAH
DENVER
COLORADO
Colorado Springs
Pueblo
St. Joseph
Kansas City
TOPEKA
KANSAS
Wichita
SACRAMENTO
Stockton
San Francisco
Oakland
Fresno
CALIFORNIA
Las Vegas
Bakersfield
SANTA FE
Albuquerque
NEW MEXICO
Amarillo
OKLAHOMA
Tulsa
OKLAHOMA CITY
Los Angeles
Anaheim
San Diego
Yuma
ARIZONA
PHOENIX
Tucson
Las Cruces
El Paso
Fort Worth
Dallas
TEXAS
AUSTIN
Houston
San Antonio
MEXICO
90
94
84
15
5
80
70
25
35
40
10
20
PONY EXPRESS
NATIONAL HISTORIC TRAIL
N
0
100
200 Miles

Russell, Majors, and Waddell built their business seemingly overnight. They bought 400 horses, chosen for strength and speed. They set up 184 relay stations, approximately one every 10 miles, where horses could be swapped out and riders could rest. Managers were hired to run the stations, supervise security, and oversee the care of the horses.

Most importantly, 100 or so young men signed up to ride into history. Applicants had to be able to ride a horse. They had to be skinny because, like today's racing jockeys, every extra pound the horse carried wasted energy that would otherwise be put toward speed. And they had to be fit: young men were considered more able to meet the physical demands of the job, which included riding an average of 75 to 100 miles per leg. At "swing stations," riders could swap a spent horse for a fresh one, hoisting their mailbags to the next horse and continuing on. At the end of each assigned leg, riders rested at so-called home stations, but the mail kept moving: the mailbag was passed on to the next horse and rider. Day and night, the mail went forward, even if that meant a rider occasionally had to ride 20 hours on a double shift. For all this, the riders were paid $100 a month (the equivalent of $2,800 a month today: not great pay considering the risk to life and limb, but far better than the wage for unskilled labor at the time, which was between $0.43 and $1 a day).

Horses carried no more than 165 pounds. Of those, 125 pounds were allotted to the rider, clothes included. Another 20 pounds went for the saddle and ancillary equipment: a revolver, a mandatory Bible (on which each rider had sworn not to drink, cuss, or brawl with other Pony Express employees), and, most importantly, the custom-designed mochila, which carried the mail itself. Designed to be quickly taken on and off the saddle, the mochila was hung over the saddle's horn and cantle and kept in place by the weight of the rider. The mail—which took up the remaining 20 pounds—was stashed in pockets that were sewn onto each of the four corners of the mochila.

Unfortunately for the entrepreneurs of the company, not to mention American legend, timing can be everything when it comes to business. Just 10 weeks after the Pony Express began operations, Congress passed a bill instructing the secretary of the treasury to subsidize building a transcontinental telegraph. Almost immediately, newly formed companies—the Overland Telegraph Company of California and the Pacific Telegraph Company of Nebraska—started construction. The death knell for the Pony Express had been rung.

Nonetheless, the Pony Express continued to operate until the last telegraph wires were strung, carrying the mail across the continent at the breakneck pace of nearly 200 miles a day. Finally, on October 26, 1861, the last wire connection was made and San Francisco and New York City were in direct telegraph contact. The Pony Express was officially terminated—though the letters and newspapers already en route on that day were safely carried and delivered in November.

THE ROUTE

Unlike the California Trail, which sprawls into a network of side trails, alternates, offshoots, and cutoffs, the Pony Express National Historic Trail is a fairly direct affair, with only a few minor variants.

The Pony Express started from the Missouri River at the company's offices and stables in St. Joseph, near Kansas City. It joined the westbound wagon trails near Fort Kearny, from which it followed the same Platte-North Platte-Sweetwater River route around the north rim of the Great Divide Basin and over South Pass.

West of the Continental Divide, the Pony Express route followed the southern alternate of the California Trail, heading southwest to Salt Lake City and then splitting off to the south across Nevada. The trail then followed the Carson River to Lake Tahoe, swung around the south side of the lake, and continued to Sacramento. From there, mail was usually carried to San Francisco by riverboat.

FOLLOWING SPREAD:
Reconstructed toll bridge over Rock Creek, Rock Creek Station State Historical Park, Nebraska (top left); Wagon remnants beside a granite marker designating the site of the Kiowa Pony Express Station, Nebraska (bottom left); Buttes near site of Red Buttes Pony Express Station, Wyoming (right)

OPPOSITE: View from cliffs of Echo Canyon, above Weber Pony Express Station, Utah

RIGHT: Simpson Springs Pony Express Station, Utah (top); Herd of wild horses near Simpson Springs Pony Express Station, Utah (bottom)

FOLLOWING SPREAD: Old ranch posts along the Pony Express Trail, Utah (top left); Foundation remnants of Carson Sink Station near Carson Lake, Nevada (middle left); Lone oak tree in grasslands near Pony Express Trail, California (bottom left); Ruins of Sand Springs Pony Express Station, Nevada (right)

LIVING THE HISTORY

Today's national historic trail passes through different state, local, and federal land-management units, as well as private and tribal lands, which offer different kinds of recreation experiences: auto touring, hiking, biking, and horseback riding on various trail segments. In California, Colorado, Nevada, Utah, and Wyoming, the Bureau of Land Management manages much of the route. In addition to the sites and experiences suggested here, many of the sites pertaining to the Oregon, California, and Mormon Pioneer Trails also contain information and exhibits about the Pony Express route, especially on the eastern side of the Continental Divide.

Annual Pony Express Re-ride, Entire Route

Perhaps the most direct and authentic way to experience the Pony Express is to ride it. Or, at least, part of it. Each year, the National Pony Express Association organizes a re-ride of the entire 1,966 miles. The reenactment between St. Joseph and Sacramento goes westbound one year and eastbound the next. Just like in the days of the real Pony Express, riders travel as a relay, averaging about 10 miles per hour.

The relay continues day and night until the mail is delivered. The only difference is that the 650 riders participating in the reenactment ride much shorter legs than the real Pony Express riders. Riders must be members of the association. Don't ride? Don't have a horse? Send a letter and join one of the chapters. Re-riders carry 1,000 to 1,200 pieces of mail in the mochila, which is passed from rider to rider (and horse to horse) from one end of the trail to the other. For those who can't see the actual reenactment, the annual re-ride can be followed online.

Patee House Museum, St. Joseph, Missouri

The Patee House was one of the best-known hotels west of the Mississippi River; among others, guests included Oscar Wilde, who had come to St. Joseph to give a lecture, and the family of Jesse James, who stayed there during the investigation of his death in a nearby house. At different times, it was also a Civil War military headquarters, a women's college, an epileptic sanitarium, a shirt factory, and the headquarters and eastern terminus of the Pony Express. Today, it is a national historic landmark and museum owned by the Pony Express Historical Association. The Patee House Museum focuses on the history of communications and transportation, with locomotives, a train depot, a Model T Ford, antique cars, trucks, fire trucks,

a 1921 race car, antique telephones and radios, and a wagonmaker's blacksmithing tools.

Pony Express National Museum, St. Joseph, Missouri

Pike's Peak Stables in St. Joseph, Missouri, is where Pony Express riders started from on the first leg of the relay that would take mail nearly 2,000 miles across the continent in 10 days. Today the stables are part of the Pony Express National Museum, which interprets the short history of the legendary mail service. Hands-on exhibits give visitors the chance to pump water from an old well, use a telegraph machine, sort mail, and affix a mochila to a saddle. In the "Family Life on the Frontier" exhibit, kids can dress up as pioneers and experience what life was like on the 1800s frontier via living history props and activities. A 60-foot diorama takes visitors along the route of the Pony Express, demonstrating the diverse environments through which the riders galloped: plains, mountains, arid mesas, plateaus, and basins.

Hollenberg Pony Express Station, Kansas

This small historic site includes the most intact surviving station of the Pony Express. Built in 1858 to serve Oregon- and California-bound emigrants, in 1860 it became a Pony Express home station, where riders switched mounts and caught a night's sleep before taking off again. During its operating years, the building served as a family residence, with a shop, tavern, and loft where riders could sleep. A stable and blacksmith's shop tended to the horses. Exhibits include displays about westward expansion, American Indians, commerce, settlers, trail life, and the Pony Express. Outside, a hiking trail winds around the grounds, which include a garden with native grasses and plants.

Riding the Route, Eureka County, Nevada

Check out a section of the Pony Express Trail where you can ride, hike, or drive part of the original route. A 53-mile section of trail runs through Bureau of Land Management lands, past the remains of five Pony Express stations from Dry Creek to Diamond Springs (19 miles north of the town of Eureka, where descendants of Pony Express riders and station masters still live). This is a dirt road, and cell phone coverage is spotty. Characterized by sagebrush-covered rolling terrain, the mountains and valleys are home to coyotes, livestock, wild horses, burros, mule deer, and sage chickens.

Opposite: Reading of the oath before the Annual Pony Express Re-ride in St. Joseph, Missouri; *Above, left:* Hollenburg Pony Express Station State Historic Site, Kansas; *Above, right:* Patee House, Missouri

Iditarod Trail

2,300 MILES ➤ ALASKA

Nome, Alaska, winter of 1925: if you lived there and needed to be somewhere else, you were going to have to travel by dogsled. Located two degrees south of the Arctic Circle on the Seward Peninsula, Nome is a small city of around 4,000 people that juts into the Norton Sound of the Bering Sea. In 1925, it was even smaller, with a population of only 450 Native Alaskans and about 1,000 settlers of European descent. About 10,000 more people, most of them Native Alaskans, lived in the outlying areas.

Elsewhere in America, modern transportation in the form of trains, planes, and automobiles was busy taming large distances, but in Alaska, distances were longer and temperatures colder. There were no roads across the frozen tundra, planes couldn't fly, and ships couldn't break through the iced-over Bering Sea. If you lived there over the long arctic winter, you had two choices: harness up the sled dogs, or stay home.

Nome's population was not only isolated, but also vulnerable. Native Alaskans lived close to American settlers, but they had no resistance to European diseases—a fact that was starkly demonstrated during the 1918–1919 influenza outbreak, when about 50 percent of Nome's Native Alaskans died.

In January 1925, they were faced with something even worse. In December 1924, diphtheria had been diagnosed; a month later, an outbreak was confirmed. The disease was spreading rapidly to a population that had no resistance, the city's supply of diphtheria antitoxin had expired, and the requested replacement had not arrived before winter set in. Health authorities estimated that the fatality rate among the region's indigenous population could be close to 100 percent.

Mitch Seavey and his dog team leaving Elim and heading toward White Mountain on his victorious 2017 Iditarod race

With reports of confirmed cases flowing in, there was only one solution and it was seemingly impossible: to deliver the serum by dogsled, traveling more than 674 miles through snowbound wilderness in the bitter cold and almost endless darkness of the arctic winter. Perhaps most challenging of all, health authorities estimated that the serum could last only six days under the conditions on the trail. It was a terrible, impossible solution. But it was also the only hope.

The result is remembered as the Great Race of Mercy. More than 150 dogs and 20 drivers (Native Alaskans, American settlers, and Europeans) participated in the relay. Battered by windchill as low as 85 below zero and by 80-mile-an-hour wind gusts, they raced over frozen tundra lit by the moon and the northern lights. The first vials of antitoxin—just enough to treat the already infected patients—reached Nome in five-and-a-half days, breaking the previous speed record by half. Later, a second shipment arrived to protect the remaining population.

The run prevented a full-fledged epidemic. It also brought vaccination to the attention of the American public. And it introduced Alaska and dogsledding to an international audience, creating the biggest canine celebrities of the day. Media attention, newspaper articles, and a statue in New York's Central Park all paid tribute to the heroes—and also created feuds as to which individual dog deserved the lion's share of the canine credit.

That single event would have been enough to earn any trail a place on a roster of historically important trails, but the Iditarod National Historic Trail is about much more than that. The Serum Run, extraordinary

Fairbanks

A4

Yukon River

Nome

Kaltag

Unalakleet

ALASKA

Alaska Range

A4

McGrath

Iditarod

Flat

Rainy Pass

A1

Kuskokwim River

Eagle River

Anchorage

Girdwood

A3

Seward

IDITAROD

NATIONAL HISTORIC TRAIL

0   100 Miles

N

as it was, would not have been able to take place without the trail network that had been developed first by the Native Alaskans and later by the gold miners and those who supplied them during Alaska's last great gold rush. It is that network that is celebrated by the Iditarod Trail.

During the early years of the 20th century, the Iditarod gold district was the third-richest placer-mining district in all of Alaska. This was the last big gold rush in Alaska; indeed, it was the largest last gold rush in the United States. Prospectors representing an array of nationalities and races heeded its call to riches. Today, Iditarod is a ghost town, but for the heady boom years, it and nearby Flat—the center of gold-mining activities—comprised the third-largest population center in Alaska. Its modern conveniences rivaled those of any pre–World War I boomtown: newspapers, wireless, telephones, and entertainment ranging from social clubs to sports teams.

Prospectors flooded in, and gold was shipped—carried by teams of dogsleds—a ton at a time. Drivers and their dog teams were hired by banks such as Wells Fargo to move the gold from the mines near Iditarod to the seacoast at Seward. Interestingly, there was never a successful robbery of one of these so-called gold trains.

The trail network was also expanded to connect Seward in the south to Nome in the north; in bypassing Fairbanks, the Nome Government Trail reduced the overland distance winter mail was hauled by 500 miles. The Seward-to-Nome Trail connected local and regional trails, and filled significant gaps between Interior Alaska and Southcentral Alaska, particularly with a 250-mile section over the Alaska Range between the Kuskokwim River and Cook Inlet. In addition to dogsleds, streams of miners trudged the trek on snowshoes, peering across the treeless tundra to spot the next trail marker. Approximately every 300 to 500 feet, three small tree limbs were lashed together into a tripod to point the way. Travel was also made possible by an informal but vital system of private roadhouses built at approximately 20-mile intervals. These roadhouses are the basis of the public shelters and safety cabins found along the trail (and throughout Alaska) today.

As is true of all gold rushes, the Iditarod gold rush had a beginning—and an end. World War I led to the depopulation of the countryside as prospectors left Alaska to join the armies of nations near and far. After the war, winter aircraft travel in the 1920s improved to the point of functionality, contributing to the demise of long-distance freight hauling by sled dog teams. But not to the demise of the legend. The Iditarod also shares its name with the iconic modern-day endurance dogsled race, which was established to bring attention to Alaska's culture of dogsledding.

Dogsledding may have enabled the gold rush and brought serum to Nome, but in Alaska, the culture of dogsledding goes back much further—to the Native Alaskans. Thousands of years in this challenging environment created a culture superbly adapted to snow, ice, wind, cold, and nights that last for months. Like so much in Alaska, the enormity of the land magnifies the challenges of the environmental extremes, and Native Alaskan culture devised technologies for thriving in a landscape that boasts the highest mountains, the biggest wilderness, and the longest nights

Bronze statue of Iditarod trail pioneer Jujiro Wada, Seward Waterfront Park, the southern terminus of the Iditarod Trail in the United States. Snowmageddons and storms of the century mean nothing to Native Alaskans; a snowpocalypse is simply the way life is.

In the arctic, creative use has always been made of the available technologies and supplies: animal furs for warmth, ice and snow for caves and igloos, snowshoes and sled dogs for travel. Today, equally creative use is made of modern technologies: Alaskans have Gore-Tex and military "bunny boots" to keep them warm; they use Tyvek and tin roofs for insulation and housing; snowmobiles and bush planes take them from one place to another. But while new may have replaced old in daily life, dogsledding still looms large in the culture and imagination. In the Alaska before bush planes and snowmobiles, sled dogs were not pets; they were a lifeline.

The national historic trail thus commemorates the traditional Native Alaskan travel routes across the interior as well as the role of dogsledding through more recent Alaskan history, including the gold rush, when indigenous dogsled routes doubled as gold miner highways. As adventurers from "outside" flooded the Alaskan interior in search of hoped-for riches, they used both the old Native Alaskan trails as well as the newer routes developed by the Alaska Road Commission. The design of the dogsleds was adapted to meet new needs of transporting mail and supplies (the sleds in today's Iditarod races are therefore different from the original American Indian designs). But the fundamental purpose remained the same: for centuries, dogsleds enabled travel and trade—even survival—across a snowbound landscape during the brutal arctic and subarctic winters.

It is appropriate, then, that much of the Iditarod is almost exclusively used in winter, unique in the National Trails System. In most of the northern and interior sections, travel is restricted to the months when swamps and marshes are frozen and when the trail has enough snow to be traversed by dogsled or, in a nod to the modern age, snowmobile. Like all national historic trails, the Iditarod is commemorative, but it is also uniquely a living trail, used today by rural Alaskans as an overland travel route between communities and for recreation and competition in everything from dogsledding to snowmobiling. The Iditarod is synonymous with adventure and the role man's best friend has played in Alaskan history—it is a living system of trails used for transportation, connection, and outdoor adventure.

In granting approval for the certification of the Iditarod as a national historic trail, the US Senate noted that it offered "a rich diversity of climate, terrain, scenery, wildlife, recreation, and historic resources in an environment largely unchanged since the days of the stampeders. It is the isolated, primitive quality of this historical environment that makes the Iditarod National Historic Trail proposal unique. Nowhere in the National Trails System is there such an extensive landscape, so demanding of durability and skill during its winter season of travel. On the Iditarod, today's adventurer can duplicate the experience and challenge of yesteryear."

THE ROUTE

Like most of the national historic trails, the Iditarod National Historic Trail is a network of connecting routes. The main trunk trail follows the originally surveyed 938-mile mail route from Seward to Nome. In addition, the trail contains 1,400 miles of side, connecting, alternate, and parallel routes that were used to link remote communities and historic sites. The Iditarod thus sprawls all over the Alaskan interior, from the Kenai Peninsula south of Anchorage to the Bering Sea at Nome. The interior town of Iditarod, after which the trail network is named, is now a ghost town.

The route is used for a variety of outdoor recreation purposes, but the most famous current use is the annual Iditarod Sled Dog Race, which goes from Anchorage to Nome using two different 1,000-mile routes, which alternate from one year to the next in order to bring the race to different communities on different branches of the trail. Alaska's trend of warming winters sometimes forces race organizers to move either the starting point of the race or the race route itself, as snow allows. Other notable sporting events that use the trail include the Iron Dog Snowmobile Race, and ultraendurance races such as the Iditarod Trail Invitational and the Iditasport Ultramarathon, where racers enter in a variety of categories and distances to run, hike, ski, or bike.

Iditarod route along what is now known as Johnson Pass Trail, Chugach National Forest

OPPOSITE: Footbridge over Raven Creek Gorge, Crow Pass Trail, which follows the historic Iditarod route, Chugach State Park

RIGHT: Dall sheep, Crow Pass Trail, Chugach Mountains, Chugach National Forest (top); Crystal Lake Cirque from Crow Pass Trail, Chugach National Forest (bottom)

FOLLOWING SPREAD: Steam car in Flat ghost town (top left); Sled dog resting at Tanana Checkpoint (middle left); Fish wheels on shore of the Yukon River (bottom left); Iditarod dog team arriving at Huslia Checkpoint (right)

LIVING THE HISTORY

On almost all of the other national scenic and historic trails, bragging rights for toughness go to the traveler who can conquer the route in winter. Not so here: on much of the Iditarod, summer travel is the most challenging season. While some of the southern Iditarod near Anchorage and between Seward and Knik can be explored any time of year (given the right gear and skill set), in the northern and interior sections of the trail, summer travel is not recommended because the trail tundra turns into a swampy, mosquito-infested bog once the ice and snow melt. Therefore, much of the recreation on the Iditarod is a cold and snowy affair: dogsledding, snowmobiling, cross-country skiing, snowshoeing, and fat biking. Depending on where and when a visitor is exploring, traveling companions might include moose, caribou, brown bears, bison, wolves, seals, and Dall sheep. The trail offers outstanding opportunities for solitude and adventure in a huge and untamed landscape. It also demands a high level of outdoorsmanship as well as gear and clothing for severe winter conditions.

Iditarod Trail Sled Dog Race Headquarters and Museum, Wasilla, Alaska

Located at the race headquarters, the Iditarod Trail Sled Dog Race Museum has a variety of exhibits detailing the stories—both past and present—of this iconic Alaskan event, which was founded to honor the history and culture of dogsledding in Alaska. Displays include artifacts from the 1925 serum run, the history of the "Last Great Race," and the national historic trail, including a replica of an Iditarod Trail public shelter cabin. Visitors have opportunities to talk to Iditarod mushers and meet sled dog puppies; in addition, summer visitors can go on a training-dog-cart ride.

Ceremonial Start of the Iditarod Race, Anchorage, Alaska

The Iditarod Trail Sled Dog Race is run every year in early March. Teams generally take eight to 15 (or more) days to cross approximately 1,000 miles from Anchorage to Nome. At the ceremonial start in Anchorage, mushers and their teams are announced to the crowd, and dignitaries and donors ride in the sleds to cross the starting line. The timed race begins the next day with the official "restart" in Willow, unless winter conditions (or the lack of them) force the race to move farther north.

Dream a Dream Dog Farm, near Wasilla, Alaska

Two Iditarod veterans offer visitors a chance to see the workings of a sled dog kennel up close and personal. Guests can tour the kennel year-round to learn how sled dogs are reared and trained. Activities include educational programs, guided trail walks, sled dog rides, and lessons in mushing—the art of driving a dogsled.

Chugach National Forest and Summer Mountain Hiking, near Anchorage, Alaska

Several sections of the trail in the mountains near Anchorage are passible in summer. The Chugach National Forest is restoring and developing more than 180 miles of the Southern Trek of the Iditarod Trail between Seward and Girdwood. The Chugach National Forest on the Kenai Peninsula and Chugach State Park near Anchorage offer opportunities to explore ecosystems of the northernmost temperate rain forest, including alpine tundra and wet lowland meadow ecosystems, and to learn about the gold rush era in Alaska.

From Seward's Iditarod Monument, a paved bike path leads north along Resurrection Bay. Just north of the city of Seward, a four-mile, mostly flat section of the Iditarod Trail leads to Bear Lake; in winter, it is a groomed cross-country ski trail.

A popular multiuse route near Girdwood, the Johnson Pass Trail affords alpine views, waterfalls, lakes, and a strenuous workout over its 24-mile, one-way length. The trail is popular with bicyclists and backpackers in summer and with snowmobilers, skiers, and fat bikers in winter.

A network of trails in Girdwood leads to and around the Iditarod Trail. From Alyeska, the three-mile Winner Creek Trail offers well-maintained access to the Iditarod. Also part of the same network, the popular and challenging Crow Pass Trail follows the historic Iditarod to the Eagle River Nature Center in Chugach State Park, where visitors can see spawning salmon during late summer.

Summer Beach Hiking, near Nome, Alaska

Visitors to Nome can hike east along the trail near the Bering Sea coast for approximately 30 miles. Gold fever brought thousands of hopefuls here to pan for nuggets in nearby creeks. But when gold was discovered mixed in with the sand on Nome's beaches, thousands more pitched their tents here. Look down! The dream lives on: just offshore, recreational gold miners still try their luck, dredging the sands. From Safety Sound, the Iditarod Trail leads through the Alaska Maritime National Wildlife Refuge. This 3.4-million-acre refuge, which spreads all over Alaska's enormous coast, was established to conserve marine mammals, seabirds, and other migratory birds. It protects some 40 million seabirds, representing more than 30 species. In the fall, the sea begins to freeze, and winter brings out ski-planes, dogsleds, and snowmobiles.

Winter Adventure and Safety Cabins, Alaskan Interior

The northern part of trail is still used for snowmobile travel between towns as well as all manner of backcountry winter recreation. Larger towns and cities near the route—Anchorage, Seward, Girdwood, Eagle River, and Wasilla in the south and Nome in the north—can be used as staging areas for a wilderness adventure. But in the interior, services are few and far between, so arrangements for transportation, lodging, and support, such as food and fuel, should be made in advance. The Bureau of Land Management maintains two remote, long-distance segments of the trail with five Iditarod National Historic Trail Safety Cabins open to the public to provide shelter from the elements. The cabins carry on the tradition from the mail route days, when mushers relied on roadhouses that were scattered throughout the trail system. Travel from village to village can be done on snow machines or dogsleds, stopping at the public safety cabins along the way. One of the fastest-growing uses on the trail is fat biking, a technology that was developed on and for the Iditarod Trail, and which has since spread across the world. Rentals are readily available in Anchorage. Multiple long-distance fat-bike race events follow the Iditarod Trail from Anchorage to McGrath and Nome, attracting an international field annually.

Top: Ceremonial start of the 2017 Iditarod in Anchorage; *Middle:* Bronze sculpture titled *Trail Blazers* at the southern terminus of the Iditarod Trail in Seward; *Bottom:* Crossing the Eagle River along the Crow Pass Trail, Chugach State Park

PART FOUR

AMERICAN DIVERSITY

———— ★ ————

How we understand the history of the United States depends on whose stories we read. Stories of conquerors are also stories of the conquered. Some heroes are also villains; some monuments cast shadows. No country's myths are free of darkness. American history is no exception. • The trails in this section have little in common except that they represent the stories of cultures and people that are outside the mainstream of European American cultural identity. The "divine right" that allowed Manifest Destiny to roll like a juggernaut across the continent had a profound effect on other, non-European peoples. For every story of mint juleps on a plantation porch, there is a story of enslavement. For every pioneer who started a western farm, there is an American Indian banished to a reservation.

Enslavement, cultural erosion or eradication, second-class citizenship, segregation, and forced removal and relocation are also the stories of American history.

The four national historic trails in this section consider some of these stories. To its credit, the National Trails System tells these tales not from the perspective of the dominant culture, but from the perspective of the cultures to which they belong.

Let's begin with the trail that tells the oldest story. In Hawai'i, the Ala Kahakai National Historic Trail contours around the Big Island, following the paths used by Hawaiians before European contact. Polynesians sailed to Hawai'i more than 1,000 years ago. The culture that evolved from their original settlements developed in relative isolation, becoming something that retains some of its Polynesian roots but is also unique to Hawai'i. The first European to arrive was James Cook in 1778. The means by which the independent kingdom of Hawai'i became an American state include colonial economic maneuvers, land grabs, an overthrow of government, and annexation, which were followed by political and economic discrimination and cultural erosion. Between then and now, the indigenous population of Hawai'i has dropped to one-third of its original number. (According to the 2010 census, the population of Hawai'i was 1.4 million, 371,000 of whom identified as Native Hawaiian in combination with one or more other races or Pacific Islander groups, and 156,000 of whom identified as solely Native Hawaiian.) Despite this grim history, today's Ala Kahakai Trail spends most of its time not on the postcontact depredations, but on celebrating the connections Hawaiians still have with their ancestors, their culture, and their landscapes.

On the American mainland, two trails tell stories of incursions on American Indian lands that ended in brutality and atrocities. The Cherokee of the Southeast Appalachians and the Nez Perce of the Northwest were unlikely tribes to be enmeshed in some of the most devastating conflicts with the American government. Both tribes had reached out to European Americans. The Nez Perce had helped Lewis and Clark, quite possibly saving the entire expedition from disaster. The Cherokee emulated some aspects of European culture, developing their own written language and adopting

PREVIOUS SPREAD: Eagle Cap reflected in small pond in Lostine Meadows, Nez Perce Trail, Eagle Cap Wilderness, Wallowa Mountains, Oregon

Arch at Nāpu'uonā'elemākule, Ala Kahakai Trail, Hawai'i Volcanoes National Park, Hawai'i

elements of European American business, trade, law, and religion. Ironically and patronizingly, they were one of five tribes characterized by the American government as "civilized." None of that mattered when it came down to gold, land, and American settlement. The ensuing forced resettlements were different in nature, but equally brutal—one was an evacuation march; the other a war precipitated by an attempted escape from confinement in a reservation. They are commemorated in the Trail of Tears National Historic Trail and Nez Perce (Nee-Me-Poo) National Historic Trail.

Finally, there is the Selma to Montgomery National Historic Trail—the only trail in the system (so far) that commemorates African Americans, and the only trail that follows a protest movement. At 54 miles, it is the shortest national historic trail and also the one that commemorates the most recent historic event. It follows the route of the 1965 Voting Rights March, generally considered one of the seminal events that led to the passage of the Voting Rights Act in the summer of 1965.

The stories in this chapter take place across different times and in vastly different parts of the country. What they have in common are elements of tragedy, resilience, cultural conflict, and survival that demonstrate the many complex layers that underlie American history.

Rural scene along the Trail of Tears near Trail of Tears State Park, Missouri

Ala Kahakai Trail

175 MILES ➤ HAWAI'I

Imagine for a moment the audacity of voyaging across the entire Pacific Ocean in a wooden canoe powered by winds, sails, and a steering paddle, guided only by the stars and the currents. The ancient Polynesians did exactly that. To call them a seafaring people is an understatement: their mastery in seamanship and navigation initiated an era of voyaging that put settlements on virtually every habitable Pacific island from New Zealand to Hawai'i.

The story of the Ala Kahakai National Historic Trail thus begins more than 1,000 years ago, when voyaging canoe migrations departed a region of islands in the central South Pacific and traveled to what is today known as the Hawaiian archipelago. These Polynesian voyagers were the first human settlers on any of the Hawaiian Islands. The Ala Kahakai Trail commemorates traditions that date to the state's earliest Polynesian settlements and that have changed and evolved over time.

The Ala Kahakai is a 175-mile-long coastal route that celebrates traditional Hawaiian culture; it has been in continuous use since the Polynesians arrived on Moku o Keawe, also known as the Big Island. Following the path of least resistance along natural contours of the land, the trail crosses more than 200 *ahupua'a,* the Hawaiian name for mountain-to-sea land divisions that were allocated according to a system of land use dating back to Polynesia.

The volcanic islands of the Pacific are characterized by steep slopes and fertile valleys, which are watered by freshwater streams that tumble to the ocean. The Polynesians divided their land units into slices that started in the central mountain ridges and

Mahai'ula Bay along the
Ala Kahakai Trail

Hawi

250

Kawaihae

Honoka'a

Waimea

19

200

190

Hilo

200

HAWAI'I

Pāhoa

130

Kailua

Kalapana

11

Pahala

Nā'ālehu

11

ALA KA HAKAI
NATIONAL HISTORIC TRAIL

N

0   20 Miles

descended from the ridges to the sea—from *mauka* to *makai*. Each *ahupua'a* was ruled by a chief. On the eastern side of the island, boundaries between *ahupua'a* often followed the natural lie of streams and riverbeds. Trails along these drainages made for ease of travel, as following a stream up or down a mountain was often easier than climbing up and over the steep slopes that divided one drainage from another.

To the west and the north of the island, the lay of the land provided fewer obvious valleys and drainages; but here, too, the land was divided to encourage a measure of equal opportunity. Each parcel traversed as many of the island's climate zones as possible to give its inhabitants access to the different types of lands, resources, and microclimates needed to be self-sufficient: fresh water; land for farming staples such as taro, sweet potato, or coconut; and wood for building canoes and houses. As with contemporary zoning, the *ahupua'a* system ensured that land parcels had access to transportation arteries, in this case the ocean. Whenever possible, no parcels were landlocked. In some areas, stone walls, which can still be seen in South Kona and Ka'u, were built to divide *ahupua'a*; the boundaries often changed over time to reflect changes in resources.

The Ala Kahakai Trail adds a new perspective to the National Trails System. The national historic trails cover a wide range of terrain and usages: trails through forests, over mountains, and through prairies and deserts; trails along rivers and across snow; trails intended for horsemen, mule trains, wagons, dogsleds, and canoes. The Ala Kahakai adds volcanic rock and sandy beaches to the list of environments. And, like the Iditarod, the Ala Kahakai brings a distinct local flavor to the national historic trails. Unlike most of America's other national historic trails, these were not trails of European migration or conquest; rather, they were trails of local settlement, made by indigenous people for indigenous people. As such, they led around the island, to places where people lived and worked and fished and prayed. They gave access to the essential inlets, coves, and fishponds, and they connected the *mauka-makai* trails that led to the various *ahupua'a*.

Some sections of the Ala Kahakai follow trails that emerged with use over time; other sections of the path were carefully constructed to ease the way through hard volcanic terrain. Parts of the trail traverse fields of *'a'ā*, which translates to "stony rough lava" (transliterated as "aa," it makes for a useful Scrabble word). *'A'ā* consists of ankle-twisting chunks of pointy, jagged rock, so ancient trails through *'a'ā* were cleared of large stones to make a footpath. In the 1800s, curbed, straight overland trails were built by the Hawaiian Kingdom government to provide for travel by horse and mule and to facilitate movement of trade goods such as cattle to ports for export.

In contrast, *pāhoehoe* lava flows are smooth: imagine a lava-lamp blob that flattened and hardened as it flowed over the ground. The surface of *pāhoehoe* is smooth but can also be slippery, especially near the ocean, where it is washed by tides and ocean spray. Over time, thousands of human feet followed each other as they found the easiest path. Today, indentations worn into the smooth rock show where the ancients walked.

Elsewhere, strategically placed stepping stones helped humans on foot cross a landscape of uneven rock. However, what works for humans does not always work for horses or mules; the same stones that gave humans a good grip could be slippery for hooves. In the 19th century, some of these stones were removed on trails where pack animals were now used; later still, modern paved roads were overlaid on some of the original trail segments.

The Ala Kahakai is a dynamic, changing trail. In many areas, the national historic trail includes segments of the ancient Ala Loa, which predate the first contact with westerners in 1778. Archaeological artifacts, fishponds, traditional trail construction, remains of ancient and historic dwellings, and sacred sites all provide a connection between the present and the past. The range of ecosystems and natural features—anchialine ponds, cliffs, ravines, streams, near-shore reefs, estuarine ecosystems, native sea turtle habitats—introduce contemporary visitors to the environments and resources that were the foundation of ancient Hawaiian culture. Managed as a partnership between descendant communities, kama'aina, land-management agencies, and local stakeholders, the Ala Kahakai demonstrates the idea that trails are a network that connect Hawaiians with places that are important not only in the present, but also in the times of their ancestors.

THE ROUTE

The Ala Kahakai National Historic Trail includes portions of historic trails known as the Alanui Aupuni (Hawaiian Kingdom Government Road), King's Trail, or Ala Loa (Long Path) that once encircled the entire island. These trails run just inland of the coast of the island through Hawai'i's famous lava fields. They also connect to the trails that run from the mountains (*mauka*) to the sea (*makai*). The trail network connects communities, cultural and historic sites, and diverse ecological environments. Like many of the national historic trails, the Ala Kahakai does not currently offer walkers a continuous, connected hiking route. Sections are opened as they can be managed and protected.

The trail corridor extends from 'Upolu Point (the northernmost point of the island of Hawai'i, near Kohala), and then follows the western coastline of the Big Island to Ka Lae (South Point), passing many of the Big Island's famous resorts as well as three national historic sites and parks. From Ka Lae, it hooks northeast to finish at Waha'ula at Puna, near the eastern boundary of Hawai'i Volcanoes National Park.

The entire Ala Kahakai Trail corridor comprises segments of many Big Island trails on both public and private land. Shoreline access points lead to sections of trail that connect to some of the island's best beaches, particularly along the west coast. Ala Kahakai segments can also be accessed from the four national parks on the island of Hawai'i: Pu'ukoholā Heiau National Historic Site, Pu'uhonua O Hōnaunau National Historical Park, Kaloko-Honokōhau National Historical Park, and Hawai'i Volcanoes National Park.

Ala Kahakai Trail heading
south toward Manō Point

OPPOSITE: Ala Kahakai Trail heading toward Puakō Point

RIGHT: Pāhoehoe lava flow, north of Kīholo Bay (top); Wave blowhole in coastal lava flow, Manō Point (bottom)

FOLLOWING SPREAD: Coastline near Humuhumu Point (left); Ala Kahakai Trail, Kaloko-Honokōhau National Historical Park (top right); Green sea turtle on beach, Kona Village Resort (middle right); Ala Kahakai Trail, Puʻuhonua O Hōnaunau National Historical Park (bottom right)

LEFT: Kanonone Waterhole, Pōhue Bay (top); Ala Kahakai Trail along coastline of Mahana Bay (bottom)

OPPOSITE: Ala Kahakai Trail, Pōhue Bay

LIVING THE HISTORY

The management of the Ala Kahakai National Historic Trail is an unusual mix of federal and local. The trail works closely with descendant families with cultural ties to historic sites on the trail, Native Hawaiian organizations, nonprofits, state and county governments, and the local community to support community-based management and preservation of trails, as well as enhancing connections to the trail. Carrying capacities along the coast, a sensitive ecology, and the presence of sacred sites complicate management challenges. As a result, trail sections are opened to the public when they are actively managed in order to preserve the cultural and ecological values of the site. The National Park Service, the Ala Kahakai Trail Association, state park management teams, the Hawai'i Island Land Trust, the Trust for Public Land, Aloha Kuamo'o 'Aina, Kohala Lihikai, County of Hawai'i, and the local community have all been involved in acquiring easements and protecting trail segments, including archaeological sites, ancient fishing villages, and important ecological resources.

Ala Kahakai State Trail, South Kohala, Hawai'i

This trail section is a state trail under the Nā Ala Hele Trail and Access Program. A 15-mile section of trail is managed by the state of Hawai'i with the cooperation of resorts, homeowners' associations, and the Ala Kahakai Trail Association. It begins at Pelekane Bay and runs from Spencer Beach Park at 'Ohai'ula south to 'Anaeho'omalu Bay. The three-mile section from Spencer Beach Park to Hāpuna Beach State Recreation Area is extremely popular and marked with trail signs and interpretive information. The trail mostly follows the ancient route along the coastline through both public and private lands, providing access to numerous beaches. It also provides access via the Malama Trail to the Puakō petroglyph field near Holoholokai, where 1,200 petroglyphs show aspects of ancient Hawaiian life, including paddlers, sailors, marchers, dancers, family groups, animals, and gods. While this section of trail provides access to some of Hawai'i's most pristine shoreline ecosystems—including the anchialine fishponds that were so important to ancient Hawaiian fishing—the trail receives limited maintenance and the path can be rough.

Pu'ukoholā Heiau National Historic Site, Hawai'i

Just north of Spencer Beach Park, Pu'ukoholā Heiau—the great red-stone temple of Kamehameha the Great—contrasts with the dark waters of Pelekane Bay. Kamehameha built the temple to appease the war god Kūka'ilimoku, hoping to seal his kingship against an upstart rival. Offshore, a ruined temple underwater receives daily visits from resident sharks. The Ala Kahakai Trail passes through the park. No swimming or sunbathing is allowed on this beach.

Pu'uhonua O Hōnaunau National Historical Park, Hawai'i

The laws of traditional Hawaiian culture were based on a system of *kapu*, which governed everything from breaking social taboos to gathering the wrong food in the wrong season. The penalty could be death. But those convicted had one chance at life—the *pu'uhonua*. A sacred place with carved images and a temple that might contain the bones of chiefs, the *pu'uhonua* was a "place of refuge." If a prisoner could escape and find their way to one of these sacred places, the penalty would be lifted. The Ala Kahakai Trail follows the coast past today's Pu'uhonua O Hōnaunau National Historical Park, which was once such a place of forgiveness and sanctuary. Visitors are asked to respect that this is a sacred site, not a recreational one. Beach chairs, towels, mats, beach umbrellas, coolers, picnicking, and beach and ball games are all prohibited, as are commercial filming, nudity, pets, weddings and wedding photography, and smoking.

Kaloko-Honokōhau National Historical Park, Hawai'i

Just north of Kailua-Kona, the 1,160-acre Kaloko-Honokōhau National Historical Park preserves and interprets many nearly intact sites associated with traditional Native Hawaiian culture. More than 200 archaeological sites in the park include ancient house platforms, religious temples and stone mounds, fishponds, petroglyphs, lava tube shelters, and parts of the Ala Kahakai Trail. A 12-mile

section of the Hawaiian Kingdom Government Road, the Mamālahoa Trail, runs north toward Kekaha Kai State Park. This rugged stretch of trail crosses lava fields, breathtaking beaches, a combination of sharp and jagged lava and fossilized coral rock, and Kua Bay before reaching Kukio Beach in front of the Hualalai Four Seasons Resort.

Hawai'i Volcanoes National Park, Hawai'i

The trail ends at Hawai'i Volcanoes National Park, where visitors can sometimes—if Pele, the Hawaiian goddess of volcanoes, is in the right mood—stand on some of the island's most ancient trails and watch the newest landscapes of Hawai'i being formed by volcanic activity. Eruptions from the park's two active volcanoes—Kīlauea (one of the most active volcanoes in the world) and Mauna Loa (at 13,679 feet,

the world's most massive shield volcano)—sometimes close visitor centers, roads, and trails, and ensure that at every visit the land will look a bit different. Designated an international biosphere reserve, Hawai'i Volcanoes National Park contains diverse environments from beaches at sea level to tropical-alpine forests and rain forests to the stark and otherworldly Ka'ū Desert, comprising dried lava, volcanic ash, gravel, and sand. Sections of the Ala Kahakai Trail can be accessed from the park, which includes more than 130,000 acres of wilderness that allow visitors to experience the land as the ancient Hawaiians might have seen it.

Opposite: Pu'ukoholā Heiau National Historic Site;
Above: Ki'i (wooden statues) over the rebuilt temple at Pu'uhonua O Hōnaunau National Historical Park

Trail of Tears Trail

5,045 MILES ➤ NORTH CAROLINA · GEORGIA · TENNESSEE · ALABAMA
KENTUCKY · ILLINOIS · MISSOURI · ARKANSAS · OKLAHOMA

Chief John Ross House,
Rossville, Georgia

OPPOSITE: Original segment of
Trail of Tears, Village Creek
State Park, Arkansas

In 1830, Congress passed the Indian Removal Act, which authorized President Andrew Jackson to negotiate land exchanges with the American Indians of the southern states. But "negotiate" is the wrong word; a more accurate word is "coerce." As a result of that coercion, tens of thousands of Choctaw, Muscogee Creek, Seminole, Chickasaw, and Cherokee people were forced to leave their ancestral homes and relocate west of the Mississippi River. The Trail of Tears National Historic Trail commemorates the forced removal of the Cherokee from their southeastern ancestral homeland in 1838.

Blame it on greed and gold. In 1828, gold had been discovered in Dahlonega, Georgia; in 1829, America's first major gold rush began. Georgians wanted free rein to exploit the forests and farmlands and search for gold—all on land that belonged to other people. Those other people were the five "civilized" tribes—Choctaws, Muscogee Creeks, Seminoles, Chickasaws, and Cherokee—so called because they had adopted such supposedly civilized (code word for "white American") practices as Christianity, centralized government, a written constitution, literacy, commerce, wealth accumulation, intermarriage with white Americans, and the enslavement of Africans. But however many of these practices the American Indians had adopted, they had not abandoned their traditional culture, and that culture was inextricably connected to the land.

Therein lay the problem: being a "civilized" American Indian meant nothing when it came to land and money. The demands from white settlers were inexorable: even before the American Revolution, they wanted the land, and they wanted the American Indians off of it. The American Indians negotiated their land rights under American law—sometimes in treaties, and sometimes via court cases, one of which went all the way to the Supreme Court. But to no avail: over the next few years, worn down by unceasing pressure, violence, and the threat of worse to come, most of the major tribes reluctantly agreed to be relocated to Indian Territory in present-day Oklahoma.

By 1835, the Cherokee people—or, at least, a majority of them—were the holdouts. One faction, called the Treaty Party, considered removal to be inevitable; they argued that their best hope for favorable resettlement terms lay in acquiescence rather than

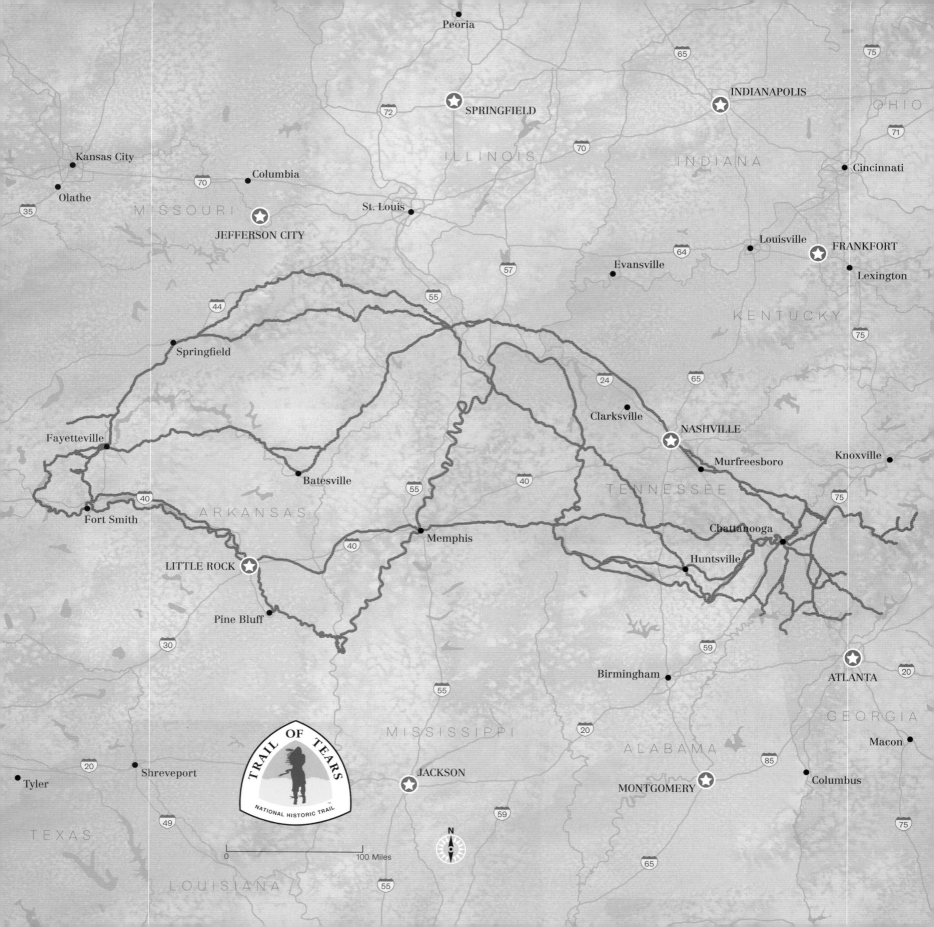

Peoria

INDIANAPOLIS

SPRINGFIELD

ILLINOIS

OHIO

71

65

75

Kansas City

Columbia

Cincinnati

INDIANA

70

Olathe

35

St. Louis

MISSOURI

JEFFERSON CITY

Louisville

FRANKFORT

57

Evansville

64

Lexington

KENTUCKY

44

75

Springfield

24

Clarksville

65

NASHVILLE

Fayetteville

Batesville

Murfreesboro

Knoxville

55

40

TENNESSEE

Fort Smith

40

Memphis

Chattanooga

75

LITTLE ROCK

40

Huntsville

Pine Bluff

30

59

Birmingham

ATLANTA

20

55

GEORGIA

TRAIL OF TEARS
NATIONAL HISTORIC TRAIL

MISSISSIPPI

ALABAMA

Macon

Tyler

Shreveport

20

85

JACKSON

Columbus

49

MONTGOMERY

N

0   100 Miles

59

TEXAS

LOUISIANA

65

55

75

resistance. So in late December 1835, representatives of this faction signed the Treaty of New Echota, even though they were not authorized to act on behalf of the tribe. The treaty—which was unlawful in the eyes of the majority of the Cherokee and the recognized leaders of the tribe—was nonetheless ratified by Congress in March 1836.

The treaty drove a wedge—sometimes a violent one—between the mainstream Cherokee majority, who opposed removal, and the Treaty Party, who thought it offered the best outcome. The exact nature of that outcome was realized in 1838, when troops of the US Army and various state militia arrived to forcibly evict more than 16,000 Cherokee from their homes in Tennessee, Alabama, North Carolina, and Georgia. First, the Cherokee were corralled into hastily constructed emigration camps, where many died while waiting to begin their journey. Then they were organized into detachments for travel. With insufficient food, equipment, medicine, and clothing, they were relocated on various routes by wagon, train, steamboat, horse, or on foot from the forested mountains of their southeastern homelands to the arid plains and prairies of Oklahoma. Along the way, drought, road conditions, illness, starvation, and the harsh winter killed thousands. The relocation was completed by March 1839. Historians debate the exact number, but the generally accepted figure (and the figure given by the Cherokee Nation) is that as many as 4,000 people died on the 1838 evacuation—1,000 on the march and another 3,000 as a result of injuries and illnesses sustained on the journey. The survivors became today's Cherokee Nation, which has more than 300,000 tribal members, split between a small band of about 15,000 in the southern Appalachians, who are descended from those who evaded the forced relocation, and the vast majority, who live in Oklahoma and are descended from those who survived the march. It is the largest of the 567 federally recognized tribes in the United States.

THE ROUTE

The Trail of Tears National Historic Trail begins in the ancestral lands of the Cherokee in northwest Georgia, northeast Alabama, and the North Carolina-

Tennessee borderlands area. Cherokee living in the southern Appalachians (to the south and west of what is now Great Smoky Mountains National Park) were corralled into removal camps. Those roundup routes form the eastern part of the national historic trail.

From 10 removal camps in Tennessee and one in Alabama, the Cherokee were organized into detachments for travel, each averaging roughly 1,000 people. Four detachments were floated by barge on the Tennessee, Ohio, Mississippi, and Arkansas Rivers, a harsh journey with a high fatality rate. After that, land routes were used instead, and the remaining detachments were marched on one of three main trails. A northern route arced through southern Illinois and Missouri, where the refugees endured a harsh winter of heavy snows, freezing rain, and bitter cold. Two other routes took a slightly more southern path; these were led by Cherokees who had been put in charge of managing part of the exodus. All four of the major land and water trails, plus alternates and variations used by the 17 different travel detachments, are part of today's national historic trail, each with its own historic sites and markers.

Cherokee Removal Memorial Park at Historic Blythe Ferry, Tennessee

FOLLOWING SPREAD: Arkansas River from Toad Suck Park, Arkansas

Source of Big Spring, a campsite for Cherokee who were forcibly removed, Kentucky

FOLLOWING SPREAD: Remnants of a road (top left) and a road sign (bottom left) commemorating Centerville, a town that has vanished, Kentucky; Ohio River, Elizabethtown, Illinois (right)

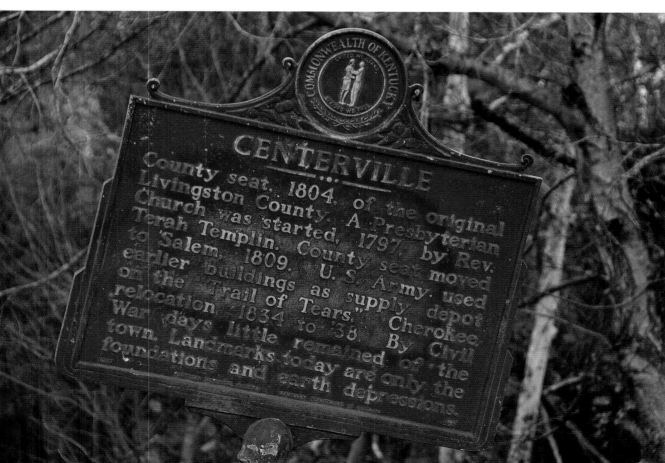

COMMONWEALTH OF KENTUCKY
UNITED WE STAND
DIVIDED WE FALL

CENTERVILLE

County seat, 1804, of the original Livingston County. A Presbyterian Church was started, 1797, by Rev. Terah Templin. County seat moved to 'Salem, 1809. U. S. Army used earlier buildings as supply depot on the "Trail of Tears," Cherokee relocation 1834 to '38. By Civil War days little remained of the town. Landmarks today are only the foundations and earth depressions.

LEFT: Grantsburg Swamp, Trail of Tears, Shawnee National Forest, Illinois (top); Maramec Spring, a campsite for many of the Cherokee detachments, Missouri (bottom)

OPPOSITE: Mantle Rock, Mantle Rock Nature Preserve, Kentucky

LIVING THE HISTORY

The Trail of Tears Trail is one of the best interpreted of the national historic trails, with scores of historic sites and museums that explain and commemorate different aspects of the trail. Sections of the trail can be retraced on foot, by vehicle, over water, by bicycle, or on horseback. The trail tells a story of suffering and intolerance. But it also tells a story of survival.

Museum of the Cherokee Indian, Cherokee, North Carolina

Operated by the Eastern Band of Cherokee, this museum displays 13,000 years of Cherokee history. Exhibits take visitors from the age of the mastodons to the present day. The story is told through computer-generated animation and special effects with lighting, audio, and holograms, along with life-sized figures, artwork, and priceless artifacts. The Trail of Tears is one of the museum's major interpretive themes.

New Echota State Historic Site, Calhoun, Georgia

In 1825, the Cherokee national legislature established New Echota as its capital. Over the next 13 years, its tribal business included a court case that went to the Supreme Court to protest incursions on Cherokee land, the signing of the contested treaty that was used to appropriate Cherokee lands east of the Mississippi River, and, finally, the collection of Cherokee for removal to what is now Oklahoma. The visitor center houses interpretive exhibits and a film. Original and reconstructed buildings include the council house and courthouse, the print shop (the Cherokee operated the first American Indian newspaper using their own syllabary and language), and homes, stores, smokehouses, and barns.

Great Smoky Mountains National Park, North Carolina and Tennessee

Before it was a half-million-acre national park, the Great Smoky Mountains were the homeland for thousands of Cherokee, who called these ancient mountains Shaconage, meaning "land of blue smoke." Running along the spine of the Appalachian Mountains on the North Carolina-Tennessee border, the park gives visitors an opportunity to experience the natural landscape very much as the Cherokee might have (especially those visitors who leave the roads and take to the park's trails). The Appalachian National Scenic Trail runs the length of the park, following the ridge that is the border between North Carolina and Tennessee. The Oconaluftee Visitor Center and Mountain Farm Museum,

located at the east end of the park by the town of Cherokee, North Carolina, focuses mainly on pioneer farm life but includes Cherokee history in several of its exhibits.

The Hermitage, near Nashville, Tennessee

Although Andrew Jackson had stepped down as president by the time the Cherokee were forcibly removed, his policies were instrumental in setting the Trail of Tears in motion for the Cherokee and the other tribes of the southeastern United States. The Hermitage contains Jackson's home and garden, his tomb, and various sites related to slavery, farming, and the natural environment. There is also a modern visitor center with exhibits pertaining to his life and presidency, including his American Indian policy.

Tennessee River Museum, Savannah, Tennessee

The Tennessee River was the primary water route for approximately 2,800 Cherokee who were sent to Oklahoma by river during the summer of 1838. A timeline tells the story of the Trail of Tears. The museum takes a sweeping view of the Tennessee River's history from dinosaurs to the dam technology and river management of the Tennessee Valley Authority. Other exhibits cover archaeology, European American pioneers, and the Civil War on the river, along with more focused displays on the development of steamboats, bridges, ferries, and the mussel industry.

Sequoyah Birthplace Museum, Vonore, Tennessee

Sequoyah (also known by his European name, George Gist) was born around 1770 to a Cherokee mother and a European American father. He is best known for creating a system of writing for the Cherokee language—a remarkable feat in that he worked alone and had no experience with literacy in any language. His entirely original syllabary contained 85 characters, each representing a different syllable. The system was adopted and used so successfully that the Cherokee literacy rate was higher than that of European Americans in the same region at the same

time. The museum exhibits trace American Indian history in the Southeast, beginning with the Paleoindian Period. Artifacts, maps, videos, and visual displays interpret Cherokee history and the Trail of Tears.

Trail of Tears Commemorative Park, Hopkinsville, Kentucky

This historic park is on the site of an 1838–1839 encampment. It is the burial site for two Cherokee chiefs who died during the removal: Fly Smith and Whitepath. A visitor center and museum has two rooms of exhibits interpreting the Cherokee Nation, the Trail of Tears, and various American Indian tribes and their respective removal histories. An annual intertribal powwow takes place the weekend after Labor Day, where American Indians gather to share and celebrate their heritage with one another as well as with interested non-Indians, who can learn about traditional dances, crafts, and storytelling.

Fort Smith National Historic Site, Fort Smith, Arkansas

The US Army built and maintained the fort here between 1817 and 1825, and used it again from 1838 to 1871. In the winter of 1838–1839, several Cherokee detachments passed through on their evacuation to Oklahoma. In addition, other southeastern tribes—such as the Creeks, Chickasaws, Choctaws, and Seminoles—were forcibly moved through the region during the 1830s and 1840s. This National Park Service property has a visitor center with a major display illustrating the Cherokee and other American Indian forced migrations. The park also contains a variety of buildings and exhibits from the days of frontier justice: two jails, a courtroom, gallows, and exhibits on the US deputy marshals, the military, and outlaws.

Cherokee National Museum, near Tahlequah, Oklahoma

The Cherokee National Museum is a long, natural stone building in the center of the Cherokee Heritage Center complex. Artifacts, archival material, and displays interpret

the Trail of Tears, including the conflicts, negotiations, and events that led to the Treaty of New Echota, the removal itself, and the resettlement in Oklahoma. Additional temporary exhibits explore other aspects of American Indian history, art, and culture. A reconstructed 17th-century village and late 19th-century Cherokee community show how life was lived in those eras.

Opposite: New Echota State Historic Site, Georgia; *Above:* Trail of Tears memorial near the gravesites of Chief Whitepath and Chief Fly Smith, Hopkinsville, Kentucky

Nez Perce (Nee-Me-Poo) Trail

1,170 MILES ➤ MONTANA · WYOMING · IDAHO · OREGON

Horse pasture and Wallowa Mountains, Oregon

OPPOSITE: Hells Canyon from near Buckhorn Spring, Wallowa-Whitman National Forest, Oregon

During the Corps of Discovery Expedition of 1804–1806, Meriwether Lewis described the Nez Perce as "the most hospitable, honest, and sincere people that we have met with in our voyage." The Nez Perce would have cause to regret that hospitality.

Perhaps the relationship was doomed from the beginning, starting as it did with a misunderstanding. Nez Perce—the erroneous name given to the tribe by French trappers—means "pierced noses," which was not the common custom of the Nimiipuu, as they called themselves. The name has since been transliterated several ways—Nimeepou, Niimíipuu, Nee-Me-Poo—and means "the people."

Fast-forward 50 years from Lewis and Clark. Routes to the American West were now open; railroads brought thousands of people a year to every corner that offered the next great opportunity for wealth. And, each year, more and more American Indians were displaced—negotiated and renegotiated out of their homelands, and then relocated and forced onto reservations. In 1855, it was the Nez Perce's turn. They signed the Treaty of Walla Walla, which gave the tribe formal title to 7.5 million acres of their ancestral lands and the right to continue to hunt, fish, and graze in the lands they had ceded to the US government.

And then, in 1860, gold was discovered on the Salmon and Clearwater Rivers. Thousands of miners and settlers poured in, and—as happened so many times—the treaty became worth less than the paper it was written on. US commissioners forced a renegotiation, though it was less a renegotiation than a land grab. They reduced the size of Nez Perce lands by three-quarters. Even that wasn't enough. Over the next 17 years, more and more homesteaders and squatters arrived, demanding ever more concessions, until the Nez Perce lands had shrunk to a tenth of the original settlement.

In 1877, a band of about 1,000 Nimiipuu found themselves at a crossroads: they had remained off the reservation, which put them in conflict with settlers, the US authorities, and even their own people. Illegal settlement from whites and American Indian resentment had turned into escalating violence. Settlers killed American Indians, American Indians retaliated by killing settlers, and the US Army set about forcing the remaining Nez Perce onto the shrunken lands

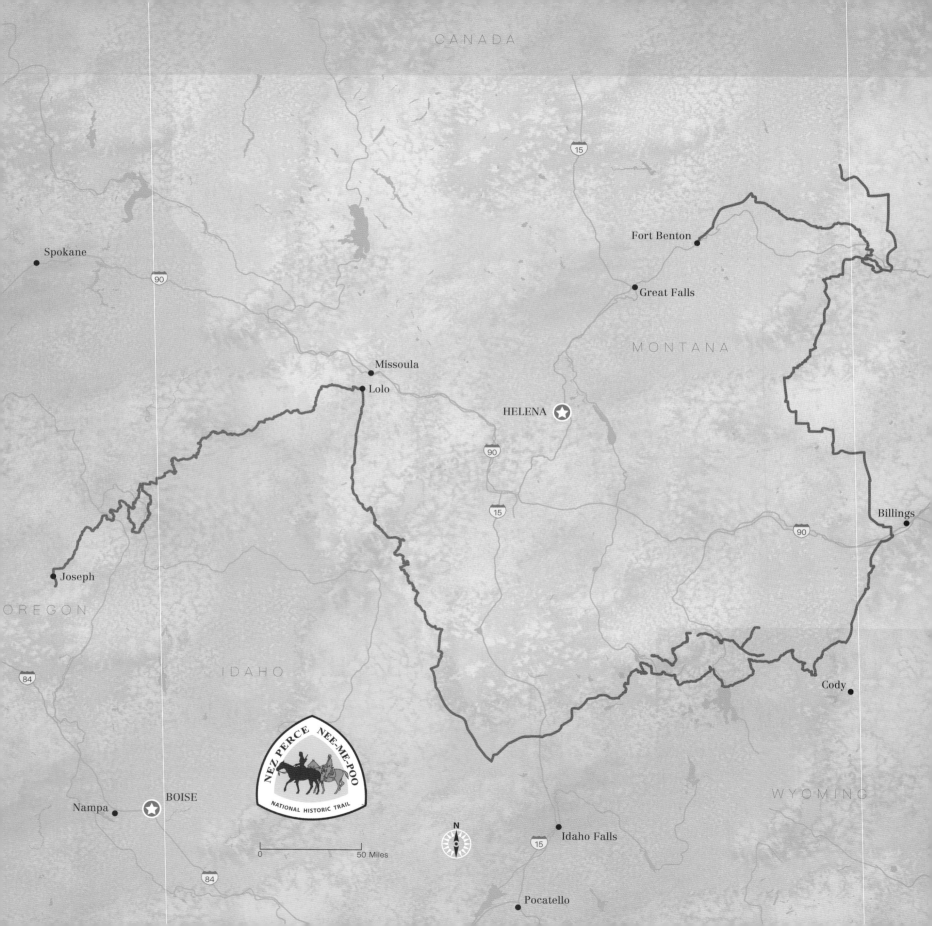

CANADA

MONTANA

IDAHO

WYOMING

OREGON

Spokane

Fort Benton

Great Falls

Missoula
Lolo

HELENA ⭐

Billings

Joseph

Cody

NEZ PERCE NEE-ME-POO
NATIONAL HISTORIC TRAIL

Nampa

BOISE ⭐

Idaho Falls

N

0   50 Miles

Pocatello

reserved for them. Some acquiesced, some initially refused. But even as these holdouts tried to find a solution and move toward the reservation, violence broke out. Realizing that a peaceful solution was becoming more and more unlikely, the band of "non-treaty" Nez Perce fled across some 1,200 miles of the American West, pursued by the US Army. So began the Nez Perce War.

It was an armed retreat: 250 warriors and 750 women, children, and elders hoped to outrun the US Army and find somewhere to continue living their traditional lifestyle. They first sought refuge with the Flathead and the Crow, but both refused, wanting nothing to do with the conflict. So the Nez Perce set their hopes on escaping to Canada.

They almost succeeded. After 128 days of retreat punctuated by battles, the Nez Perce were within 40 miles of safety at the Canadian border. The trek had been brutal: women and children were exhausted and starving, the sick and elderly were cold and dying. And now, in late September, the weather was changing. In northern Montana, an early winter storm stopped the Nez Perce and allowed the better-equipped US Army to catch up with them. When the Battle of Bears Paw was over, nearly 300 Nez Perce men, women, and children managed to escape and make thier way into Canada. The rest—418 survivors, most of them women and children—surrendered.

Chief Joseph negotiated the terms of surrender. Although he was not primarily a warrior, he had been identified as the leader by the US Army. In reality, though he did fight, his main leadership role was nonmilitary; he was responsible for managing the logistics of camp, travel, and horses, and for protecting the women and children, especially during battles. Regardless, as the long flight—and fight—drew to an end, he was the only chief left.

Historians debate the accuracy of the famous translation of Chief Joseph's speech that has filtered through history, but the meaning was clear as he summarized the sorrow and heartbreak that was the flip side of the European American settlement of the western territories. "Hear me, my chiefs!" he said. "I am tired; my heart is sick and sad. From where the sun now stands, I will fight no more forever."

The surrendering Nez Perce were banished first to Kansas and then to Oklahoma, where they were kept for seven years, many of them dying in the hot, unfamiliar, hated landscape. In 1885, the survivors were allowed to return to their shrunken reservation in Idaho—except Chief Joseph, who was sent to the Colville Reservation in Washington State.

In 1877, *The New York Times* ran an editorial: "On our part, the war was in its origin and motive nothing short of a gigantic blunder and a crime."

THE ROUTE

The Nez Perce (Nee-Me-Poo) National Historic Trail follows the approximately 1,170-mile route of the Nez Perce as they fled and fought the US Army. The flight path took the tribe across three distinct ecoregions, which are still in evidence today. Rolling grasslands of shortgrass prairie dominate the Palouse of central Idaho and the Missouri Basin east of the Continental Divide. In the plateaus along the Columbia and Snake Rivers, sagebrush steppes cover lava fields with gray-green shrubs. And in the northern Rocky Mountains of Montana and Idaho, high-elevation conifer forests and alpine meadows blanket the sky-piercing peaks.

The trail begins at Wallowa Lake in northeast Oregon, where the Nez Perce headed east, following the Clearwater and Lochsa Rivers across central Idaho. After crossing the Continental Divide at Lolo Pass in the Bitterroot Mountains, they continued south through the Bitterroot and Big Hole Valleys, where one of the major battles of the war took place. (The Lewis and Clark National Historic Trail, Continental Divide National Scenic Trail, and Nez Perce National Historic Trail all intersect at the Big Hole National Battlefield.)

At Bannock Pass near Leadore, the Nez Perce recrossed the Continental Divide into present-day Idaho. Continuing south and east, roughly parallel to the Continental Divide, they entered Yellowstone National Park at West Yellowstone and trekked across to what is now the east entrance, taking tourists temporarily hostage as they went. From there, they turned north into Montana for a final push to Canada. The trail ends near the Bears Paw Mountains, where the last battle took place.

FOLLOWING SPREAD: The Nez Perce used caves such as these for food storage, Wallowa-Whitman National Forest, Oregon (top left); Cold Springs Road descending to Joseph Creek near the Oregon-Washington border (middle left); Tolo Lake, Nez Perce National Historical Park, Idaho (bottom left); Hunter Peak over Bitterroot River Valley, Montana (right)

OPPOSITE: Big Hole National Battlefield, Montana

RIGHT: Bannack Ghost Town, Bannack State Park, Montana (top); Sculptures at Camas Meadow, Nez Perce National Historical Park, Idaho (bottom)

FOLLOWING SPREAD: View west of Tower Junction, Yellowstone National Park, Wyoming (left); Nez Perce sculpture at Dead Indian Pass, Wyoming (top right); Sunlight Creek Gorge near Clarks Fork Canyon, Wyoming (middle right); Near Cow Island, where the Nez Perce crossed the Missouri River in their attempt to evade the US Army, Upper Missouri River Breaks National Monument, Montana (bottom right)

LIVING THE HISTORY

Today, the history of the Nez Perce is commemorated by both a national historic trail and a national historic park. The national historic park is unique in that its 38 sites are spread over four states. Many of the sites in the park commemorate the Nez Perce War of 1877, but some are associated with other periods of Nez Perce history. The Nez Perce National Historic Trail mainly focuses on the route the fleeing "non-treaty" Nez Perce took to escape entrapment on a reservation. Some of the sites overlap.

Nez Perce National Historical Park Sites, Nez Perce Reservation, Idaho

Of the 38 sites in the Nez Perce National Historical Park, 26 are located on or close to the Nez Perce Reservation on the tristate border of Idaho, Oregon, and Washington. The museum at the Nez Perce National Historical Park visitor center in Spalding, Idaho, displays a collection of artifacts including clothing, tools, weapons, and ceremonial objects. From the visitor center, several hiking trails lead to sites that reveal aspects of Nez Perce life during the 19th century, including residences, a store, a church, a mission, a cemetery, a gristmill, and a sawmill. Other nearby sites include battlefields from the 1877 war, overlooks, and sites from long before Europeans even dreamed of a continent across the ocean. At Buffalo Eddy on the Snake River, hundreds of petroglyphs and a few pictographs contain images that may date from 4,500 years ago.

Auto Touring, Entire Trail

The states of Oregon, Washington, Idaho, Wyoming, and Montana have designated more than 1,500 miles of federal, state, and county roads as the Nez Perce National Historic Trail Auto Route. These roads closely follow and are sometimes contiguous with the official national historic trail, which follows the exact course traveled by the Nez Perce in 1877 as they fled from Wallowa Lake, Oregon, to the site of their defeat at Bear Paw Battlefield near Chinook, Montana. The autoroute offers several different variations depending on the type of traveler. (These variations are why the mileage is longer.) Routes are given for mainstream travelers (in average street cars, on paved roads and highways); rugged or adventurous travelers (in four-wheel-drive vehicles recommended for more rugged or remote roads, including high-quality gravel roads); and intrepid travelers (high-clearance, four-wheel-drive vehicles recommended for even more remote gravel and dirt roads). Detailed guides for each of the eight sections of the auto-touring route are available online and at visitor facilities along the trail.

Bitterroot Valley to Yellowstone National Park, Idaho, Montana, and Wyoming

From the Bitterroot Valley to Yellowstone National Park, the Nez Perce fled along what is now the Idaho-Montana border, crossing the Continental Divide three times before entering Yellowstone in western Wyoming. National Forest Trail 406 offers an opportunity to hike on the exact route of the Nez Perce and the US Army, starting about 6 miles south of Sula, Montana, near the Indian Trees Campground, east of Route 93. This 3.1-mile-long trail was also used by William Clark on his 1806 return journey from the Pacific Ocean, and is also part of the Lewis and Clark National Historic Trail. For hikers who want a longer experience, the Continental Divide National

Scenic Trail runs through spectacular high-mountain country south of Chief Joseph Pass, as well as through the Anaconda Pintler Wilderness to the north, making for the possibility of a multiday—or multiweek—adventure.

Yellowstone National Park, Wyoming

The Nez Perce crossed Yellowstone National Park from west to east, sometimes following what are now park roads, and sometimes following what have become backcountry hiking trails. The Continental Divide National Scenic Trail crosses Yellowstone on a slightly different route,

but offers today's hikers a chance to see what passage through this landscape would have been like before roads and cars. Detailed autoroute maps from the Forest Service show the routes of the US Army and the Nez Perce, as well as the scouting parties for each, through the park.

Bear Paw Battlefield, near Chinook, Montana

A moderately difficult 1.25-mile self-guided interpretive trail leads through the battlefield (ranger-led tours are also available if arranged in advance). In the nearby (by western

standards—it is 16 miles away) town of Chinook, the Blaine County Museum tells the story of the battle and the surrender of those final few days. The museum's exhibits include a 20-minute multimedia presentation, artifacts from the battlefield, and photographs and military gear from the late 1800s.

Opposite: Buffalo Eddy Petroglyphs along Snake River, Nez Perce National Historical Park, Idaho; *Above:* Annual commemoration of the Battle of Bears Paw, Nez Perce National Historical Park, Montana

Selma to Montgomery Trail

54 MILES ➤ ALABAMA

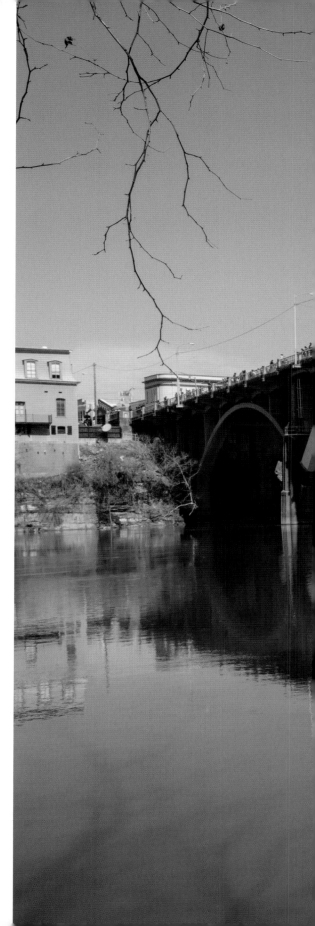

Names tell us something about a place. Sometimes they describe an environment, real or imagined: Magnolia Avenue, Oak Street, Garden Drive, Breezy Hill Road. Or they relate a bit about something that happened there: Wall Street, Front Royal, Harpers Ferry, Keep Tryst Road. And, of course, they give us the names of heroes: Washington Square Park, Madison Avenue, Jefferson Davis Memorial Highway.

That last one—the Jefferson Davis Memorial Highway—also has another name. When Highway 80 passes through Alabama it becomes the Selma to Montgomery National Historic Trail. Its designation as a national historic trail honors the more than 8,000 people, mostly African Americans, who in 1965 marched along this route to protest the suppression of their right to vote, and the 25,000 protestors who ultimately gathered at the Alabama State Capitol to demand reform. Along the way, on side roads off the highway, there are other place names: Frederick Douglass Road, Langston Hughes Drive, Harriet Tubman Road, Ida Wells Way, the Rosa Parks Museum. Coming full circle, less than a mile from the Rosa Parks Museum are the Jefferson Davis Apartments (the majority of whose inhabitants, it should be noted, are African Americans).

The confusion—over what is valued, commemorated, remembered, revered—doesn't end there. On arriving in Montgomery, Alabama, on a crosswalk that leads to the state capitol building, painted footsteps mark the path of the 1965 marchers. Sitting just opposite the crosswalk is another monument, this one erected in 1942 by the Sophie Bibb Chapter of the United Daughters of the Confederacy: Jefferson

Edmund Pettus Bridge
in Selma

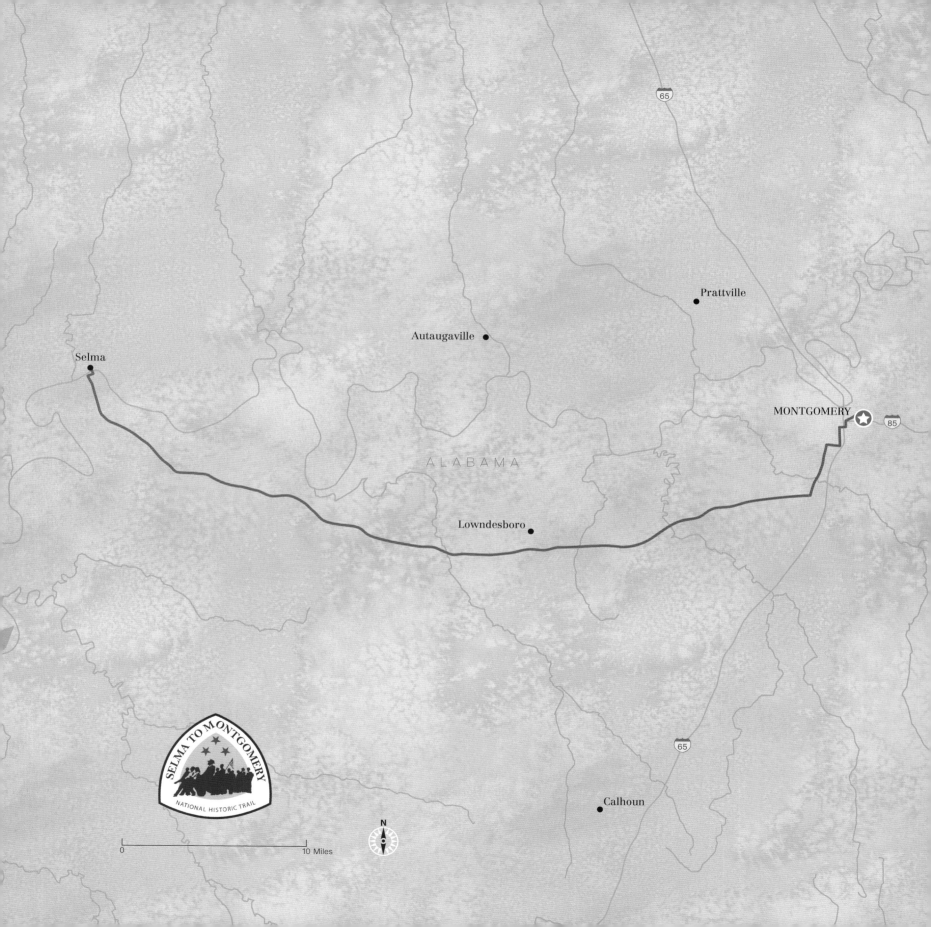

Selma

Autaugaville

Prattville

MONTGOMERY

ALABAMA

Lowndesboro

Calhoun

SELMA TO MONTGOMERY
NATIONAL HISTORIC TRAIL

0   10 Miles

N

Davis—yes, again. This monument commemorates his inauguration as president of the Confederate States of America.

These Alabama place names—on streets, buildings, and monuments—tell a confusing story of collision, reconciliation, and continuing conflict. Inscribed in the unyielding, permanent media of metal and stone, they announce who values what. The seal of the city of Montgomery puts the conflict front and center: in the middle of the seal, inside a six-pointed star, are the words "Cradle of the Confederacy." A white circle surrounding the star contains the words "Birthplace of the Civil Rights Movement."

It is that second claim that is celebrated by the National Trails System. The Voting Rights March from Selma to Montgomery was one of the most decisive actions in the African American fight for equality.

The Civil Rights Act of 1964 had made discrimination illegal based on race, but it did not get African Americans over the hurdles they faced when trying to register to vote in the Jim Crow South. For example, in Lowndes County, through which the marchers passed, 81 percent of the population was black and 18 percent was white. No black people were registered to vote; 2,240 whites were registered—representing 118 percent of the actual white population. Apparently, dead whites and whites who moved away could stay on the voter rolls. Blacks, no matter how alive and present, could not.

To protest the situation was—literally—a death-defying act in the Deep South. Protesters—mostly black—were bludgeoned, teargassed, firehosed, and murdered for demanding their constitutionally guaranteed rights to vote, attend school, or even walk on the same sidewalks, sit at the same lunch counters, or use the same water fountains and bathrooms as whites. Even a full 100 years after slavery officially ended, Jim Crow laws held millions of African Americans in legal and emotional chains. Hundreds of local and state ordinances undermined the civil liberties of African Americans at every turn. For instance, a 1964 injunction in Selma made it illegal for more than three people to meet and talk about civil rights or voter registration.

For 600 people to gather to protest voter suppression was therefore not only an act of courage,

but also an act of defiance that involved enormous, even fatal risk. But in March 1965, courage and defiance were called for. Selma's African American community was reeling from the murder of a black civil rights protestor named Jimmie Lee Jackson by a white law enforcement officer. On March 7, 1965, those 600 people left the Brown Chapel AME Church in Selma, intending to walk to the state capitol building in Montgomery, 54 miles away. The walk was a protest march: a public reaction to the murder that attempted to bring a grieving, angry community together to focus attention on positive change rather than violent reaction.

That first march did not last long. On what came to be known as Bloody Sunday, police officers standing on the county line just over the Edmund Pettus Bridge beat the marchers back with batons and teargas. The violence was televised nationwide. Two days later, marchers tried again in a second attempt that turned out to be largely symbolic. By prearrangement, Dr. Martin Luther King Jr. had agreed to turn back the march in order to await a judicial decision

Jimmie Lee Jackson
gravesite near Marion

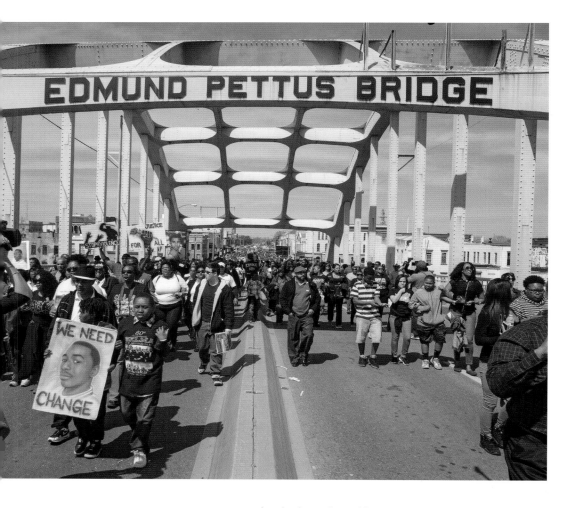
EDMUND PETTUS BRIDGE

they created a mass that could no longer be ignored. Standing on a flatbed truck in front of the capitol building, King had this to say:

Last Sunday, more than eight thousand of us started on a mighty walk from Selma, Alabama. We have walked through desolate valleys and across the trying hills. We have walked on meandering highways and rested our bodies on rocky byways. Some of our faces are burned from the outpourings of the sweltering sun. Some have literally slept in the mud. We have been drenched by the rains. Our bodies are tired and our feet are somewhat sore . . . They told us we wouldn't get here. And there were those who said that we would get here only over their dead bodies, but all the world today knows that we are here and we are standing before the forces of power in the state of Alabama saying, "We ain't goin' let nobody turn us around."

The words resonate, as does the lesson: the power of community can effect meaningful change. In August 1965, President Lyndon Johnson signed the Voting Rights Act into law.

In Selma, place names continue to give evidence of a conflicted history. At the intersection of what was formerly Jefferson Davis Avenue and Martin Luther King Street, visitors might take a moment to consider the history that has been and is still being made here.

THE ROUTE

The Selma to Montgomery National Historic Trail was established by Congress in 1996 to commemorate the routes, people, places, and events significantly linked to the Selma voting rights movement and the three voting rights marches that took place in 1965.

From Selma, the 54-mile-long national historic trail crosses the Edmund Pettus Bridge and runs east along US Highway 80, which is also known as the Jefferson Davis Memorial Highway. It passes through Dallas, Lowndes, and Montgomery Counties before ending at the Alabama State Capitol in Montgomery. Campsites where the marchers slept are marked along the way.

Walking across the Edmund Pettus Bridge in Selma as part of the 50th anniversary celebration of the 1965 Voting Rights March

OPPOSITE: Brown Chapel AME Church in Selma

that he hoped would give protection to the marchers. So, at the second march, the protestors once again turned back at the county line.

Finally, two weeks later, on March 17, the hoped-for court decision came through, giving permission for the march. The Alabama National Guard was federalized and ordered to protect the marchers. King once again led the protesters—out of the church, across the bridge that arcs high over the Alabama River, down the Jefferson Davis Memorial Highway, and into history. By the time they reached the capitol, the 8,000 marching protestors had swelled to 25,000 men, women, and children—mostly African American, but with some white supporters. Many had hiked the 54 miles in blistering street shoes. But as those 25,000 people crowded around the capitol,

PREVIOUS SPREAD: Paintings to celebrate the 50th anniversary of the 1965 Voting Rights March in Selma (all)

LEFT: Commemoration marchers passing the Rosa Parks Library and Museum in Montgomery (top); Monument to the 1965 Voting Rights March in Montgomery (bottom)

OPPOSITE: State Capitol Building in Montgomery

LIVING THE HISTORY

The 54 highway miles between Selma and Montgomery do not fit the typical definition of the word "trail." For modern-day travelers, this trail is not especially walkable. There is often no shoulder, and cars and trucks fly past belching fumes and spitting gravel. But in the context of the national historic trails, it makes perfect sense. The national historic trails are about the routes that connect people, places, and historic movements. Few protest marches have had the impact that this one did: a straight line of cause and effect led from the march to the Voting Rights Act of 1965. Most visitors experience the trail by car, stopping along the way to study the historic sites. The few who do walk the entire distance are not doing so for a recreational experience, but for a deeply personal encounter with history. If they travel as independent individuals, they do so at the considerable cost of personal vulnerability and physical discomfort, not to mention the mental stress of constantly reacting to the sounds of speeding cars and trucks.

Walking the Trail, Selma, Alabama

For those who want an immersive experience, Selma, Alabama, hosts an annual Jubilee in which thousands of people commemorate Bloody Sunday and gather to consider contemporary civil rights and social justice issues. Participants walk across the Edmund Pettus Bridge to commemorate the Voting Rights March. Once every five years, a full reenactment of the entire walk takes place, with Jubilee participants leaving the chapel, crossing the bridge, and continuing all the way to the Alabama State Capitol in Montgomery. The value of experiencing the walk in concert with social justice advocates and descendants of the original marchers brings the trail to life.

Selma Historic Sites, Alabama

The Selma Interpretive Center at the foot of the Edmund Pettus Bridge has museum exhibits, a small bookstore, and a view of the bridge. Almost next door are the Slavery and Civil War Museum and the Old Depot Museum; across the bridge is Selma's National Voting Rights Museum and Institute, along with a memorial to some of those who died

during the civil rights movement. The Martin Luther King Jr. Street Walking Tour brings visitors past some 20 sites associated with events in the voting rights movement, including the Brown Chapel AME Church (the starting point for the protests, it was later designated a national historic landmark in 1982), the First Baptist Church (headquarters of the Student Nonviolent Coordinating Committee), and the Martin Luther King Jr. Monument.

Trail Campsites, Alabama

Most visitors to the national historic trail drive the route, stopping in small southern towns to enjoy local cooking and views of the surrounding farmlands and to investigate the historical markers along the route. These include the four campsites along the route, most notably the City of St. Jude Historic District. This Catholic social services complex was the site of the last encampment and the "Stars for Freedom" rally, where musicians such as Harry Belafonte, Tony Bennett, and Peter, Paul, and Mary performed for the marchers.

Lowndes Interpretive Center, White Hall, Alabama

About midway along the route between Selma and Montgomery, the Lowndes Interpretive Center offers an expansive view of the civil rights movement, with exhibits about the Voting Rights Act as well as civil rights events throughout the nation. A 25-minute film gives an overview of the events of 1965. The center is built on the White Hall tent city site. When black tenant farmers began registering to vote after the Voting Rights Act was signed into law, white landowners punished them by throwing them off their land, resulting in "tent cities" that would house dispossessed black families, often for months or even years. A memorial just a few miles away honors Viola Liuzzo, a mother and voting rights advocate from Michigan, who was shot and killed by members of the Ku Klux Klan.

Montgomery Historic Sites, Alabama

Two sites in Montgomery are integral to the Voting Rights March. The Dexter Avenue King Memorial Baptist Church was the staging area for the concluding rally. The Alabama State Capitol was the destination for the marchers. Montgomery had been important in the civil rights movement for at least a decade before the Voting Rights March. Several other sites and museums commemorate this history, including the Rosa Parks Museum (built on the site where she was arrested on the bus in 1955), homes and churches associated with Martin Luther King Jr., the Freedom Rides Museum, the Civil Rights Memorial Center, the National Memorial for Peace and Justice, and the National Center for the Study of Civil Rights and African-American Culture.

Opposite: Bridge Crossing Jubilee headquarters in Selma; *Above, left:* First Baptist Church in Selma; *Above, right:* Martin Luther King Jr. memorial in front of Brown Chapel AME Church in Selma

PART FIVE

OTHER VOICES

★

In the broadest sense, all Americans came here from somewhere else. The English, Spaniards, and French thought they had discovered a "new world." But what was new to them was old to those who already lived here—and even they had come from elsewhere. Polynesians crossed the Pacific Ocean by boat to settle the Hawaiian Islands. Asians migrated across Siberia to cross the Bering Sea and find themselves on a whole new continent, where they would one day become known as Native Americans or American Indians—though, if we take a technical long view, they were neither. And later, Africans were forcibly brought across the Atlantic on the brutal Middle Passage. • Starting not long after the 13 colonies broke away from England to establish the great American experiment, immigrants from all

the world's countries—about 190 at present count, depending on whom you argue with—made their way here, settling in the Little Italies and Spanish barrios and Chinatowns and Japantowns and Greektowns and dozens of other ethnic enclaves of American cities. A large part of our domestic history is the story of how these disparate cultures have moved and interacted, both peacefully and in conflict.

The 19 national historic trails only scratch the surface of these stories. The current roster leaves out many important movements and events. The Spanish Southwest is honored with four trails, but the explorations of the early French, the Dutch settlement of New Netherland, and the Pilgrims and Puritans of New England are all missing. The civil rights movement is honored, but trails that trace the stories of slavery or the Underground Railroad are noticeably absent. There is nothing about women's suffrage, nothing about the construction of the transcontinental railroads, and, perhaps most startling of all, nothing about the entire Civil War.

In this section, we explore other trails that fill in some of the gaps in our history. Some of these trails are part of the National Trails System, inscribed as national recreation trails; many of them offer opportunities to hike, paddle, bike, or ride horses along routes of historic significance. Some of the routes have been developed by local history associations; others are recognized as historic sites by the National Park Service. Two are national scenic trails with strong historic components.

FREEDOM TRAIL
Massachusetts

Boston marks the beginning of the Revolutionary War. Its famed Freedom Trail, marked by red lines on the sidewalks of downtown Boston, winds past some of the key historic sites in the city. Only 2.5 miles long, the Freedom Trail can be walked in a mere hour or two, but its sites, parks, and museums can easily devour a day or more of a visitor's time. The trail connects 16 historically important sites, including the Old South Meeting House (where the Sons of Liberty organized a "tea party"); the Boston Massacre Site; Faneuil Hall (a forum and market dating back to 1741); the Paul Revere House; the Old North Church, where two lanterns were hung to spread word that the British were coming by sea; and many other sites.

PREVIOUS SPREAD: Sunset from atop Mangum Indian Mound, Natchez Trace Trail, milepost 45.7, Mississippi

Freedom Trail emblem, Boston, Massachusetts (left); Dorchester North Burying Ground, African American Trail, Boston, Massachusetts (right)

AFRICAN AMERICAN TRAIL PROJECT
Massachusetts

The American history of slavery as a legal institution begins in Massachusetts. Although the first slaves in what would become the United States arrived in Virginia in 1619, it was Massachusetts that formally defined and legalized slavery in 1641. But Massachusetts was also among the first states to condemn slavery in what would become one of the most important legal cases in the state's history. In 1783, Elizabeth Freeman (also known as Mumbet) and another slave known as Brom brought a suit for freedom against their owner, John Ashley. Massachusetts courts declared that "the idea of slavery is inconsistent with our own conduct and [the Commonwealth's] Constitution." The African American Trail Project, based at Tufts University, maps African American history across Massachusetts and through the centuries, from the first slaves to the ongoing contemporary struggles for racial justice. At current count, 236 historic sites from Boston to the Berkshires commemorate individual African American leaders, writers, artists, and thinkers, as well as events in history that impacted African Americans.

BARTRAM TRAILS
Florida, Georgia, North Carolina, and Alabama

Naturalists, authors, and explorers, John Bartram and his son, William, roamed North and South Carolina, Georgia, Florida, Alabama, Mississippi, Louisiana, and Tennessee between 1773 and 1777. They catalogued the plants and animals, drew pictures of what they saw, wrote evocative descriptions, and took copious notes. William Bartram's book, *Travels*, documents the flora and fauna, as well as interactions with American Indians. The Bartram Trail in Putnam County, Florida, seamlessly combines the idea of a traditional trail (built and maintained for travel) with the idea of historical conservation. It reestablishes and conserves sites related to Bartram's travels on the St. Johns River and makes them accessible both in primitive form—as he would have experienced them by boat and on foot—and in modern form—trails that can accommodate bicycles and automobiles. In northern Georgia and North Carolina, the Bartram Trail is a 115-mile

national recreation trail that follows his approximate route through the southern Appalachians. And in Alabama, the 200-mile Bartram Canoe Trail allows visitors to explore the Mobile-Tensaw River Delta system as Bartram would have—by canoe and kayak.

MISSISSIPPI BLUES TRAIL
Mississippi

The blues is the bedrock of American popular music. Everything from jazz to country to rock has borrowed from and been inspired by this art form. And the blues itself is derived from the disparate elements of western musical harmony accompanying melodies and stylings that have their origin in African American field songs, and, even earlier, in songs from Africa. The blues is music, but it is also a kind of historic document: a litany of stories and emotions with their roots in the Jim Crow era of segregation and deprivation. The Mississippi Blues Trail includes more than 100 historic markers honoring iconic bluesmen such as Robert Johnson, W. C. Handy, Charley Patton,

I-84 bridge and casino riverboat on the Mississippi River, Natchez, Mississippi

and B. B. King. The trail is rich with opportunities to get up close and personal with the music. Sometimes it comes in the form of sheer luck, perhaps a chance performance in a local blues joint by one of the few remaining old-timers. Sometimes it is the contemporary blues found in clubs like Morgan Freeman's Ground Zero in Clarksdale. The many music museums along the trail share more of the story: the Gateway to the Blues Museum in Tunica, the B. B. King Museum and Delta Interpretive Center in Indianola, the Greenwood Blues Heritage Museum and Gallery, the Official Delta Blues Museum in Clarksdale, and the Cottonlandia Museum in Greenwood (where Robert Johnson is buried). And, for a full immersion, tour the sites along the trail and then end at the Bridging the Blues fall festival, a several-week constellation of music events anchored by the King Biscuit Blues Festival in Helena, Arkansas, and extending throughout the Delta to Memphis, Tennessee.

C&O CANAL TOWPATH
Washington, DC, and Maryland

The C&O Canal was the realization of an idea originally proposed by George Washington as a way to open trade routes to the as-yet-unknown west. Built between 1824 and 1850, it operated until 1924. The old towpath is now a 185-mile hiking and biking trail, with campsites every few miles. On its way to Cumberland, Maryland, it passes the historic town of Harpers Ferry, West Virginia, site of John Brown's raid, and, just up the hill in neighboring Bolivar, a small Civil War battlefield. Its Paw Paw Tunnel was considered a 19th-century engineering marvel. The towpath starts in Washington, DC, contains a tiny section of the Appalachian National Scenic Trail, and is the core of the 800-mile Potomac Heritage National Scenic Trail. Biking, hiking, and horseback riding are permitted.

CHILKOOT TRAIL
Alaska and British Columbia, Canada

Running smack across the US-Canadian border, the Chilkoot Trail is a historic 33-mile route originally used by 19th-century prospectors moving from Dyea (near Skagway, on Alaska's southeast coast) to Bennett, British Columbia, in Canada, and from there

to the Yukon goldfields of the 1890s. The trail is in the Klondike Gold Rush International Historical Park, managed jointly by the United States and Canada. Rising from sea level in the coastal rain forest, the trail climbs to 3,500 feet at Chilkoot Pass—a brutal, treeless, snow-covered elevation at such a high latitude. Backpackers have it easy compared to the so-called stampeders (the name given to the miners who first crossed the pass). Before stampeders were permitted to cross the pass, the Canadian government required them to have a year's worth of supplies to survive on the frontier; the list of required essentials added up to two tons per man. Most of the men ferried their possessions, going up and down the pass as many as 80 times to carry more and more loads, weighing 50 to 60 pounds each, up and over. And, like modern hikers starting a thru-hike with too much of the wrong stuff, they sometimes abandoned nonessentials. Today, the cold air of the alpine pass has preserved some of these artifacts, giving the Chilkoot Trail the claim of being the world's longest outdoor history museum. Today's hikers generally take three to five days to complete the hike, traveling south to north (the direction in which

OPPOSITE: Paw Paw Tunnel, C&O Canal Towpath section of the Potomac Heritage Trail, Maryland (bottom)

ABOVE: C&O Canal near Spring Gap, Maryland

FOLLOWING SPREAD: Boardwalk section of the Chilkoot Trail (left) and placer pan from the gold rush (right), Klondike Gold Rush National Historical Park, Alaska

the prospectors traveled) and passing through three distinct ecosystems: the coastal rain forest, a high alpine section, and the boreal forest. The hiking season extends from late May through early September. Only 50 backpackers are allowed on the trail each day.

CIVIL RIGHTS TRAIL
15 states and Washington, DC

Not all wars are fought on battlefields. In the 1950s and 1960s, the battle for civil rights was fought at churches, courthouses, and schools, primarily in the southern states. The Civil Rights Trail was established in 2018 to identify, interpret, and preserve important civil rights landmarks, especially places where activists sought equal access to public education, public transportation, and voting rights. From school desegregation to lunch counter sit-ins to bus protests to the Selma to Montgomery Voting Rights March (itself a national historic trail), the Civil Rights Trail commemorates a historic movement that is still relevant and ongoing. Important civil rights heroes such as Martin Luther King Jr., Rosa Parks, and Medgar Evers are commemorated. In Montgomery, Alabama, a memorial by Maya Lin honors 41 people who lost their lives fighting for civil rights between 1954 and 1968. The trail also includes stops at museums and institutes that study and interpret various aspects of the movement, including the National Museum of African American History and Culture, the Birmingham Civil Rights Institute, the National Center for Civil and Human Rights in Atlanta, and the Mississippi Civil Rights Museum in Jackson. The Civil Rights Trail tells visitors that "what happened here changed the world." Indeed it did. It also reminds us that continuing battles for racial justice are still needed to change the world even more today.

CIVIL WAR TRAILS
Maryland, Virginia, West Virginia, Tennessee, North Carolina, and Pennsylvania

The Civil War Trails project began in 1994, when a group of historians linked travel routes to important Civil War sites in Virginia around Petersburg (the site of nearly 300 days of fighting during the last year of the war) and Appomattox (where Robert E. Lee surrendered). With the enthusiasm of historians and grassroots history buffs, the project grew to include more than 200 interpretive sites by 1999—and more than 1,550 sites today. The sites represent both the great campaigns of the war and smaller, less famous battlefields in Maryland, Virginia, West Virginia, Tennessee, and North Carolina (as well as the Confederate incursion into Pennsylvania and the Battle at Gettysburg). A series of detailed trail maps and brochures guide visitors from one site to the next by car, bike, and sometimes on foot, following in the footsteps of the soldiers.

NATCHEZ TRACE NATIONAL SCENIC TRAIL
Tennessee and Mississippi

The Natchez Trace National Scenic Trail took a wrong turn somewhere in the maze of the National Trails System: it is much more a national historic route than it is a recreational hiking trail. The Natchez Trace Parkway is a national park—drivable by automobile from Nashville, Tennessee, to Natchez, Mississippi—that closely parallels the original trace. The original Natchez Trace was used as a trading and travel route, first by ancient American Indian cultures following

OPPOSITE: Antietam National Battlefield, Maryland

BELOW: Burnside Bridge, Antietam National Battlefield, Maryland

FOLLOWING SPREAD: Alligator resting on log, Cypress Swamp, Natchez Trace Trail, milepost 122.0, Mississippi (left); Sunken Trace, Natchez Trace Trail, milepost 41.5, Mississippi (right)

buffalo and later by trappers and traders bringing goods from the eastern United States to the Mississippi River, where they could be taken to New Orleans by boat. Some of the original trace is still on the ground (often in ruts that have sometimes been eroded to a depth of several feet.) The parkway passes numerous historic sites, dating from ancient American Indian cultures to the use of the trace as a pioneer travel and trade route to the building where Meriwether Lewis died, a victim of either suicide or foul play and politics (historians don't know for sure).

NEW ENGLAND NATIONAL SCENIC TRAIL
Connecticut and Massachusetts

One of the newest of the 11 trails in the National Scenic Trails System, the 215-mile New England Trail begins at Long Island Sound and traverses Connecticut and Massachusetts, passing some 40 towns along the way, many of which contain colonial historical landmarks. Much of the trail follows the Mattabesett, Metacomet, and Monadnock Ridges, including old American Indian travel ways and ridges and forests where Metacomet, an American Indian leader also known as King Phillip, fought the New England European settlers in one of the deadliest wars in colonial history.

ROUTE 66
Illinois, Missouri, Kansas, Oklahoma, Texas, New Mexico, Arizona, and California

It went by other names: the Will Rogers Highway, the Main Street of America, the Mother Road. The history of Route 66 parallels the history of the automobile in America, starting in 1926. At 2,448 miles long, it was one of the first true interstates, running from Chicago, Illinois, to Santa Monica, California. It caught the popular imagination: it was a Dust Bowl route of despair and escape in John Steinbeck's *The Grapes of Wrath*, a place for kicks in the song "Route 66," and the star of its own eponymous television series. Today, some portions of the road in Illinois, Missouri, New Mexico, and Arizona have been designated the Route 66 National Scenic Byway, with historic sites along the route. Parts of it are now designated as the Bicycle Route 66, starting with a 358-mile section between Baxter Springs, Kansas, and St. Louis, Missouri. Proposals to make the entire span of the route a long-distance bicycle trail are underway.

TRAIL OF THE ANCIENTS
Colorado and Utah

The Trail of the Ancients is a 480-mile national scenic byway that highlights the archaeology and culture of the American Indian people of the Southwest in southern Colorado and Utah, crossing the Colorado Plateau of the Four Corners Region. The region has been occupied for at least 10,000 years. Most of the sites are on or near paved roads, but some of the roads are dirt or gravel. The natural landscape is also suitable for hiking and biking, with red rock and sandstone formations, canyons, and snowcapped mountains. Along the way are Canyon of the Ancients National Monument (in Colorado: more than 6,000 archaeological ruins over 183,000 acres), Hovenweep National Monument (in Colorado: six groups of Ancestral Pueblo villages), Edge of the Cedars State Park (in Utah: Anasazi ruins), and Natural Bridges National Monument (in Utah: outstanding landscape formations). It is possible that

some sites in Arizona and New Mexico, such as Navajo National Monument (New Mexico) and Canyon de Chelly National Monument (Arizona), might be added to the trail.

UNDERGROUND RAILROAD BICYCLE ROUTE
Alabama, Mississippi, Tennessee, Kentucky, Ohio, Pennsylvania, New York, and Ontario, Canada

The Underground Railroad was a clandestine network of routes followed by American slaves seeking freedom. The 2,000-mile Underground Railroad Bicycle Route follows the main trunk of the network from Mobile, Alabama, to Owen Sound, Ontario, with a few additional spurs and alternates. Cyclists pass memorial markers to important figures, both black and white, in the fight for freedom, including Harriet Tubman, John Brown, Harriet Beecher Stowe, and countless Underground Railroad conductors—Quakers, former slaves, and ministers—who gave shelter and direction to fugitives from slavery. Also found along the route are museums, historic parks, Civil War sites, and actual Underground Railroad stations with hidden rooms where slaves took shelter. A spur trail to Cincinnati leads to numerous related sites, including the National Underground Railroad Freedom Center and the Harriet Beecher Stowe House. In northern Ohio, the Hubbard House is an Underground Railroad museum and an important benchmark: from there, escaped slaves could cross Lake Erie by boat to freedom in Canada.

NATIONAL VOTES FOR WOMEN TRAIL
New York and Nationwide

Women's Rights National Historical Park in Seneca Falls and Waterloo, New York, contains four historical properties: three homes of activists in the women's suffrage movement and the Wesleyan Methodist Church, which was the site of the Seneca Falls Convention. Associated with the park is the Votes for Women History Trail, which links sites throughout upstate New York that were important to the establishment of women's suffrage, including the Susan B. Anthony House in Rochester. Additionally, the National Collaborative for Women's History Sites has expanded the project to a national scope. The National Votes for Women Trail collects sites that commemorate and

interpret the story of women's rights—up through suffrage and beyond. Currently, the project has 44 state coordinators and more than 1,000 sites nationwide.

ZEBULON PIKE TRAIL
24 States

At roughly the same time Lewis and Clark were sending a prairie dog down the Missouri River to be delivered to Thomas Jefferson, Zebulon Pike was sailing up the Mississippi River to find its headwaters. Acting on the behest of Jefferson, he followed his river exploration with a foray westward to explore America's new borderlands with New Spain's settlements in Texas and New Mexico. Today, however, he is probably best remembered for the mountain in Colorado that bears his name. He identified it, described it, and tried—but failed—to climb it. Following the routes of his explorations, the Zebulon Pike Trail is now being developed as a possible new addition to the national historic trails. It claims 8,763 miles, 24 states, 320 counties, 109 historic sites, and countless roadside interpretive signs and markers, with sections designated for auto touring, bike routes, and hiking.

OPPOSITE: Harriet Tubman mural, Cambridge, Maryland

Bronze sculpture commemorating 19th-century activists Susan B. Anthony, Elizabeth Cady Stanton, and Amelia Bloomer, National Votes for Women Trail, Seneca Falls, New York

TRAIL INFORMATION AND ORGANIZATIONS

For more information about the 19 national historic trails and the organizations that protect and maintain them, please visit the following websites.

ALA KAHAKAI TRAIL

Ala Kahakai Trail Association: alakahakaitrail.org
E Mau Nā Ala Hele: emaunaalahele.org
National Park Service: nps.gov/alka

CALIFORNIA TRAIL

National Park Service: nps.gov/cali
Oregon-California Trails Association: octa-trails.org

CAPTAIN JOHN SMITH CHESAPEAKE TRAIL

Chesapeake Conservancy: chesapeakeconservancy.org
National Park Service: nps.gov/cajo

EL CAMINO REAL DE LOS TEJAS TRAIL

El Camino Real de los Tejas National Historic Trail Association:
   elcaminorealdelostejas.org
National Park Service: nps.gov/elte

EL CAMINO REAL DE TIERRA ADENTRO TRAIL

El Camino Real de Tierra Adentro Trail Association (CARTA): caminorealcarta.org
National Park Service: nps.gov/elca

IDITAROD TRAIL

Bureau of Land Management: blm.gov/programs/national-conservation-lands/
   national-scenic-and-historic-trails/iditarod
Iditarod Historic Trail Alliance: iditarod100.org

JUAN BAUTISTA DE ANZA TRAIL

Anza Trail Coalition of Arizona (ATCA): anzatrail.org
Anza Trail Foundation: anzatrailfoundation.com
National Park Service: nps.gov/juba

LEWIS AND CLARK TRAIL

Lewis and Clark Trail Heritage Foundation: lewisandclark.org
Lewis and Clark Trust: lewisandclarktrust.org
National Park Service: nps.gov/lecl

MORMON PIONEER TRAIL

Mormon Trails Association: mormontrails.org
National Park Service: nps.gov/mopi

NEZ PERCE (NEE-ME-POO) TRAIL

Nez Perce Trail Foundation: nezpercetrail.net
United States Department of Agriculture: fs.usda.gov/npnht

OLD SPANISH TRAIL

National Park Service: nps.gov/olsp
Old Spanish Trail Association (OSTA): oldspanishtrail.org

OREGON TRAIL

National Park Service: nps.gov/oreg
Oregon-California Trails Association: octa-trails.org

OVERMOUNTAIN VICTORY TRAIL

National Park Service: nps.gov/ovvi
Overmountain Victory Trail Association (OVTA): ovta.org

PONY EXPRESS TRAIL

National Park Service: nps.gov/poex
National Pony Express Association: nationalponyexpress.org

SANTA FE TRAIL

National Park Service: nps.gov/safe
Santa Fe Trail Association: santafetrail.org

SELMA TO MONTGOMERY TRAIL

National Park Service: nps.gov/semo

STAR-SPANGLED BANNER TRAIL

National Park Service: nps.gov/stsp

TRAIL OF TEARS TRAIL

National Park Service: nps.gov/trte
Trail of Tears Association: nationaltota.com

WASHINGTON-ROCHAMBEAU REVOLUTIONARY ROUTE TRAIL

National Park Service: nps.gov/waro
National Washington-Rochambeau Revolutionary Route
   Association: w3r-us.org